DISRUPTING
WHITE SUPREMACY
FROM WITHIN

DISRUPTING WHITE SUPREMACY FROM WITHIN

WHITE PEOPLE ON WHAT We NEED TO DO

Edited by
Jennifer Harvey,
Karin A. Case, and
Robin Hawley Gorsline

THE
PILGRIM
PRESS
Cleveland

To the named and unnamed who went before us, with gratitude
To the many who will come after, with hope

The Pilgrim Press, 700 Prospect Avenue
Cleveland, Ohio 44115-1100, U.S.A.
© 2004 by Jennifer Harvey, Karin A. Case, and Robin Hawley Gorsline

Printed in the United States of America on acid-free paper

09 08 07 06 05 04   5 4 3 2 1

Library of Congress Cataloging-in-Publication Data
Disrupting white supremacy from within : white people on what we need to do /
    edited by Jennifer Harvey, Karin A. Case, and Robin Hawley Gorsline.
        p. cm.
    Includes bibliographical references.
    ISBN 0-8298-1607-0 (pbk. : alk. paper)
    1. Racism – United States. 2. Whites – Race identity – United States. 3. Whites –
United States – Attitudes. 4. Social movements – United States. 5. Christians
United States – Attitudes. 6. Racism – Religious aspects – Christianity. I. Harvey,
Jennifer, 1971- II. Case, Karin A., 1958- III. Gorsline, Robin Hawley, 1946-
E184.AID53 2004
305.8'00973 – dc22
                                                                    2004053543

CONTENTS

FOREWORD

ONE OF THE SPIRITUAL GIFTS to America of this collaborative book is hope for a better future where all races can enjoy one another as human beings. In these pages, we sense a turn by progressive, if not radical, religious scholars digging deep into the Christian witness and surfacing a magnificent treasure — that is, the truth that the humanity of white sisters and brothers lies in the humanity of people of color. Put differently, we discover writings strongly suggesting that segments of the white academy and church have the resources internal to themselves to change the structures and soul of white supremacy. Furthermore, because this text symbolizes white brothers and sisters of faith, it offers the white church an alternative way in making the United States a place systemically welcoming for all races. In a word, the authors offer the most cutting edge conceptual framework and most practical challenge for race, faith, and hope in the contemporary period.

However, the notion of white Americans having internal resources to racially overthrow the heresy of white supremacy is not, and has never been, a given. And the white church, at the foundational level, has not surfaced convincing evidence of its ability to redirect its proheresy policy. When pushed against the wall, the United States, like its parent countries in Europe, assumes itself a *white* country. When further crises of identity press harder, a great number of white Americans, if tradition persists, will even proclaim a white *Christian* nation. But a recounting of the historical growth of white folk on this side of the Atlantic results not from crass finger pointing or guilt whipping. On the contrary, unveiling interracial narratives assists in revealing one of the defining characteristics of what it means to be white (and a white Christian, in particular) in the fifty states of the Union.

Here we underscore the white identity of privileging historical amnesia. From the perspective of a person of color, it is amazing to watch too many white folks believe that this is their country, they worked hard to achieve what they have achieved, they labored on their own, and they deserve to monopolize wealth, income, power, privilege, and position. In accepted commonsensical terms, America at its core privileges white democracy. And it just so happened that the descendants of Christian Europe have become the normative population and dominant religion.

In contrast to this mythology induced by memory loss, California Newsreel (www.newsreel.org) has documented the norm of affirmative action for whites supported by white churches. Personally and/or structurally, all whites have the option of benefiting from the affirmative action of white supremacy. Perhaps 99.9 percent know they benefit. Perhaps 99.9 percent choose to remain silent. For instance, in the beginning, the U.S. Constitution and the Declaration of Independence focused on whites, primarily elite white males with property. The thirteen colonies and, then, the nation, in 1787 were not founded for yellow, red, brown, and black human beings. In this history, the seventeenth century saw enslaved Africans replace European indentured servants. The latter's payoff was to accept rights, entitlements, and opportunities in the divine covenant of antiblack racism.

The 1830 Indian Removal Act, carried out by the terrorism of the white U.S. Army, committed quasi-genocide by violently "relocating" Creeks and Cherokee to the Mississippi River's western shores. The white government then helped white settlers occupy these stolen lands of red peoples. The 1862 Homestead Act solidified in public policy the reality already existing in practice. Ten percent of the U.S. land mass, or 270 million acres of land stolen from Native Americans, became private homestead areas. The 1790 Naturalization Act opened the floodgates to European immigrants who could vote, be on juries, enjoy potential office, and maintain property. In California and other states, whites passed Alien Land laws to keep Asian immigrants from ownership while allocating farm land to white growers.

After the 1865 end of slavery, instead of reparations for blacks, the white federal government paid former slave masters for the loss of their human property. Here we discover a plumb line of the heresy of white supremacy — the monopolization of material wealth crafted by God for all races. White slave masters, from 1619 to 1865, accumulated assets and privileges from unpaid black bodies. The overwhelming majority of white churches actively condoned the beating, castrating, and raping of black workers' bodies. Once the racialized, monopoly accumulation of wealth took place, it was (and continues at this very moment to be) passed down to white offspring generation after generation. The sin of Christian white supremacy is that it uses language about God, democracy, freedom of speech, assembly, etc. and all other manifestations of bourgeois theology to hide white monopolization of God's creation.

The 1935 Social Security Act guaranteed a retirement income for U.S. workers, but excluded millions of black, brown, red, and yellow Americans. So, instead of passing on wealth to their children upon retirement (and eventual death), these retiring parents of color had to draw on their children's income. In contrast, centuries of white supremacist affirmative action enabled white parents to bequeath wealth and income to their next generations.

The 1935 Wagner Act, passed by a white federal government, facilitated organizing of the white working class and excluded peoples of colors. Today, in many trades, we still have the catch-22. To get a job, a person of color has to have a union card. To have a union card, one has to be white. When whites do allow nonwhites a card, better-paying trade jobs go to those with longer seniority. Furthermore, the American Dream consists of home ownership. Yet, the Federal Housing Administration, under the New Deal, linked mortgage eligibility to race. And finally, and perhaps the most materially damaging, after roughly four centuries of affirmative action for whites, today white families own about eight times the assets (i.e., wealth) of their black counterparts.

And so, to have the authors of this volume take a stand for the Good News of mutual humanity across racial and ethnic lines brings a beacon to the possible. These white sisters and brothers are going against the entire spiritual and physical legacy of white skin privileges initiated and perpetuated since the early seventeenth century. They claim that God-talk about race is neither antiblack racism (by conservatives) or suffocating hypocrisy (by liberals). These pioneers for progress have staked out a new position — whites can claim a full humanity by redefining what it means to be white. This is a foundational idea forged by an unprecedented group of faith followers. With "mustard seed" convictions and prophetic voices, they are risking the (white) perks of this world to witness for a higher calling. This book is theoretically astute and spiritually inspiring. It enables us to see what it means to claim our own humanity by acts of love for the humanity of others.

DWIGHT N. HOPKINS
University of Chicago Divinity School

ACKNOWLEDGMENTS

FROM THE START, this book was a collaborative effort, and we have many people to thank. The editors have enjoyed an extraordinarily rich collegiality among ourselves and would like to acknowledge the shared kindness, generosity of spirit, trust, and tenacity, as well as the insight and expertise, which have made this volume possible. It has been a joy working with one another, and we have learned a great deal in the process.

We acknowledge James H. Cone for his prophetic voice and for repeatedly issuing a challenge to white theologians and ethicists to take white supremacy seriously. We also thank the Religion and Social Sciences Section of the American Academy of Religion (AAR) for the original opportunity to present our work, and especially Elizabeth M. Bounds and Dwight N. Hopkins for their roles in that effort. In addition to the volume's editors, Sally Noland Mac Nichol and Aana Marie Vigen were among the original five AAR panelists, and they deserve special recognition for their vision and inspiration from the beginning of this project and throughout its production as a volume.

There are a number of people who were critical dialogue partners with us as we discerned how best to develop the original AAR panel into this collection of essays. We are grateful to the following people for sharing their time, knowledge, and wisdom: Elizabeth M. Bounds, Patrick Cheng, James H. Cone, Ibrahim Farajajé, Mary Foulke, Dwight N. Hopkins, Ada Maria Isasi-Díaz, Sylvester A. McIntosh Johnson, Mab Segrest, and emilie m. townes. While not all of their feedback is represented in these pages, what *is* here has made the work stronger than it would have been without their help.

We are grateful also to all the contributors for providing excellent material to work with, for exploring these issues with vulnerability and truthfulness, and for their enduring commitments to make their work and scholarship powerful sites of resistance to white supremacy.

We thank Pilgrim Press for taking the risk of trusting relatively junior scholars with this important project. In particular, we thank our editor, Pamela Johnson, without whose gracious guidance this work would not have come to be.

Jennifer Harvey thanks my doctoral advisor, emilie m. townes, who consistently provides that not-always-comfortable balance of challenge and support. I thank especially my partner, Michelle Billies, for her patience and support during many arduous hours, but, even more, for being a critical, courageous, and conscientious thinker and activist in her own right. Our near-daily engagements on these issues were integral to this project.

Robin Gorsline thanks Ibrahim Farajajé, Delores S. Williams, James H. Cone, Sally Mac Nichol, Renée Hill, Mary Foulke, Kristin Klein-Cechettini, my husband, Jonathan Lebolt, and our daughters, Emily, Meg, and Robin Gorsline for their unsparing support and challenge to be the most persuasive and active anti–white supremacist I can be.

Karin Case thanks Beverly Wildung Harrison and Carol S. Robb, who introduced me to white feminist liberationist ethics; dissertation advisor emilie m. townes, who listened as I struggled to articulate issues of whiteness for the first time; Ruth Garwood, Sally Noland Mac Nichol, Teresa Delgado, and Traci C. West, who have shared their journeys with me; Philip J. Mayher, for assistance at a crucial point in writing; and especially my husband, Kevin McIntosh, for his support, encouragement, and insight and for walking this road with me daily.

DISRUPTING WHITE SUPREMACY FROM WITHIN

INTRODUCTION

JENNIFER HARVEY, KARIN A. CASE,
AND ROBIN HAWLEY GORSLINE

RECENTLY, A PASTOR CONFESSED that although communities of color compose approximately 40 percent of the city, his church almost exclusively draws congregants from white communities. A parishioner from a different congregation complained, "We have tried reaching out to people of color. They just don't seem to want to come to our church." Another pastor was told by a white congregant that he does not allow his adopted daughter — born to biracial parents — to refer to herself as "Black." "She's my daughter now," the father says. Stories like these are repeated daily by white pastors and church leaders. They are rightly the cause of much concern among leaders of both denominations and seminaries.

Despite the changes wrought by the civil rights struggles of the 1950s, '60s, and '70s, churches in the United States are still largely divided by race. This is not to say there have been no significant gains in racial justice and interracial understanding since the Civil Rights Movement, but eleven o'clock on Sunday morning remains the most racially segregated hour of the week. Moreover, white Christians continue to seem baffled by race and its significance — a state of confusion that has damaging effects as it is lived out in our personal, social, and institutional relationships. Mainline Protestant denominations have repeatedly focused on issues of racial reconciliation and pursued programs for multicultural understanding.[1] The deep racial separations that divide the Christian community as a whole,

3

however, are mere symptoms of a much more insidious and seemingly intractable problem: white supremacy.

Why does race continue to divide us? Why can't Christians, of all people, overcome the pervasive effects of racism? The contributors to this volume propose that a fundamental part of the answer to these questions lies in the unwillingness of *white* people to admit, understand, and confront the power of white supremacy in our lives.

White supremacy permeates and distorts every aspect of life. It permeates the practice and study of Christian theology and ethics, as well as the religious lives of Christian churches and the people within them. By use of the term "white supremacy" we do not mean the activities and ideologies of supremacist groups, such as the Ku Klux Klan, although these groups pose a genuine danger in the United States. Here, instead, we understand white supremacy more broadly as a system of individual, institutional, and societal racism in which whiteness — that is, "white" bodies, and cultural and social practices associated with those deemed "white" — are seen as normative and superior, and through which white people are granted advantaged status of various kinds. White supremacy has obviously had and continues to have devastating effects on peoples of colors. And, because we benefit from that which simultaneously harms others, it deeply malforms us as white people.

In the pages that follow nine white scholars wrestle with the role that white supremacy plays in our individual and communal lives; in the institutions in which we work: churches, colleges, seminaries, and social service agencies; and in our nation. We do so because we believe that until white people acknowledge our complicity in maintaining white supremacy and take responsibility for dismantling it, the racism most of us claim to oppose will maintain its stranglehold on us all. We assume that to confess and analyze this power is one step in the larger work of disrupting white supremacy's pervasiveness. We believe this is work to be pursued by those in the theological academy, and by pastors and laypeople.

We are by no means the first to claim that racism is, fundamentally, a white problem. Rather, this book is a collaborative act performed in the spirit of attempting to take responsibility in one small way in our particular contexts. Specifically, it engages in theological and ethical reflection, from a Christian liberationist perspective, on the problem of white supremacy and the relationship, role, and responsibility of white people to, in, and for it.

At the heart of our attempt is James Baldwin's counsel to white people: to "do your first works over." In Baldwin's words:

> ... to reexamine everything. Go back to where you started, or as far back as you can, examine all of it, travel your road again and tell the truth about it. Sing or shout or testify or keep it to yourself: but know whence you came.[2]

In the 1960s, during a time of great racial upheaval in the United States, Baldwin's thundering voice offered perhaps the clearest analysis of the white sickness permeating the national soul. His was a third voice, along with that of the Rev. Dr. Martin Luther King Jr. and Malcolm X, insistently and powerfully calling for racial change. The particular gift of Baldwin was his acute analysis of the *character* of white America. That his analysis — which felt to many like an indictment — was coupled with clear statements of love for white people made it all the more powerful.

Baldwin was clear that white people suffer from a racial sickness. He recognized our inability to see ourselves not only as U.S.-Americans but also, at core, as *white people*. He challenged us to overcome our inability or unwillingness to recognize that we, as white people, have created and are maintaining a deadly system to the detriment of ourselves and everyone else, and he insisted that it is *our* failure that lies at the root of our racial sickness. Baldwin was adamant that in the United States, white people, especially, must learn to understand the true history of our country and the white supremacy on which it stands. This, he claimed, was imperative work in order for us to be released from the devastating effects of white supremacy on who we are as white U.S.-Americans and to participate in creating a nation in which racial justice, rather than injustice, is the norm.

Baldwin's prophetic challenge to white U.S.-Americans informs the work we take up in this volume. Recognizing and responding to white supremacy requires that we go back to discover our racist pasts — every white person has one. We must face our well-manicured and carefully hidden places of racist feelings and attitudes that, despite our best efforts, continue to permeate our minds and shape our actions. Taking an honest inventory of our racialized lives opens new life-giving possibilities. As Baldwin knew from his years as a youthful preacher, confession is good for the soul.

Baldwin understood, however, that true redemption — to use Christian theological language — requires more than confession; people who seek salvation must change. Moreover, opposing white supremacy requires more than inward, personal change. Beyond facing our pasts and confessing our complicity in white supremacy, change means active involvement in dismantling the structures that sustain it.

White supremacy has retained its power for so long, in part, by functioning as standard operating procedure and disguising itself as the way things are "supposed to be." For white people, therefore, the process of change is usually difficult. Moreover, it requires self-examination, for which we are often poorly equipped.

Change is not a linear process, nor work to be pursued in isolation. Instead, it is a journey that unfolds over time and best takes place in the context of relationships. Each of the contributors to this book has been pushed and challenged by others. It has often been persons of colors — colleagues, friends, mentors, and role models — who have urged us first and most persistently to confront our own participation in the mechanisms of white supremacy. We write this book, then, as a part of our own processes: as white people engaging in an ongoing, ever unfinished, and never very neat process of increased awareness and commitment, and as scholars attempting to incorporate our learnings into our work. We write in the hope of providing to other white folks a resource for their journeys. Most importantly, we write as fellow sojourners on the way who have discovered that we are stronger and more resilient when the journey is shared.

HOW THIS PROJECT CAME TO BE

The inspiration for this collection of essays originated in the context of the theological academy, specifically out of the American Academy of Religion (AAR).[3] In November 2001, Dr. James H. Cone, the earliest and most influential articulator of Black liberation theology, gave a major plenary address at the AAR annual meeting in Denver, Colorado, entitled "Theology's Great Sin."[4] In his address, Cone charged that more than thirty years after the emergence of Black liberation theology, white theologians have failed, overwhelmingly, to make racism a starting point of our theological reflection.

In an attempt to respond to Cone's challenge, five junior scholars, who had been doing critical reflection and praxis-oriented scholarship on white supremacy and whiteness, composed a panel. It was entitled "Doing Our First Works Over: White Theologians and Ethicists Talk about Race," and was presented at the AAR meeting in Toronto the following year.

The collaborative and dialogical process that characterized our panel and the development of this book is methodologically critical to our praxis as scholars and activists. We have sought to embody accountability and responsibility to scholars and communities of colors and to one another as white people working for social change. This has meant speaking our truths as clearly as we are able; testing our beliefs and perceptions with a wide circle of trusted friends and colleagues; confessing the limits of our understanding; admitting when we were stuck or unsure how to proceed; and *especially* seeking input from those whose perspectives are different from our own. In these ways, we hope to move beyond the limits of our individual understanding into the broader project of liberation. These practices have not only informed the shape of this book: we also understand them to be part of the change we are trying to create. We describe in some detail, therefore, the processes and considerations that determined the present shape of this project.

When Pilgrim Press approached us to consider developing the work of the panel into a book, we were excited, in part, because of our passionate desire to instigate change in a white supremacist world. We were eager to address such important matters from within, and in response to, the churches and academic institutions in which we live and work. In part, we were drawn to this project because each of us knows that the journey of seeking to stand against (and trying to figure out *how* to stand against) the very systems that insulate and unjustly benefit us is perplexing at best. While each of us has come to this point in our lives from different places, we recognize that sharing what we have learned and are continuing to learn as white people seeking to live an anti-racist praxis is one way to contribute to disrupting white supremacy. We are confident that many white Christians committed to working for racial justice are yearning for companionship along the way.

Given the nature of Cone's challenge, responding to his call initially as a group of white scholars seemed a straightforward choice. However, with the opportunity to publish a book came more difficult questions about the nature of the volume. Should it remain a collection of works by white scholars or be developed into a multiracial work on whiteness and white supremacy? As the original panelists began to conceptualize a larger project beyond the scope of the original panel, we saw the need for a volume in which white people address white supremacy and its impact on our lives. We also wrestled, however, with the limitations and dangers of such a volume.

First, the larger work of speaking truth to power from within the beast of white supremacy needs to be recognized as a *multiracial* endeavor. Each of us comes to the work of social change with particular insights and passions and from distinct social locations. Disrupting white supremacy is necessarily a coalitional project. All of our energies and perspectives are needed to build the vision and sustain the practices necessary to do so. Moreover, we are indebted to persons of every race and through many generations who have dared to speak and act on their convictions. As white people, however, we are especially indebted to the sustained efforts of peoples of colors in the struggle for liberation. Indeed, most of the contributors to this volume have come of age as scholars challenged and nurtured by movements among Black, Latina feminist, and womanist activists and scholars in the United States, and liberation activists and scholars from around the globe. This indebtedness must be consistently acknowledged.

Second, we understand that as white persons, we are insulated from the harshest impacts of white supremacy. Thus, we often understand its pervasiveness, function, and urgency the least. We take Kathleen Neal Cleaver's critique of white feminists seriously. Cleaver challenges, "[N]o one can speak truth to power until they know what is true."[5] Not only does our insulation produce a flawed understanding, it sometimes means that even in our best attempts to engage in anti-racist analysis and praxis, we may unwittingly reinscribe the very things we claim to oppose. Each of these issues is of utmost concern in the venture of publishing a book of this nature.

Amid these concerns, however, we also recognize that peoples of colors have *long* done their part in this multiracial endeavor to disrupt white supremacy. In addition to living vital resistance, they have told white people over and over, and with increasing precision and moral urgency, for more than two hundred years what it is like to live under this system of domination. They have repeatedly showed us the ways in which we remain complicit. Scholars of colors have engaged this project in their intellectual work, while repeating the call for white responsibility in terms similar to Baldwin and Cone.

Meanwhile, on the whole, those of us who are white have not yet done the work necessary to enable our genuine and sustained participation in dismantling white supremacy. We have not confessed its impact on our souls, acknowledged its devastating effects on peoples of colors, nor taken our own steps to abolish it. These are moral and practical prerequisites for relationships of solidarity with peoples of colors.

We bore all of this in mind as we discerned the appropriate contours of this phase of our participation, as white theologians and ethicists, in the multiracial project of disrupting white supremacy. In our discernment, we initiated conversations regarding the nature of this volume with numerous colleagues, and particularly with colleagues who are engaged in liberationist-oriented intellectual work as scholars of colors. We asked specific questions about what kinds of work would be most useful from white theologians and ethicists at this time, and whether and how the racial identities of the contributors should matter. The responses we received varied, but, overwhelmingly we heard reiterated the continuing need for white scholars to do our own work on whiteness and white supremacy as one step toward creating the conditions under which we might come together in genuine multiracial dialogue, coalition, and solidarity.

It became clear to us, therefore, that despite the inherent limitations and potential pitfalls of a volume of white voices, the immediate and pressing project before us was to respond to white supremacy out of our specific social locations as white people. Ultimately we determined that the shape of this book should remain consistent with the nature of its origins: a response to a critical moment in the theological academy, in which persons of colors once again said that white folks must speak.

This is a volume, then, in which white theologians and ethicists, pastors, activists, and scholars analyze white supremacy *from the precise points* at which our bodies are socially located. Social transformation is wrought through concrete actions, commonly through communities of people working together over the long haul, but the work of justice can only be sustained where there is vision. Good social theory, or critical analysis, helps us understand the roots of the problem and can indicate the types of action that may be effective.

The critical analysis of white supremacy contained in this book, we hope, makes one contribution to such understanding. No book, of course, will eliminate white supremacy, yet breaking the relative silence by white people remains an important step, and one that needs to happen again and again until the silence is no more.

LIBERATION THEOLOGY AND ITS CHALLENGES FOR WHITE THEOLOGIANS AND ETHICISTS

Cone's indictment of white theology and ethics contains several insights critical to the effort to undermine white supremacy from within. Two of these inform the major theoretical agenda of this book as a whole, which is variously pursued in the individual chapters. First, white supremacy pervades the theological enterprise. As such, it distorts the work of (white) theologians and ethicists who fail to take it seriously as a starting point. Second, in order to take white supremacy seriously as a starting point — to address it honestly and fully — white theologians and ethicists must attend overtly to our social location as white people.

A basic tenet of liberation theology is the recognition that human oppression and injustice have ontological significance. This significance rarely is taken seriously by the oppressor. Moreover, the mechanisms of white supremacy encourage white people to perceive it as normal and assume we are the norm. We are, thus, particularly prone to assuming that white reality is the *only* reality, and that the differing experiences and perspectives of others are unconnected to our own. This allows us to maintain an oppressive system while denying complicity in its operation.

For liberation theologians and ethicists, all talk about God is interested talk. A fundamental question for liberationists is, therefore, in *whose* interest is God-talk being pursued? Theologians from many communities — Black, womanist, feminist, Latin American, Asian, African — have been working for decades to engage in God-talk that privileges overtly the experience of the oppressed in order to create theologies that reject the pernicious effects of dominant theology done in the interest of the oppressor and to articulate theologies *interested* in justice and liberation. However, white theologians and ethicists have rarely undertaken parallel work, examining our experiences in order to discern how the theology we write is in the interest of the status quo (namely, white dominance) and how it damages not only these others but also ourselves.

Fundamental issues of how knowing, thinking, believing, and living are organized — questions of epistemology, hermeneutics, and praxis — are implicated in the maintenance of white supremacy. White supremacy permeates theological and ethical reflection done by white people, not because we ascribe to overtly racist beliefs, but because white supremacy, in its institutional and social forms, structures how we think, know, and live. This does not mean white people should not be writing theology or reflecting ethically. Rather, it means we must ground our work self-consciously in the reality of white supremacy and in the struggle to overcome it. Critical engagement with epistemology, hermeneutics, and praxis must attend both to the impact of white supremacy on our lives and to what is required to dismantle it. White theologians and ethicists too must undertake *interested* God-talk; our God-talk must include critical self-reflection on our connections with, and contributions to, oppressive power.

One major task of this volume, therefore, is the attempt to begin with racism; to make our relationship as white people to white supremacy an overt starting point for theological and ethical reflection. Several of the chapters in this book address racism issues in more detail. Robin Gorsline analyzes the pervasiveness of white normativity in (white) theology. Karin Case examines how the distortions in white peoples' self-perceptions are implicit to the way white supremacy is structured and sustained. Becky Thompson, Aana Vigen, and Sharon Welch each address issues of praxis in the context of taking seriously dominant social location and our connections to oppressive power.

Second, as liberation theologians and ethicists have insisted on the ontological significance of oppression and justice, they, along with scholars in other disciplines, have constructed epistemological frameworks through which difference and particularity are the starting points for theory. These frameworks take issue with discourses that presume to articulate justice in universal terms and by way of abstract principles. They are suspicious of claims to "objective" truths.

For example, in *Black Womanist Ethics,* Katie G. Cannon demonstrates that the presumedly universal "virtues" espoused by dominant ethics — "self-reliance, frugality and industry" — obscure the social truth that no matter how much peoples of colors might embody such qualities, they will not, in a racially subordinating landscape, attain economic equality. And, besides being behaviors compelled by capitalism, the methodological choice to valorize such "virtues" results in the abjection of real communities if and when they do not conform to such ideals.[6] Cannon's response is to construct a methodology for ethics that "starts with experience instead of with theories of values or norms."[7]

The epistemological and methodological shift toward privileging particularity and experience (both individual and communal) poses a challenge for members of dominant groups. How can the particularity of our lived experience as members of dominant groups illuminate and further the project of human liberation? A partial answer is that we must consider all the facets of our social location as we are always manifoldly located selves. We are impacted by complex matrices of privileges and exclusions, and trajectories of power. Laurel Schneider and Elizabeth Bounds explore the complexities of race, sex, and gender, and race and class, respectively, in order to analyze the complicated ways in which oppressive power dynamics intersect in our identities.

Still, the dominant aspects of social locations create an epistemological conundrum. White feminists, for example, have grounded their theory and praxis in the experience of being female in a patriarchal order. And, after decades of being challenged by feminists of colors, white feminists increasingly have understood the imperative of specifying their racial location. But what does such specification mean? Is naming the particularity of being a white feminist a claim to be just another voice in a diverse multicultural mix that includes Native American and Latina feminists? Is it a confession about one's racial status in a white supremacist social order? Or does it delimit the breadth of one's truth claims?

The implications of these questions are demonstrated in the dialogical space between womanist and feminist ethicists. Womanists locate themselves in the particularities of Black women's experiences. Moreover, inherent in the very identification "womanist" is a critique of "feminist," which, at worst, represents a falsely universalized "we," or essentializes "white" into woman. In this context, "white" remains the unspoken norm whenever the "feminist" is invoked without white particularity being named. Obviously, however, it is not the case that white feminists should ground themselves in the epistemologies, culture, and politics of *white* hegemony. So, what does particularizing white racial identity mean? This problematic exists because of the real impact of being socially located in a position of dominance in an unjust social order. In this sense, "being white" in a white supremacist order must be scrutinized as part of the work of considering our role in and responsibility for disrupting white supremacy.

Those of us who are white cannot simply decry racial injustice in our theology and ethics without locating such denunciations in the particularities of what it means for us to be white in the U.S. social order and amid its global manifestations. Rather than affirmation of a "universal" theological imperative for justice, critical interrogation of our social location itself is an intrinsic part of the work of taking white supremacy seriously as white scholars. This interrogation is a second task of this book. As Karin Case suggests, one aspect of taking seriously the urgent questions raised in the preceding example is clarity about what "white" means, what "white" is, and what being white has to do with white supremacy. Jennifer Harvey takes up this task by engaging the construction of white as a racial category through historical analysis in order to make an ethical argument about political and moral transformation of white communities.

THEORETICAL FRAMEWORK: SOCIAL CONSTRUCTION

Because white theologians and ethicists have largely failed to take white supremacy seriously as a point of departure in our theorizing, the critical frameworks necessary to interrogate white social location and white supremacy in our fields of Christian religious studies are underdeveloped. In the last decade, theoretical frameworks essential for critical scrutiny of race, racism, and whiteness have been substantially more developed in other scholarly fields including history, sociology, psychology, educational theory, African and African American studies, and critical race theory. The emergent critical consensus is that race is a social construction, and these disciplines have explored in various ways the processes by which race and whiteness, in particular, are constituted.

Rather than assuming that race is something natural, biological, fixed, or essential, therefore, this volume operates within a theoretical framework of constructionism. Race may be evident to the eye, but there is no DNA, no genetic marker, no fixed or predictable "difference" that can be employed legitimately to categorize persons according to race. Indeed, the insistence that race *is* essential has played an intrinsic part in white supremacist claims about various racial groups. For example, according to Reginald Horsman, during colonization of what became the United States, English colonists first articulated their political "destiny" — namely, the reasons they were "entitled" to take Indigenous peoples' lands and commit genocide — through notions of being God's chosen people. From the Revolutionary War forward, this sense of destiny became expressed in racialized terms and legitimized through (pseudo-)biology. Because they were "anxious to justify the enslavement of the blacks and the expulsion and possible extermination of the Indians," writes Horsman, "the

American intellectual community... fed European racial appetites with scientific theories stemming from the supposed knowledge and observation of blacks and Indians."[8] Observation of "others" was accompanied by (mythological) notions of white Americans' descent from an ancient and eminent "Anglo-Saxon" political heritage, and claims for "a distinct 'American' race, composed of the best Caucasian strains."[9] Biological essentialism thus has been the ideological grease of white supremacy's wheels and has led to all kinds of social atrocities.

In the twentieth century, biological notions of race were thoroughly discredited in the sciences and other scholarly disciplines.[10] The focus has shifted greatly to recognizing and studying race as a social and political reality. Various attributes of human physicality have been *given* meanings, and race, in the process, becomes recognizable, through being referenced in the sociopolitical realm.

In the context of a white supremacist social order, human differences are given both ideologically supremacist meanings and concrete material meanings. For example, when the book *The Bell Curve* purported to make claims about "natural" differences in intelligence among racial groups, in fact it was making ideologically supremacist claims of what it "means" to be white, Black, or Latino/a.[11] In addition, unjust economic and political processes (many of which employ the kinds of ideological supremacy just noted) result in real entrenched disparities in wealth and income between white peoples and peoples of colors. Thus, both ideological supremacist meanings and concrete material meanings reference bodies and co-construct race.

Ian Haney López gives this helpful definition:

> ...race must be understood as a *sui generis* social phenomenon in which contested systems of meaning serve as the connections between physical features, faces, and personal characteristics. In other words, social meanings connect our faces to our souls. Race is neither an essence nor an illusion, but rather an ongoing, contradictory, self-reinforcing, plastic process subject to

the macro forces of social and political struggle and the micro effects of daily decisions.[12]

In short, the theoretical framework of this volume includes recognition that people are categorized racially in the interest of various social and political projects.[13] Thus, for example, when we say "white" we do not evoke either a positivistic or an essential sense of the term. Instead, because white supremacy is the structure within which racial categorizing is done, we recognize that how race is understood in theory is of great importance, and that the various meanings of racial constructs and processes by which they are produced are intrinsically important sites of inquiry. Moreover, individuals and communities have lived and continue to live various agencies in response to the processes that construct race. Such agency is, itself, imperative to keep in view as it testifies to the power of resistance to disrupt white supremacy and is part of the heritage and social memory out of which anti-racist praxis in the future must continue to emerge.

Each of these implications for operating out of a constructivist framework will be touched upon in turn. Jennifer Harvey pursues in more detail the implications and dangers of theorizing race as a social construct. Laurel Schneider and Elizabeth Bounds investigate crucial facets of the processes through which race is constructed: sex/gender and economics. Sally Mac Nichol insists on the importance of remembering and recounting the histories of those who have lived as powerful and resistant anti-racist agents from the site of white identity.

LANGUAGE AND THEORY

For the sake of clarity, it is important to establish working definitions for the terms the reader will encounter throughout this book, and the operating assumptions that inform them. There may be nuances in how each author uses particular terminology, but the working definitions we provide here are generally shared by the authors of individual chapters.

Peoples of Colors and White People(s)

Because U.S. social reality is thoroughly racialized in both its construction and practice, it is necessary to use racial labels to describe it, as well as the social locations and experiences of people who inhabit this world. Using racial categorizations and identifications is also essential for describing, with precision, the axes along which white supremacy functions. At the same time, just as the construct "race" arises within the context of white supremacy, so also does the language used to describe racial groups. It is a challenge, therefore, to use racial terms without evoking or reinscribing domination.

Throughout this volume, we strive to use language that has descriptive clarity and illuminates the dynamics of white supremacy, while honoring the rights of persons to name themselves. Racial designations can serve many purposes. Sometimes they reflect the processes of domination — as when powerful groups exercise control through naming "others." Conversely, racial categories and labels may be deployed in the processes of resistance and struggle — as when oppressed peoples name themselves or redefine names they have been given. Racial labels reflect complex patterns of domination and struggle.

In this volume we use the term *white people(s)* to refer to those who are accorded white advantage in U.S. society — usually, but not always, persons of European ancestry. This category is intended as a description of social location within the system of white supremacy and is not intended to describe innate, biological, essential, or fixed characteristics of persons. The term *peoples of colors* is used to refer collectively to those who are targeted by the system of white supremacy — usually, but not always, persons of African, Latin American, Asian, and Native American ancestry. These collective labels are not meant to erase the significant differences in culture and history between and within diverse groups, nor to refer to innate, biological, essential, or fixed characteristics of persons.

Like the term *white,* the term *peoples of colors* is intended to evoke the social context of white supremacy, in which persons are situated and rewarded differentially along a binary axis of white/ not-white. We find such language to be necessary for scrutinizing white supremacy's actual function — namely, white supremacy variously advantages white people(s) while it disadvantages those who are not white. At the same time, we recognize that use of such a binary runs the risk of reifying it conceptually — namely, creating a kind of "white/other" paradigm — that runs absolutely counter to our intent. Our use of the plural nouns (peoples) and adjectives (colors), is, thus, an attempt both to honor the diversity within this theoretical grouping as well as to avoid reifying white/nonwhite as much as possible.

We have attempted in our analysis to avoid theorizing that reinforces the white/Black dualism toward which much racial analysis in the United States tends. Because race is a sociopolitical reality, racial formations in the United States are continually changing. Virulent anti-immigrant policies and ideologies, for example, are a particularly pernicious manifestation of white supremacy: part of the dominant white/nonwhite racialization process, as well as revelatory of how deeply notions of whiteness are bound up with what it means to be U.S.-American. To theorize in terms of a racial dualism blurs needed theoretical clarity about how multifaceted and complex white supremacy is. More importantly, it threatens to erase the shared and distinct experiences with white supremacy among South Asian, Latino/a, East Asian, Native American, Pacific Islander, and many other communities.

At the same time, there are reasons that analyses in the United States tend toward a white/Black dualism, which are important to understanding the particular power of white supremacy here. Because the enslavement of African peoples was a deep part of U.S. national formation and Jim Crow a *very* recently legally sanctioned system of racial stratification, the Black/white bifurcation in U.S. society remains particularly potent. This bifurcation affects language. For example, as editors of this volume, we decided that the word "white," when referring to white people, would not be capitalized, while the word "Black," when referring to African Americans, would. We did so because we believe that people of African descent have made the "black" created by white supremacy into a resistant, lively, and creative identity, while people of European descent have not done so in regards to our "whiteness." In this regard Black and white are not parallel, and thus representing them differently in language is appropriate. At the same time, there is no one right way to decide these questions and any choice creates other problems. Thus, Elizabeth Bounds and Laurel Schneider urged that neither "white" nor "black" be capitalized — or, that both be. They did so because they understand both terms as social constructions, constructions that condense a complex and problematic — and interrelated — history. Capitalizing either term risks masking this construction, and thus obscuring this history, by seeming to refer to an actual color or racial essence. This conversation helps us, as white people, to better understand our personal racial and social locations as they are affected by white supremacy, and to make thoughtful choices about naming ourselves and others.

Our sense is that the ongoing powerful role of "color" in U.S.-American life, as it pertains to African American communities and growing out of this history, remains a fraught issue requiring careful consideration within analysis of white supremacy. Moreover, our experience has been that white people are sometimes more willing to engage in dialogue about racial issues in relation to non–African American communities than about those that arise from our national history involving African Americans. Indeed, we are sometimes more quick to speak about the dangers of not reifying a binary racial analysis than we are to speak about our own relationship to white supremacy. All of these issues remain important in work analyzing white supremacy, even if they seem to lend themselves toward binary theorizing.

As important here, the genocide and colonization of Native peoples is equally formative of U.S. national origins. It has been (to non-Native peoples) a less "visible" force in structuring racialized life in the United States because of the mechanisms by which white supremacy and U.S. imperialism pursued Native American subjugation: namely, though genocidal policies and forced assimilation. Moreover, this invisibility — which works in the interest of white supremacy — in relation to Native peoples, and the subsequent nonrecognition of the implicated relationship between white U.S.-Americans and Native Americans, has also created a situation in which the relationship of Native peoples to processes of racialization remains undertheorized.[14] These forms of domination further demonstrate the importance of theoretical clarity about how white supremacy works in relation to differently racialized groups, as well as speaking to the importance of history in all analysis that engages white supremacy in the United States.

We cannot and do not address all of these complex issues in relation to language and theory in this volume. However, language issues need to be kept visible because we are aware, and the reader should be aware, of the various urgent issues that the use of language creates, obscures, helps, and perpetuates in terms of domination and resistance. We recognize that theory is limited, that even the best cannot capture nor make sense of all realities. At the same time, we believe that maintaining a keen awareness of theoretical issues is a vital part of the effort to end white supremacy. A central point of theory — that we hope is evident at various points in this book — is that whiteness is not monolithic. Tremendous variation in culture, ethnicity, class, and experiences is represented within the category "white." However, in our effort to conceptualize across a broad spectrum, it seems unavoidable that at times this term, like others, will be made to appear more fixed than it is. We have tried to be aware of our own situational biases and to correct for them, but inevitably such efforts fall short.

White Supremacy and Racism

We use the term "white supremacy" throughout this volume to refer to the dominant form of racism in the United States, and we do so with great intentionality. bell hooks has persuasively argued that white supremacy is a better expression of the exploitation of peoples of colors than "racism" because it overtly names the link between the discriminations of racism and the privileges held by whites (including the privilege to ignore our own race).[15] Moreover, white supremacy names an integrated system of individual, institutional, societal, and civilizational racism in which whiteness — "white" bodies, "white" persons, cultural and societal practices associated with those deemed "white" — is seen as normative and superior. In a system of white supremacy, whiteness relates to being granted advantaged status, while persons seen as not-white are perceived as deviant or inferior, and commonly denied access to the opportunities and resources that similarly situated "white" persons are granted.

Another assumption that informs the theoretical framework of this book is that white supremacy is *saturating*. It affects us at every level of social organization, from the most intimate family unit to the largest nation-state and multinational corporation. As a system, white supremacy involves concrete material practices and elaborate systems of symbolism and signification which privilege whiteness. Material practices and symbolic representation act simultaneously and in mutually reinforcing ways to produce and maintain white power, white normativity, and white dominance.

For example, language, metaphor, literature, film, and other forms of visual, verbal, and nonverbal symbol systems in the United States often present "darkness" (and all things not-white) as deviant, evil, inferior, suspect, imperfect, ugly, or dirty. Simultaneously, whiteness is co-constructed as pure, desirable, normative, good, beautiful, trustworthy, or clean.[16] Such symbol systems and significations deeply shape and form social consciousness. While inequality is established through material practices, often including force and violence, and supported by the legal codes, all of these mechanisms are reinforced and even encouraged by white supremacist conditioning of our consciousness.

Many well-intentioned white people find it difficult to understand how we are implicated in the system of white supremacy, since we do not consciously or intentionally discriminate against anyone. It is important to emphasize that white supremacy is pervasive, systemic, and multifaceted. It is so permeating that we all participate in it: no white person is exempt. White supremacy functions on at least five distinct and interrelated levels, described cogently in the work of James Scheurich and Michelle Young. Scheurich and Young identify these levels as: *covert* (individual), *overt* (individual), *institutional, societal,* and *civilizational* racism. Both overt and covert racism function at the level of individual attitudes and behaviors and have, at their core, prejudiced beliefs. *Covert racism* is not expressed in public, while *overt racism* "is a public, conscious, and intended act by a person or persons of one race with the intent of doing damage to a person or persons of another race."[17]

Both *institutional racism* and *societal racism* function at the level of social and organizational structures. They are encoded and embedded in the norms and practices of entire organizations and segments of society. Scheurich and Young specify:

> Institutional racism exists when institutions or organizations . . . have standard operating procedures (intended or unintended) that hurt members of one or more races in relation to members of the dominant race. Institutional racism also exists when institutional or organizational cultures, rules, habits, or symbols have the same biasing effect.[18]

Societal racism is similar, but exists on a broader scale. It occurs when "prevailing societal or cultural assumptions, norms, concepts, habits, expectations, etc. favor one race over one or more other races."[19]

Institutional and societal forms of racism tend to be much less visible to members of the dominant group, often appearing to be "natural" or inevitable.[20] Perceiving the bias inherent in our own norms and practices requires concerted effort to make visible white norms so that they can be seen as socially constructed, contingent, and mutable.

Civilizational racism occurs on the level of our broadest and most normative assumptions — assumptions that "construct the world and our experience of it," and are so deeply embedded as to be customarily unconscious to most members of a civilization.[21] These include how we know, how we perceive and name the world, and what counts as "real." Dominant groups commonly project themselves and their set of assumptions onto all of society and, in fact, all of "reality." As philosopher Sandra Harding observes, the beliefs and practices of *civilizational racism* "are the most difficult to identify because they structure and give meaning to such apparently seamless expanses of history, common sense, and daily life that it is hard for members of such 'civilizations' even to imagine taking a position that is outside them."[22]

All five aspects of white supremacy interact dynamically and reinforce one another in complex ways. In general terms, the contributors to this volume see the systemic and structural forms as primary. The emphasis of this volume, thus, is on analysis of *institutional, societal,* and *civilizational* racism. Individuals can and must take concrete action to resist these totalizing systems, and the chapters in these books include work that tries to suggest some ways in which we may do so.

Still, the macro level of white supremacy always affects us acutely on the personal level. The recognition that none of us is able to escape the larger systemic operations of white supremacy has two major implications. First, even as we take responsibility for how we think and act personally, the structural and systemic levels remain operative; this reality lends greater urgency to institutional, societal, and civilizational racism. Second, how we see, think, and act deeply impacts our abilities to resist and challenge racism at the structural and systemic level; this reality makes attention to the individual (covert and overt) learnings about race and racism very important as well. Throughout this volume, then, various contributors focus on the complex interplay between personal and communal formation within, and structural manifestations of, white supremacy. Thus, for example, Robin Gorsline engages the institutional and civilizational aspect of racism in addressing the white supremacy inherent to the theological enterprise. Karin Case gives attention to the ways in which institutional, societal, and civilizational racism deeply form resultant self-understandings of white people. Becky Thompson explores the imbrication of white supremacist phenomena of U.S. colonialism and imperialism with the experience and expectation of white privilege among individuals. Aana Vigen articulates elements needed to mitigate the pervasive effects of individual and societal racism in engagements between white peoples and peoples of colors. Sharon Welch describes pedagogical practices in the classroom that can assist in making people more aware of and self-conscious about the impact of all of these levels of racism for teaching.

INTERSTRUCTURED SYSTEMS OF DOMINATION

Given the many possible theoretical approaches to analyzing systems of oppression and domination, we note here two additional assumptions about white supremacy that are key to our analysis. First, white supremacy has its own etiology and internal logic. Second, white supremacy interlocks with other systems of domination to reinforce itself and create complex patterns of benefit and exclusion.[23] It is important to maintain clarity about both of these dynamics, because analysis of how white supremacy functions generates specific strategies for change. It is equally important to understand the complex interplay of these systems with each other, for they compound each others' effects, creating deeper and more enduring structures of benefit and exclusion.[24]

Principal systems of domination in addition to white supremacy include patriarchy, capitalism, and colonialism as well as the related systems of heterosexism, Eurocentrism, able-bodyism, and the like. The genesis of each system and the particular ways in which they are related to each other are matters of considerable debate among theorists. For the purposes of this collection, we claim that white supremacy is a powerful force in its own right, not something which is merely derived from another form of oppression. If we were to completely do away with patriarchy, colonialism, or economic oppression in society, white supremacy would still exist. At the same time, white supremacy is so completely interstructured with other forms of oppression that disrupting any one system has repercussions for the others and, in fact, it would be impossible to eradicate one without eradicating the others.

The historical development and contemporary manifestations of white supremacy are shaped by other systems of benefit and exclusion: White supremacy in the U.S. context takes its particular form because of and through the history of European colonial conquest, our particular brand of capitalist economy, and the pervasiveness of patriarchy. All of these dynamics are complexly interwoven, resulting in interstructured systems of domination.[25]

Each system is analytically distinct and possesses its own peculiar dynamics, yet each is intimately connected with the dynamics of other forms of oppression. By way of illustration, we might consider the effects of white supremacy in the lives of a wealthy African American man, a middle-class Chinese American woman, and a working-poor white woman. In the case of the African American man, for example, the "advantages" afforded by class privilege and gender privilege may act as somewhat of a buffer to the harshest effects of white supremacy. In the other cases, two or more systems of domination (racism and patriarchy for the Chinese American woman; capitalism and patriarchy for the white woman) coincide to compound oppression. Patterns of colonial conquest, economic exploitation, and the privileges and exclusions of patriarchy affect each of these individuals in distinct and related ways, yet the way in which their "race" is constructed and perceived by others remains salient.

PROMISES AND DANGERS OF THE PROJECT

As we have indicated throughout this introduction, and as identified in many of the chapters within the book, serious impediments — of our own making — have long existed to white people practicing liberative ways of being in and with multiracial communities. The analysis in this book, we hope, contributes to developing needed understandings and methods for critical self-reflection by white people that might make our ways of being, acting, thinking, and speaking more likely to facilitate our participation in challenging white supremacy, alongside the communities who have done so for so long.

The decision to proceed with a collection of works by *white* scholars takes seriously the need for transformative anti-racist analysis and praxis by those very persons who benefit from white supremacy. Significantly, it claims white social location as a site of resistance to racism. This is one important promise of an anti–white supremacy project, constructed from the particularity of white scholars' racial location.

Still, to publish such a collection creates several salient problematics, many of which have already been articulated. As we close, we note several issues about which we urge the reader, of whatever racial identity, to remain attentive. These issues are salient as she or he explores the pages of this book, and as she or he considers what the analyses herein may (or may not) portend for her or his own ongoing life praxis in relation to white supremacy.

First, white peoples' efforts to dismantle white supremacy are always accountable to and forged in conversation and coalition with peoples of colors. Even though this project has attempted to embody such processes and commitments explicitly, it is inevitable that this work is limited precisely because it is a work by white scholars. The very promise of such a volume — a response to the moral urgency of white people taking on white supremacy — is inextricable from a danger inherent to it — that our understandings are flawed. The various analyses in this text make clear that our particular social location means that inherent to the work of resistance is the difficult attempt to recognize distortions in our own understanding. Yet, the very nature of such a situation renders such a process, including that which has created this book, ever incomplete and imperfect.

Second, our opportunity to publish and the chance that we will be taken seriously — *perhaps* more seriously than scholars of colors (though sometimes scholars of colors are cast as experts on race, while being proscribed from being authorities on anything else!) — are inextricably bound up in white privilege. Moreover, as the white-dominated publishing industry increasingly valorizes work on whiteness, there is the constant danger that a focus on *whiteness* may become merely solipsistic and abstract, rather than part of a genuine effort to disrupt *white supremacy* and transform society.

Finally, a volume that contains white voices alone runs the risk of reproducing a tendency endemic to white supremacy: namely that white folks presume that we can set the agenda and act autonomously, independent of the perspectives and agendas articulated by communities of colors. The challenge for white people is to be responsible for doing our own work (and not to ask peoples of colors to do it for us or to depend on others to identify what our work must be). Simultaneously, we must be receptive and responsive listeners, so that we do not proceed simply from our own agendas, which inevitably will be imbued with self-interest as well as the distortions of understanding caused by white supremacy.

Discourse about racism by white people remains, especially among white Christians, overwhelmingly concerned with reconciliation and "inclusion," and, especially among white theologians and ethicists, is characterized by too quick and too abstract a call to solidarity. Peoples of colors have stated unambiguously that repentance and reparations precede reconciliation and that solidarity is anything but a self-evident possibility. The tasks facing peoples of colors and white people in resisting white supremacy are different. A major critical task facing us, as white people, is to engage in repentance and reparations that help create discursive and material conditions from which a deeper multiracial dialogue and solidarity can emerge. One promise of this project, then, is that by addressing the issues we explore in this volume, we will help identify routes through which we, as white people, can more honestly and honorably join in a desperately needed dialogue among ourselves and with peoples of colors in order to create new forms of action and solidarity against white supremacy.

The work we as white people have before us to overcome the immoral and unjust conditions that keep us separated from peoples of colors is substantial and particular. We approach the way ahead committed to creating the change necessary to undo these conditions, but we proceed with humility, recognizing the enormity of the task before us, as well as the risks to all peoples should we fail.

NOTES

1. Many Protestant denominations have created church-based curricula focusing on issues of race. See, for example: United Church of Christ, *A New Church/ A New World: A Racial Justice Resource of the United Church Board for Homeland Ministries–Division of the American Missionary Association* (Cleveland: United Church of Christ, n.d.). Careful study of these resources would be necessary to assess how effectively they teach about issues of white supremacy. In any case these curricula are not systematically implemented and, therefore, may have little effect on the established culture and structure of these denominations. A number of individual denominations, most often as a result of advocacy by communities of color within the denomination, have adopted various formal resolutions in subsequent decades, however, which denounce racism, apologize for historical racial atrocities (such as slavery), as well as offering concrete recommendations for structural change. Also, see the National Council of Churches of Christ in the U.S.A., *Policy Statement: On Racial Justice* (New York: National Council of Churches, 1984).

2. James Baldwin, "Introduction," *The Price of the Ticket: Collected Nonfiction, 1948–1985* (New York: St. Martin's/Marek, 1985), xix.

3. The American Academy of Religion (AAR) is the principal professional organization for scholars and teachers in the fields of religious studies and theology. The annual meeting of the AAR, usually attended by more than seven thousand scholars in religion and theology, is significant not only for its impact on scholarly thought, but also because it directly impacts the teaching of religion and theology in colleges, universities, and seminaries where pastors are trained.

4. Cone's influential career began with the publication, in 1969, of *Black Theology and Black Power.* His extensive publications and dedicated teaching since then have had a major impact on the development of Black liberation theology, and other liberation theologies in the United States and in the Two-Thirds World. The lecture at

the AAR can be found in James H. Cone, "Theology's Great Sin: Silence in the Face of White Supremacy," *Union Seminary Quarterly Review 55*, no. 3–4 (2001): 1–15.

5. Kathleen Neal Cleaver, "Racism, Civil Rights, and Feminism," in *Critical Race Feminism: A Reader,* ed. Adrien Wing (New York and London: New York University Press, 1997), 40.

6. Specifically, she writes that the assumptions contained in the values with which traditional Protestant ethics begin ultimately imply that the Black community is "either immoral or amoral" rather than that the integrity or truth of the ethical categories should be subject to question. Katie G. Cannon, *Black Womanist Ethics* (Atlanta: Scholars Press, 1988), 2.

7. Ibid., 5.

8. Reginald Horsman, "Race and Manifest Destiny: The Origins of American Racial Anglo-Saxonism," in *Critical White Studies: Looking Behind the Mirror,* ed. Richard Delgado and Jean Stefancic (Philadelphia: Temple University Press, 1997), 140.

9. Ibid.

10. After World War II, as a response to the atrocities of the Nazis, social scientists and biologists from across the globe gathered in 1949, 1951, 1964, and 1967 "to disprove the claims of racial science.... They concluded: 'For all practical purposes "race" is not so much a biological phenomenon as a social myth. The myth of "race" has created an enormous amount of human and social damage.'" Kenan Malik, *The Meaning of Race: Race, History and Culture in Western Society* (New York: New York University Press, 1996), 15.

11. Richard J. Herrnstein and Charles Murray, *The Bell Curve: Intelligence and Class Structure in American Life* (New York: Free Press, 1994).

12. Ian Haney López, "The Social Construction of Race," in *Critical Race Theory: The Cutting Edge,* 2nd ed., ed. Richard Delgado and Jean Stefancic (Philadelphia: Temple University Press, 2000), 165.

13. Michael Omi and Howard Winant call this phenomenon "racial formation projects." See Michael Omi and Howard Winant, *Racial Formation in the United States: From the 1960s to the 1990s,* 2nd ed. (New York: Routledge, 1994), 56.

14. A point made by Dr. Andrea Smith, in conversation with one of the authors of this chapter, on May 13, 2003.

15. bell hooks, quoted in Trina Grillo and Stephanie M. Wildman, "Obscuring the Importance of Race: The Implication of Making Comparisons between Racism and Sexism (or Other Isms)," in *Critical Race Feminism,* 45.

16. See Toni Morrison, *Playing in the Dark: Whiteness and the Literary Imagination* (New York: Random House, Vintage Books, 1992), for an important treatment of this subject.

17. James Joseph Scheurich and Michelle D. Young, "Coloring Epistemologies: Are Our Research Epistemologies Racially Biased?" *Educational Researcher 26,* no. 3 (1997): 5.

18. "For example, if an institution's procedures or culture favor Whites for promotion, such as promotion to full professorship...[or] If a school's standard pedagogical method is culturally congruent with the culture of White students but not with the cultures of students of color." Ibid.

19. For example, "if the socially promoted idea — through the media, through legal practices, through government programs — of what a good family is, is primarily drawn from the dominant culture's social, historical experience, that is societal racism." Ibid., 6.

20. Social arrangements which appear to members of the dominant group to be "natural" are often erroneously attributed the status of scientific truth. The most extreme form of this is biological determinism that appears repeatedly as a way of justifying the superior social status of "white" people.

21. Scheurich and Young, "Coloring," 7. Here Scheurich and Young are following Michel Foucault (they cite *Discipline and Punish: The Birth of the Prison,* trans. Alan Sheridan [New York: Vintage Books, 1979] and *Madness and Civilization: The History of Insanity in the Age of Reason,* trans. Richard Howard [New York: Vintage Books, 1965]) and Edward Said (*Orientalism* [New York: Vintage Books, 1978]).

22. Sandra Harding, *Is Science Multicultural? Postcolonialisms, Feminisms, and Epistemologies* (Bloomington: Indiana University Press, 1998), 14.

23. Feminists of color were those most responsible for introducing the concept and engaging in analysis of oppression as interstructured. See Cherríe Moraga and Gloria Anzaldúa, eds., *This Bridge Called My Back: Writings by Radical Women of Color* (New York: Kitchen Table: Women of Color Press, 1981); Barbara Smith, ed., *Home Girls: A Black Feminist Anthology* (New York: Kitchen Table Press, 1983); Gloria Anzaldúa, ed., *Making Face, Making Soul/Haciendo Caras: Creative and Critical Perspectives by Feminists of Color* (San Francisco: Aunt Lute Books, 1990); Patricia Hill Collins, *Black Feminist Thought: Knowledge, Consciousness, and the Politics of Empowerment* (New York and London: Routledge, 1991). This analysis and its emergence through painful struggles over issues of race among women of colors and white women in feminist movements is recounted in Becky Thompson, *A Promise and a Way of Life: White Antiracist Activism* (Minneapolis: University of Minnesota Press, 2001).

24. See Charles Tilly, *Durable Inequality* (Berkeley: University of California Press, 1998).

25. Patricia Hill Collins uses the terminology of "interlocking systems of oppression" and "matrix of domination." See Collins, *Black Feminist Thought,* 222ff.

One

SHAKING THE FOUNDATIONS

White Supremacy in the Theological Academy

ROBIN HAWLEY GORSLINE

I N 1970 JAMES H. CONE OBSERVED, "no white theologian has ever taken the oppression of blacks as a point of departure for analyzing God's activity in contemporary America."[1] Thirty-one years later, he restated this charge in a plenary address at the American Academy of Religion (AAR) meeting in Denver. Cone challenged white theologians, ethicists, and other scholars of religion to do what we still had not done: to make racism, what in this book we call white supremacy, a central starting point in our religious reflection.[2] No one has publicly challenged the accuracy of Cone's statement — because there is no ground from which to do so. Indeed, Cone's address in Denver brought a standing ovation from many, although not all, in the audience. To date, however, no white practitioner of Cone's discipline, systematic theology, or of Christian ethics has undertaken the work to which he and others have called us. As I show in this chapter, some white theologians and ethicists have analyzed racism and white supremacy and drawn on the work of writers of colors in their work. However, it remains true that white theologians and ethicists have not presented an anti-racist or anti–white supremacist theology or ethic grounded in the concrete reality of white racism — or in what Cone calls "the oppression of blacks" — and what we, in this book, are calling white supremacy.

What is it in the way that white scholars in theology and ethics — and pastors and priests — traditionally perceive our tasks that keeps us from serious, sustained engagement with issues and practices of white supremacy, in academy, church and society? Why is it that despite the good intentions of many, and actual attempts by a few, to combat white supremacy within the theological academy and the church — in this essay, the focus being on Protestantism — white scholars and ministers find it so difficult to make white supremacy a central concern in our work?[3] This chapter responds to these questions in two ways. First, I engage the ominous silence that has pervaded so much of the theological academy around issues of racism — its own racism and that of others. Second, I examine the work of some white theologians and ethicists who *have* engaged racism. Because most white theologians and ethicists have been silent, however, examining some of the reasons for the larger silence will be an important part of my analysis.

Part of the work of those who both benefit from, and choose to resist, white supremacy is to confess our complicity even as we proclaim our resistance. Such a practice helps to keep our focus on the materiality of that which we oppose. Thus, I wish to relate one of my own experiences of being silent. Ten years ago, I took a graduate course in gay men's literature. The class of ten white gay men and two white gay professors enjoyed all the authors we read except for African American novelist and essayist James Baldwin. During our examination of his novel, *Giovanni's Room,* the criticisms became quite harsh, and after a little while I became uncomfortable with the dismissal of Baldwin. However, I remained strangely silent. I love that novel, indeed I love Baldwin, but I did not speak in his defense. Later, I realized that I had succumbed to the potent silencing mechanism that goes on among white people when faced with sophisticated, racist commentary that appears, on the surface, to have no racist content. I vowed then to learn how to resist these mechanisms. Since that time, I have worked to understand the roots and mechanisms of white supremacy, as I have been learning new behaviors, and unlearning old ones.

THE TOPIC IS NOT "RACE"

One of the formal academy responses to Cone's address was to issue a call for papers to be presented the following year on the topic "How Can White Theologians Begin to Speak about Race?" In the ten years since that graduate literature class, with the help of Baldwin and countless other peoples of colors (and some white people), I had learned enough to see two immediate problems with the topic: first, that the subject is not "race," and second, white theologians are not just now beginning to speak about race. These two learnings are central to the larger issues addressed in this essay and in this book.

In the almost fifty years since the Montgomery, Alabama, bus boycott, there has been a variable level of interest among white theologians and ethicists about race. Some white theologians — George Kelsey, William Stringfellow, Susan Brooks Thistlethwaite, and Mary Hobgood come to mind — have written earnestly and with insight about racism. Even before, and contemporaneously with, that momentous event in Montgomery, Reinhold Niebuhr spoke eloquently in a variety of forums about the struggle of "the Negro" and the need for the rest of us to work for justice for "the Negro race." It certainly cannot be said, therefore, that it is only now that we, white theologians and ethicists, have begun to write about race or racism. Although it may seem so to many, race is not a new topic. What is new, however, are the ways in which we need to engage this topic.

In order to explore this point, I need first to engage the question of terminology. The name given to what is being studied impacts what we actually see. As white theologians and ethicists, therefore, our subject must be white supremacy, and not "race." The first reason for rejecting race as the topic is that so often the assumption among white people is that *race* is something *other* people have. Conversations about race among white people often turn out to be about *them.*

The second reason for questioning race as our topic is that race, as it is commonly understood — as a scientifically valid categorization of people based on physical characteristics — can no longer be accepted as a natural phenomenon. There is little debate among scientists anymore over the proposition that race, as a category in nature or science, does not exist.[4] At the same time, the absence of scientific support for the existence of race does not mean that race does not exist or that it has no effects. As Mary Hobgood and many others continue to point out, the category "race" actually is a social construction of racial hierarchies that sustain domination and privilege by some over others.[5] When I question, therefore, whether our topic ought to be race, I am suggesting that one cannot talk about race without talking about racial hierarchies of domination and privilege. Many theorists refer to this hierarchy as "racism"; the more acute among them call it "white racism." I choose to label this social construction "white supremacy."

By "white supremacy" I mean the operation of social practices by individuals and institutions, including political and economic mechanisms, to achieve and maintain the political, social, and economic dominance of white people and the subjugation of peoples of colors. In its simplest terms, white supremacy is the state of white people being "supreme," a state that — unless we believe in the natural superiority of white people — occurs because of human social action. White supremacy is, then, the matrix of structures, attitudes, and behaviors that keep white people supreme, on top — no matter what challenges are offered by peoples of colors (or even by some white people).[6]

These practices and mechanisms are so deeply embedded in daily life in the United States that most white people do not even notice, let alone ever think about them, nor certainly do most of us seek to change them. Indeed, the invisibility of these practices and mechanisms — invisible to white people, *not* to peoples of colors — is probably the single most important factor in the continuing potency of white supremacy. From this invisibility flows what may be the most difficult — and most important — characteristic of white supremacy for white people to understand, namely that it is self-perpetuating, not self-correcting.[7] Thus, white supremacy is both personal and institutional, and all white people collude in it (even those dedicated to fighting it).[8]

White supremacy is most commonly associated with regimes of social control and violence at the extreme rightward end of the political spectrum. This definition of white supremacy as extremist, coupled with the use of the term "racism" to describe "milder" (seemingly less extreme and more personal) forms of racial prejudice removes anti-racism as a topic of serious, mainstream political and theological debate requiring action. "Racism" is seen as an individual character flaw, a personal prejudice that requires overcoming, or at least hiding. Use of the term "racism" for the white supremacist behavior engaged in by most white people and the institutional practices sustained by white people, and restriction of the term "white supremacy" to the practices of a small group of white persons engaged in more obviously odious behaviors, privatizes white supremacy and allows a society dominated by white people to escape responsibility for our history and our present lives.[9]

WHITE SUPREMACY: IN THE AIR WE BREATHE

With this background, it becomes clearer that white supremacy permeates every aspect of the academic theological and religious studies enterprise, as well as the professional education of pastors and priests. To say that white theologians and ethicists are only now beginning to speak about race is to maintain an innocence belied by the evidence. White theologians and ethicists have been talking about race without ceasing, even when the words never leave our lips.

Cornel West and David Theo Goldberg, among others, have displayed the central role of white supremacist discourse in the rise of the modern West. West describes a "normative gaze" that relies on classical aesthetic and cultural norms developed at the advent of modernity in order to provide an acceptable authority for the idea of white supremacy through its institutionalization within scientific disciplines.[10] Goldberg claims that the "standards of Reason in modernity emerged against the backdrop of European domination and subjugation of nature, and especially of human nature...," so that there is "a coemergence in modernity of rationality and race as definitive constituents of human selfhood and subjectivity."[11] Thus, West and Goldberg push us to acknowledge that Western epistemology, especially as it has been constructed since the Enlightenment, is captive to the white supremacist constructs of human society and especially of learned discourse. This recognition deeply implicates the Western theological enterprise.

Ruth Frankenberg, in her study of the lives of a group of white women, investigates how epistemological whiteness — what Goldberg calls "methodological Eurocentrism"[12] — affects each of us more personally. Frankenberg demonstrates that what "is most 'given' about whiteness (and indeed about the relations of race in general) is the materiality of its history."[13] By this she means that not only is whiteness a social construct but that it is a personal construction as well. This combination of the social and personal is what gives whiteness an epistemological status. Our knowledge of the world is filtered through the lens of whiteness that each of us, as white people, inherits and which we then adapt to fit into our own life situations. As a result, each white person participates in making up whiteness — our own and that of others. Probing the inculturated experiences and views of her subjects, Frankenberg concludes that white people are "the nondefined definers of other people," and that "[w]hiteness appeared in the narratives to function as both norm or core, that against which everything else is measured, and as residue, that which is left after everything else has been named."[14] It is not surprising, then, that white people have trouble even trying to talk about white supremacy: our very being *as white people* depends on our not talking about it.

Our very being as white *theologians* also depends on our not speaking about white supremacy, or when we do speak about it, to do so in ways that do not result in serious, sustained conversation that results in serious dialogue with our colleagues and real social and ecclesial change. Thus, to date, few white theologians have actually written about racism, or white supremacy. A library search reveals little in the way of nonjournal treatment of the topic in the past fifty years, and even the journal articles are limited in number. Even so, it is important to note that some white theologians and ethicists have explored some issues related to white supremacy. When I began research for this essay, I expected to find little or no writing, but a few theologians have been highly critical of the racism so prevalent in U.S. society and in the church and seminaries. The inaccuracy of my initial perception reflects, I think, not so much the absence of individual efforts as the absence of a sustained conversation that would demonstrate a larger institutional commitment to wrestle with deeply troubling issues. Having now uncovered a significant body of writing — the strengths and weaknesses of which I explore here — I am forced to conclude that white supremacy depends on relative, although not absolute, silence.

Maintaining white supremacy does not require all white theologians to avoid addressing racism, or even naming white racism. Instead, *the maintenance of white supremacy requires the absence of open discussion and open dialogue that leads to widespread awareness of its awesome power to structure society.* Open consideration of the evils of white supremacy as they affect everyone — in other words, disclosure of the hidden structure beneath what we usually see — might well lead to organized, coherent, consistent efforts to dismantle white supremacy's power to structure society. This possibility is a major deterrent to discussing white supremacy within theology and the theological academy. It also is a major deterrent to discussing the evils of white supremacy within the churches.

EARLIER WHITE THEOLOGICAL RESPONSES TO WHITE SUPREMACY

As stated above, the power of this prohibition against open dialogue about white supremacy has not prevented some white theologians, ethicists, and churches in the United States from addressing racism and white supremacy. We may divide the writing into three parts.

First, beginning before World War II and continuing into the mid-1960s a number of prominent theologians, mostly neoorthodox in approach, addressed the subject with considerable energy. Second, the rise of Third World feminism, and especially Black feminism and womanism, in the 1980s, forced white feminists, theologians among them, to confront issues of "difference." Finally, changes in the structure of global ecumenical movements, continuing struggles within U.S. society around racial strife, and political activism in opposition to U.S. government policy regarding South African apartheid and imperialism in Central America created the conditions for some churches, beginning in the 1980s, to engage white supremacy with an urgency that had not been present since the 1960s.

Reinhold Niebuhr, a prominent voice in Protestant theological circles, is the best example of the first period. As early as 1932, Niebuhr wrote with characteristic realism, "However large the number of individual white [persons] who do and who will identify themselves completely with the Negro cause, the white race in America will not admit the Negro to equal rights if it is not forced to do so."[15] Niebuhr also was outspoken in subsequent years in support of the Civil Rights Movement in the United States and in the struggle against apartheid in South Africa.

Despite the value of Niebuhr's example, however, his reliance on the strict division between the individual and society obscures some of the mechanisms by which individuals and society conspire to maintain white supremacy. This aspect of Niebuhr's method has particularly serious consequences for analyzing and resisting white supremacy. Primarily it abets the idea not only that individuals need merely to change themselves and their attitudes, but also that personal change is all that they can achieve. That such limitations are not what Niebuhr intended does not erase the difficulties his perspective perpetuates. Further, Niebuhr, like many others, failed to see the deeply epistemological nature of the problem: even neoorthodox and liberal theology are so infected by white supremacy that it will take a fundamental reordering of our theological systems to overcome it.

George D. Kelsey took up Niebuhr's task in 1965, calling racism "an idolatrous faith."[16] He analyzed racism as a faith system, thus contributing to our understanding of white supremacy as a totalizing values framework. Kelsey also distinguished between white racism — understanding that it possesses both privilege and power — and other forms of racialized thinking and acting in which the less powerful — he uses the faith of the Black Muslims as an example — express their will to power in terms of faith and eschatology. His was an important book, sadly overlooked by many. A major shortcoming of Kelsey's work, however, is that he tries to stand in the middle, to adjudicate what he sees as conflicting racist claims. As a white man, he thus fails to examine his own participation in white supremacy and to share that learning with others.

In 1964, William Stringfellow, a lay theologian, attorney, and activist in the Episcopal Church, published *My People Is the Enemy: An Autobiographical Polemic,* in which he argued that the estrangement between black and white people in the United States was almost unbridgeable.[17] Stringfellow, a white man who lived and worked in Harlem for many years, spoke eloquently and passionately — even harshly — in chastising the failures of the white church. He was especially critical of the failure of its liberal wing to be changed by the actual conditions of Black people — both the condition of poverty and despair so rampant among many and the condition of revolt and rebellion rising among many as well — in the past and present. Stringfellow described the poverty created by white racism in Harlem and elsewhere and the complicity of the Christian churches in its maintenance. He concluded by asserting that the "central witness of the Church in the racial crisis is to bear the rejection of white people by Negroes," and to do so "without protest or complaint, without concern for innocence or guilt . . . in other words, in the love of Christ for the whole world."[18] His was a radical white voice, largely ignored by church leaders and members alike.

The writings of these powerful white neoorthodox voices at this early stage of theological wrestling with white supremacy offered a significant opportunity for others to begin the creation of a profoundly important dialogue. Such a dialogue might have changed the churches, and social history, had it gathered momentum. Unfortunately, none of the three was able to engage in a sustained investigation and critique of white supremacy on their own nor to develop a compelling theological vision building on that critique. Moreover, they do not appear to have understood the need for group action.

WHITE FEMINIST THEOLOGIANS RESPOND

After Niebuhr, Kelsey, and Stringfellow, for about twenty years there was a noticeable silence about white supremacy among white theologians and ethicists. The rise of feminism in the late 1960s and 1970s, however, energized in large measure by the U.S. Civil Rights and Black Power Movements, created conditions that would lead Barbara Andolsen in 1984 to write *"Daughters of Jefferson, Daughters of Bootblacks."* Andolsen analyzes the racism she identifies as endemic to white feminism and white feminist theology through a historical account of the women's suffrage movement. She tells the story of how white women abandoned their natural allies among Black women and men in the struggle for emancipation. She uses this history to sustain an argument against vestiges of the "cult of true womanhood" that remain implicit in the work of some feminists. Rejecting the implicit notion that women (meaning white women) are naturally better people than men (meaning all men), she proposes, following Rosemary Radford Ruether, that oppression based on race and oppression based on gender, and oppression based on other factors, are "interstructured."[19] Echoing Carter Heyward and Beverly Wildung Harrison, she concludes by calling for a new vision of feminist theology grounded in "right relation." Andolsen's examination of the roots of racism within white feminism is enormously helpful in understanding the present. It was not her project, however, to analyze

fully the impact of this history on feminist *theology*, and it certainly
was not her project to develop an alternative theological vision.

Perhaps the most important theological book by a white person
addressing white supremacy in recent years is *Sex, Race, and God:
Christian Feminism in Black and White,* by Susan Brooks Thistlethwaite in 1991. Thistlethwaite forthrightly struggles to understand
the role of white feminist women in perpetuating the subjugation
of African American people, especially African American women.
She takes seriously the critiques of these women, responding to the
question, "What happens when the *differences* between black women
and white women become the starting point for white feminist theology?"[20] In her effort to answer this question, she relies in very
significant ways on the insights in fiction written by Black women.
The resulting equation of white feminist racism with sin is strong
and clear.

At the same time, however, one senses that Thistlethwaite struggles
with how really to confront the past and even current practices of her
white feminist siblings. This struggle results, in part, from her chosen
location as the arbiter of difference between white and Black women,
that is, adjudicating between the "hermeneutic of suspicion of racial
privilege" and the "hermeneutic of white women's suffering." Standing in between allows Thistlethwaite to engage in personal reflection
and even confession, while simultaneously managing to speak for
both white and Black women. Further, she bases her theological reflection on the *difference* between these women, rather than on the
experience of white women *as white women* in a white supremacist
academy, church, and society as that experience is challenged and described both by Black women and a thorough analysis and description
of white supremacy. In so doing, Thistlethwaite manages to maintain
a privileged location as a white feminist scholar. She fails to make a
root analysis of the white supremacist foundations of white feminist
theology. This critique does not diminish her courage nor her obviously commendable intentions in writing. Had she written a second
book on the subject or had some other white theologian responded

directly to her important beginnings, a dialogical response might have developed and we could be even further along in understanding white supremacy theologically.

Sharon Welch, in *A Feminist Ethic of Risk,* follows Thistlethwaite in drawing on Black women novelists for evidence to support a communicative ethic of risk as an alternative to communitarian ethical systems offered by Alasdair MacIntyre and others.[21] Welch's ethic of risk grows out of her awareness that ethics must be done in communication with others outside of our own social and religious groups. She utilizes the work of five African American women novelists to highlight the moral wisdom and strength required in the face of seemingly intractable social problems. Drawing on the womanist methodology of Katie Geneva Cannon, she offers thoughtful analysis of the five novels in the first half. In the second half of the book, however, the voices of these African American women writers are noticeably quieter. As a result, it remains unclear whether Welch has brought the two traditions she describes, the African American and the Euro-American, into full communication.

Similarly, Welch turns to jazz and the blues in her more recent book, *Sweet Dreams in America.* Her effort is to develop a new ethical foundation as well as practices that will sustain movements for social change in the face of seemingly impossible odds.[22] Welch resonates with the ambiguity of jazz and blues idioms. She argues vigorously for abandoning rigidity and rules-based ethical systems in favor of more contingent strategies based, in part, on the methodology of open-ended, yet still responsible, music-making. In this book, as in her previous ones, Welch displays an awareness of the centrality of white racism in U.S. culture and is conversant with sources and movements not so obviously engaged by other white theologians.

Welch understands that the experiences of Black women and white women are marked by important distinctions. For example, she argues that the privilege marking the general social location of the latter has helped them avoid dealing with conflict. Thus, Welch proposes that "white women need an ethic of conflict," in order to avoid crumbling in the face of conflict with others, perhaps espe-cially other women. This is an important and vital suggestion for change among white feminists, and all white people. It represents an awareness of the contemporary disutility of the traditional role of white women to smooth over the conflicts brought about by white and male supremacies.

At the same time, she is aware that change is incremental and that patience is required; Welch sees that human nature is fickle and that grand narratives and calls for revolution do not produce much change. She, thus, proposes that those who desire fundamental change develop more contingent strategies — more fluid and open like jazz and the blues. Contingent strategies permit easy alteration and adaptation to particular conditions and needs. Thus, Welch draws upon an unusual source for ethics, the musical tradition of African Americans, to suggest a new nontheological ethical model. This cre-ates the possibility of an alternative to white supremacist, patriarchal theological constructions that often perpetuate top-down, controlling modes of thinking and acting. At the same time, Welch avoids sys-temic analysis of white supremacy and theological re-visioning based on it.

Feminist liberation ethicist Mary Elizabeth Hobgood has under-taken important work in seeking to display for "overprivileged" persons how we may begin the process of undoing the privilege we take for granted. In *Dismantling Privilege: An Ethics of Ac-countability,* Hobgood outlines the costs — psychic and otherwise — of unearned privilege and suggests "solidarity and alliance build-ing" as the "means for us to recover our fundamental humanity."[23] Hobgood's analysis is not limited to matters of white racism and su-premacy. However, it is clear that racialized privilege is central to her own experience and analysis, and that she fervently wishes to end it. Her connection of racism with class- and gender-based oppression, moreover, is thoughtful and clear. However, Hobgood moves rather quickly to call for alliance among all those affected, including the underprivileged. She does so, perhaps without sufficiently prescrib-ing work by the overprivileged to understand, and begin to divest ourselves of, our sense of entitlement to "credit" for not only our real work against white supremacy, but even for our good intentions.

Despite whatever shortcomings may be identified among the works of these white authors, each of them offers a wealth of information, and rich theological and ethical discourse. Unfortunately, few others have responded to or sought to build on their courageous work. Niebuhr raised the issue of white supremacy in 1932. Yet later in 1965, Harvey Cox, in the pages of *The Secular City*, avoided ref-erence to the titanic struggle for civil rights and Black power then engulfing the United States. White theologians generally have avoided engagement with the work of James Cone and the outpouring of Black theological exploration he has inspired. Two exceptions are Rosemary Radford Ruether and Robert McAfee Brown, who of-fered essays in the twentieth anniversary edition of Cone's *A Black Theology of Liberation*. Unfortunately, while acknowledging the im-portance of Cone's work, Brown seems to hold him and other angry Black people responsible for the failure of white theologians to engage in substantive discussions of racism.

Ruether's approach in her essay in Cone's book and in several texts is far more complex and substantive. This is particularly true in her early work, *New Woman, New Earth*, where her discussion of the history of oppression in the United States suffered by white women and Black women and men is nuanced and thoughtful.[24] At the same time, Ruether's efforts over the years have been marked by a failure to allow her understanding of white feminism to be changed by the lives of the Black women and other women of colors to whom she listens. This failure, as Ellen Armour has pointed out, is due in some measure to Ruether's reliance on liberal feminism, which tends to flat-ten the differences among women.[25] Despite Ruether's understanding of history, she appears to largely share Mary Daly's view that patri-archy is the fundamental sin from which all other oppressions flow. This perspective makes it difficult for either of them to actually name *racism,* or white supremacy, as a practice of white women for which they are accountable.

THE CHURCHES RESPOND

This brief survey of theologically based work against white supremacy would be incomplete and inaccurate if it ignored the work within some white churches by white people against white supremacy. Stringfellow, in 1964, took a generally pessimistic view of the churches' efforts against white supremacy. He wrote:

> The churches of white society in America have largely forfeited any claim to leadership in the relations between the races, and, to a great extent, have not even seriously understood those relations in terms of the Christian faith; their active concern in the last century has been, to an overwhelming degree, limited to the nominal pronouncements of church assemblies and ecclesiastical authorities. But few of these pronouncements have betrayed a theological understanding of the relations of the races. Mainly, they have repeated the empty dogmas of humanism and the platitudes of tolerance.[26]

Since then, and perhaps most notably, the National Council of Churches of Christ (NCCC) has attempted to reverse Stringfellow's judgment. The ongoing work of the NCCC has taken place, first, through its recognition that racism distorts efforts at ecumenical relations because it wounds the entire Body of Christ and, second, through the ongoing work of its Racial Justice Program and the Racial Justice Working Group. Also, beginning in 1952, the World Council of Churches (WCC) began trying to reconcile its vision of the global Body of Christ with the realities of social and religious life divided along racial and other lines. The WCC Faith and Order process has made significant strides in promoting a Christ-centered view that affirms all persons and seeks to undo the social and ecclesial structures that work against this view.[27]

Denominational bodies as well as state and local councils of churches have been encouraged by the WCC and NCCC initiatives to undertake anti-racism work. Some have empowered denomination-wide commissions to provide training for anti-racism trainers to work in congregations. Groups within denominations have made anti-racism a focus of their program.[28] The Minnesota Council of Churches, for example, began in 1992 to address the changing racial climate in that state, seeking to develop anti-racist initiatives in local churches. The program has evolved into a shared enterprise with the Minneapolis and St. Paul Councils of Churches, now called the Minnesota Churches Anti-Racism Initiative (MCARI). MCARI works with local churches to create means by which they may internalize and regularize capacity for anti-racism education and assessment, and participate in multicultural collaborations to combat systemic racism.[29] In their efforts to dismantle white supremacy in their own congregations and communities, many churches and other religious groups utilize the pioneering work of Joseph Barndt, a pastor and director of a program in New York City to build a multicultural church.[30]

These church-centered activities have not been undertaken in response to leadership from white theologians and ethicists. Instead, many of them have arisen because members of the groups both recognize a deep wound within their own ranks and are disturbed by the continuing racial insensitivity, injustice, and divides they see in their own communities. The peace movement of the 1980s, especially that organized in opposition to the U.S. governmental policy of imperialism in Central America, helped many churches begin to make connections between white supremacy and other public policies, including immigration. Becky Thompson's essay in this volume examines this phenomenon in detail.[31] It is significant that the initial impetus to act has not come from theological exploration in seminaries or higher church bodies so much as it has come from the personal experiences of people of faith who recognize the disconnect between what they claim to believe and the actual practice of themselves, their neighbors, their church, and their government. That white theologians have not led the way in helping churches overcome white supremacy is troubling. But if white theologians understand, as stated previously, that our very being as white theologians depends on our not talking about white supremacy in the academy or the church, we may not be surprised.

THEOLOGY AND ITS WHITENESS

Beyond the reality that white scholars have not led the way in addressing white supremacy lies a potentially more painful reality: white supremacy — the self-perpetuating, hidden, yet powerful construct shaping how white people think and act — has affected, perhaps it is more accurate to say infected, white theological worldviews. There will be some who will object immediately to this statement of the problem. They will contend that there is no *white* theological worldview. Theology, they will argue, is color-blind, and, even if it is not, they will point to Black, feminist, Asian, African, Hispanic, womanist and *Mujerista* theologies as proof that the enterprise of theology grows and changes.

It is true that these insurgent theologies signal an irruption from the "Two-Thirds World" into the "First," an irruption that has immeasurably enriched the discipline of theology. Yet, it also remains true that those who write theology — those who are *not* Black, feminist, Asian, African, Hispanic, womanist, and/or Mujerista — remain content to have *their* theology known simply as "theology"; Not white theology or "Euro-American" theology — no hyphenated label marks their location, their perspective, as less than universal. Lest the reader fall into thinking that I am speaking of a minor matter of labels, it is important to restate that labels are neither minor nor accidental; labels reflect and shape how we think. If *theologians* are writing *theology,* and Black theologians are writing *Black* theology, do we not have a clue about the content of each? Do we not have a clue about the relative social weight each carries in a profession still dominated by white people, and in seminaries and churches dominated by white people? Has any [white] *theologian* been passed by a cab, on the basis of the color of his or her skin, on the way to give a talk at a theological conference? If the [white] theologian is passed by would that theologian have reason to think it might be because of her or his race? If that had happened, would it have made any difference in the speaker's *theological* perspective?

Not only is one's worldview affected by such events, but also the absence of these events affects one's worldview. That a *theologian* never has had to think that her or his skin color, or race, might be the basis of how people act toward her or him *affects her or his theology fully as much* as does the fact that an African American theologian always has to be aware of the possibility, and the reality, of such events.[32] What is missing is often as important, and is certainly as revealing, as what is present. There is little, or no, accounting for this absence in most theology written by white people, however.

"Race" is mentioned in texts authored by many white theologians — including in works beyond those reviewed here. It is named, at least, as something that people have and that should not be ignored. It is identified as something that should not create the conditions based upon which others discriminate or oppress. Many white writers urge solidarity with those whose liberation is still being sought, contending that solidarity across lines of difference is key to carrying out the commands of the gospel. Still, even in this most heartfelt effort to create the conditions for change, the *theologian* whose work is *theology* stands in the center place, the place against which all other views must contend. In such a context, theology without any racial or ethnic modifiers remains "both norm or core, that against which everything else is measured, and as residue, that which is left after everything else has been named."[33]

I attended seminary twenty years ago. At that time, a fellow student and I made two white professors noticeably angry when we presented the views of James Cone for a class in theological method and spirituality. I shall never forget one of the professors getting red in the face as he attempted to tell us that Cone and Black theology did not constitute *real* theology, even as he assured us that he was very supportive of the struggle of Black people for civil rights. Much has changed, I know, at least at the seminary I attended and at others of a similarly progressive outlook. However, how many white professors, even today at progressive theological schools, teach Black theology for an entire semester as if it were as valid and worthwhile, and as central to Christian theology, as teaching a semester of Tillich or Moltmann or Barth?

The question of audience is crucial in writing and teaching. Those of us who are white are usually unaware of how our racial audience is selected, partly because we have never had to think about it. We assume that *people,* not Black people or white people, will buy our books and read our articles. When we proceed from this place of presumed universality — while actually writing from the place of white privilege — we protect ourselves from being interrogated honestly. We avoid being questioned and critiqued by those whose location is outside the circle of privilege. If we write from a place of assumed whiteness, it is likely that our readers primarily will be white people, and our insulation remains intact.

When I wrote my dissertation on James Baldwin and Audre Lorde, I decided that a majority of my committee had to be *not* "white." I knew that if it were not so, it would be too easy for "us," the white folks, to contain these two powerful figures within the grasp of white epistemological privilege. It is not for me to say whether or not I succeeded in avoiding this outcome, but I know that having three distinguished African American scholars and theologians on a committee of five appreciably changed the dynamic in my writing and my defense.

THE WHITE CHURCH

The inability of white theologians and ethicists to grapple adequately in our work with the fact of our racialized privilege rests in part on convenient theological amnesia. The enslavement of millions of Africans is a foundational social and religious fact of life in the United States. Many will accept that it is socially and politically foundational, but will question its religious significance. Others recognize that it is the slave experience that gave rise to spiritual traditions that helped create and still inform the Black church (as well as giving rise to musical and spiritual traditions that some white folks draw on in white churches today). What most of us may not be so quick to notice is that it also had a powerful impact on the White church.

The White church? Even use of the term is shocking. The White church? What is that? In its simplest form it is the entire Christian church that is not known as the Black church (and the Korean American church and others). I have written elsewhere about how the insistence of most of U.S. Christianity on the primacy of heterosexuality and the exclusion of queer peoples from ordination, marriage, and other religious rites constitutes a church that claims sexuality as of equal or greater importance than the gospel values of justice and peace.[34] The same may be said of white Christianity. From the early days of life on this continent down to very recent history, "race" — more precisely, white supremacy — has been of equal or greater importance than the gospel values of justice and peace. Given the paucity of pastors and leaders from among peoples of colors in most Christian denominations outside the historic Black churches and other churches in nonwhite racial/ethnic communities, *de facto* reliance on a gospel seriously infected with white supremacy continues.

It is necessary to pause here to attend to a complication in resisting white supremacy. Our resistance requires white people to attend to our participation in racism in relation to all peoples of colors, not just those labeled Black or African American. At the same time, those of us who are white U.S.-American Christians have a special history in relation to Black siblings. This relation is revealed most keenly in the existence of the Black church. To put it directly, if our ancestors had not insisted on a whites-only church, the existence of the historic Black churches would not have been necessary. If our ancestors had not blocked the ordination of and acceptance of Black leadership, it is doubtful that these leaders would have felt the need to start their own churches.[35] If our ancestors — not just those in the South — had not used the Bible to justify slavery, or had not succumbed to moral paralysis in the face of biblical ambiguity (to put the best face on it) about slavery, it is doubtful so many slaves would have felt the need to create their own churches. Frankenberg is again right: white supremacy has a very material history, and within Christianity its evidence is the necessity of the Black church. To say this in no way implies that the historic Black churches have not enlarged, and do not now enrich, Christian belief and practice. Nor is it to suggest that they do not stand on their own in full faith and organizational credit. Rather it is to point out that their founding and development highlights most powerfully the white supremacist sinfulness of the White church.

At the same time, I acknowledge that today people of goodwill do not consciously intend that white supremacy govern our decision making. Church boards and clergy — no less seminary boards and faculty — do not sit around dreaming up ways to avoid having clergy and leadership from among peoples of colors. Indeed, most leaders now claim quite the reverse, and appear to work hard for diversity. However, as noted above, the invisibility of practices and mechanisms of white supremacy contributes to its self-perpetuating character, meaning that *no one — no white person — has to do anything for white supremacy to continue.* Perhaps more troubling, we can even speak against it while continuing to collude in its maintenance and power. What is adamantly required, therefore, is real work *against* white supremacy. That means actively seeking to give up personal privilege and power based on white supremacist practices and mechanisms, and working with other white people, and peoples of all colors, to end white supremacy.

THE LANGUAGE OF WHITE SUPREMACY

The white struggle against white supremacy takes place on many fronts, one of which is language. The anti–white supremacist struggle is not the first to confront language as an issue of fundamental importance. Feminists and womanists, and their male allies, have raised serious critiques about masculinist language for God and humanity. No longer is it so easy for theological writers of any stripe to refer to humanity as "mankind." In more conservative circles, however, using male pronouns in reference to God remains not only acceptable but also a badge of faith. Those who first rejected, and those who still reject, the feminist/womanist argument contend, in part, that language is only words, that it does not constitute content, that which is most important. Thus, antifeminists can still contend that referring to God as "He" has no affect on how people see or experience God, and that speaking of "man" when referring to all human beings does not exclude women (or woman).

Similarly, theologians — and not just white ones — are often unaware of how language of "light" and "dark," particularly language that promotes enlightenment over an alternative and negative darkness, perpetuates and re-creates a cultural value of light over dark. In a Christian context, exalting Christ as the Light of the World creates a connection of holiness with light. Even when there is no explicit mention of darkness as unholy, this usage reifies the theological and cultural dualism of light over dark. This is, in part, because our Eurocentric cultural and linguistic heritage is undergirded by dualisms — male and female, white and black, straight and gay, rich and poor. In each case one of the two terms serves as the socially preferred and/or more powerful location (in these examples, the first).

The absence of attention to these linguistic questions within the white theological academy arises from both the larger lack of awareness of the pervasiveness of white supremacy and the unwillingness to tackle what are deep and troubling issues for those of us who inhabit white racial locations. Parallel to Frankenberg's observation of white people in general as "the nondefined definers of other people," white theologians function as the nondefined definers of other people's theologies.

Theology, therefore — that is, theology by white (more often male than female, although this is changing) theologians, which is not identified by any modifier that locates its author or point of view sociologically or demographically — is that which presumes to exist prior to, and after, all the theologies that are considered to be hyphenated, or partial, or special, theologies. This unidentified theology encompasses many divergent views. It is often divided by denominational considerations — and even modifiers — such as "political" or "continental" or "process" or "Barthian" or "Tillichian." However, it appears at the same time to be unfettered by any connection to particular social or cultural groups. This theology retains its central, normative, and, in Frankenberg's conception, "residual" function. In part, this is because its practitioners refuse to give it labels that might indicate the partiality of its perspective. Even within denominations, it is safe to assume that the voices behind Methodist theology, Roman Catholic theology, or Anglican theology are not speaking from a nonnormative, noncore, nonresidual location. Rather these voices inhabit that general, and rather exalted, space within the denominational theological structure known as "theology." All the "great" European and U.S.-American theologians from the past — Schleiermacher, Jonathan Edwards, Barth, Tillich, Niebuhr, among others — were not limited in their own work by any considerations of partiality. They spoke to, for, and from all of Christendom, and the others who continue to build upon and respond to them, without qualification, maintain the same privilege.

SOME IMPLICATIONS, AND SUGGESTIONS FOR MOVING FORWARD

This brief history and commentary can, I hope, give us some clues about what remains to be done. I suggest that the tasks before us can be understood as personal and communal, as well as epistemological and hermeneutical. Each white person lives out our own personal version of white supremacy, while simultaneously being deeply implicated in the larger social white supremacist structure and practices. One cannot be addressed without working on the other. Similarly, matters of what we know as white people — because white supremacy is part of the air we breathe and foundational to all our knowledge — cannot be separated from our interpretative activities. We must understand not only that white supremacy is foundational to our knowledge but that it is foundational to our work as interpreters of texts and lives, even as we engage in precise analysis that teases knowledge and interpretation apart in order to change them both. Thus, our task as white Christians is not only to confess our complicity, but to seek to understand it, and then to change it. As theologians and ethicists and religious leaders, probably unaccustomed to being students again, this work is painful and strange. And it is especially so because our teachers will be people from whom we are often unaccustomed to learn.

From what we have already adduced about the potency of white supremacy — both within our society and within each of us — the paucity and relative weakness of theological work among white people engaging white supremacy should come as little surprise. We can and do thank Niebuhr, Kelsey, Stringfellow, Thistlethwaite, Ruether, Welch, and Hobgood, among others, for their pioneering contributions. But these scholars *need more dialogue partners*. For the most part, each of them has written as if the others did not. The result of such fits and starts is that growth and change are sporadic and idiosyncratic rather than systemic and communal. The isolation many feel when confronting our complicity in white supremacy is perpetuated by scholarship that is not moored in overt understanding that the work of resistance must be shared. Until such time as there is a critical mass of interconnected writing and teaching about theological white supremacy, the relative silence in which it thrives will continue. This means that white theologians of all stripes need to engage in some theological affirmative action — perhaps giving up one cherished current or future project — in order to undertake a systematic review of our prior works, our first works, to discern what we failed to see and say the first time around. The contributions of many are required in order to create a critical mass of anti–white supremacist theologizing sufficient to create fundamental change.

Further, as white Christian theologians we must take up James Cone's advice to give up whiteness and take on Blackness, understanding the latter as "the ontological symbol and visible reality which best describes what oppression means in America" and a concept that "includes both what the world means by oppression and what the gospel means by liberation."[36] The fact that my seminary professors of twenty years ago had — and that most since then, and I myself, have had — so much trouble doing this is indicative of the power of white supremacy. In 1983 it was more "acceptable" to let this resistance show, as my two professors and others demonstrated, but the fact that we continue to resist with more subtlety and grace today is testament only to our skills of evasion. Seriously entertaining and acting on Cone's invitation — by overcoming our resistance — requires attention to both epistemology and praxis. In other words, we must simultaneously change how we think and how we live.

Every time I suggest to white colleagues, friends, and family members that we take on Blackness, I am greeted first with incomprehension and then with declarations of the task's impossibility. Some accuse me of wanting to change my skin color, suggesting by their body language that this would be a tragedy. I am accused of wanting to erase Black people by becoming one.

I continue to struggle with this myself. I am not sure if I can ever learn to live and think Black, but I do believe I can learn a lot about living and thinking nonwhite. Even writing that is an unsettling experience. I know I can never get it right by others' standards, because as I have my own version of white supremacy I also am creating my own version of nonwhiteness. I recognize that I am doing so while receiving all the automatic benefits and privileges conferred by my status as a person whose skin passes the whiteness test. Working to resist my personal white supremacy and end that of the society of which I am part — while living as a white person enjoying the automatic benefits of white privilege — requires intense listening. This listening must be both to the others I have been trained to ignore and also to my own inner struggle. Aana Vigen addresses this work directly and eloquently in her essay in this book on "white listening." In addition, as scholars and pastors wrestling with white supremacy, we have to be willing to change in ways that will allow us to appear less than perfect, less than completely in control of our subject.

I have written elsewhere about the enormous power of Enlightenment epistemological systems to sustain our inability, and our unwillingness, to think outside the box of whiteness.[37] I continue to believe that as white Christian theologians our greatest task is to dis-identify ourselves from the image of God as a *white person* (and I recognize that for many today that person remains male) deeply embedded in our psyches. Such a task is difficult, not only because it is the image we learned in Sunday school, but also because it is the image never really rebutted in seminary. It still lurks in many a soul. Just because many of us no longer are comfortable using images of God as an old white man with a beard does not mean we have erased them from our inner hearts and minds.

None of this can be done easily or quickly. That which infects us has been at work a long time. However, I suggest as a first step that every time we think of, or use, the metaphor of shining a light on something, or emerging from the darkness of ignorance or prejudice, that we reverse the image. Instead, think of the extraordinary clarity photographers achieve in the darkroom. Let us decide to go deeply into the dark ourselves and let our eyes become accustomed to the beauty of the dark and the black. Going into the dark seeking truth feels foreign, and that is itself a significant clue about how distorted our vision has become. From my own experience, limited as it is, I know that the theologian seeking to examine — and resist — white supremacy in her own and others' works is working in an arena where each discovery opens grievous social and personal wounds. That these wounds are of our own making, or, at least, are of our continuing complicity in the evil perpetrated by earlier generations, makes them especially painful. This can cause us to react with anger if not rage.

This time, however, instead of blaming the victim or looking the other way, let us try to use the power of that anger in a new "work of love,"[38] deciding to cede, piece-by-piece, what Mary Hobgood, Karin Case, and others call our unearned privilege or advantage. To really understand white supremacy and to participate in its undoing, requires, as Hobgood argues forcefully, that "we must work in coalition with subordinate others to transform social systems that are detrimental to all."[39] However, even as we move, too often prematurely, to build coalitions, we must understand that it is we, the white supremacists, not the racial Other we have participated in creating and maintaining in our fetid and all too real imaginations, who are the problem and the solution. As James Baldwin observed to his young nephew many years ago on the hundredth anniversary of Lincoln's Emancipation Proclamation, "the black person has functioned in the white person's world as a fixed star, as an immovable pillar: and as...[we] move...out of place, heaven and earth are shaken to their foundation."[40] After all the years of Black people and other peoples of colors urging us to change our ways, *now* is the time for white people, and especially white theologians, to move out of our place and shake the foundations of white supremacy.

NOTES

1. James H. Cone, *A Black Theology of Liberation* (New York: Orbis Books, 1986 [1970]), 9.

2. James H. Cone, "Theology's Great Sin: Silence in the Face of White Supremacy," *Union Seminary Quarterly Review* 55, no. 3–4 (2001): 1–15.

3. Although I cite several authors who come out of the Roman Catholic tradition, this essay is grounded in, and is primarily addressed to participants in, Protestant theological traditions. I have not made any study of these issues as they relate to various Orthodox traditions.

4. For a clear, brief summary of the debate about what "race" is, see Howard Winant, "The Theoretical Status of the Concept of Race," in *Theories of Race and Racism: A Reader,* ed. Les Back and John Solomos (New York: Routledge, 2000), 181–90. For a thoughtful examination of the politics of scientific theorizing, see Nancy Leys Stepan and Sander L. Gilman, "Appropriating the Idioms of Science: The Rejection of Scientific Racism," in *The Bounds of Race: Perspectives on Hegemony and Resistance,* ed. Dominick LaCapra (Ithaca, N.Y.: Cornell University Press, 1991), 72–103.

5. Mary Elizabeth Hobgood, *Dismantling Privilege: An Ethics of Accountability* (Cleveland: Pilgrim, 2000).

6. "White" and "Black," normally seen as fixed indicators of stable identities, are actually highly contested in their meaning and operation, depending on a host of factors in specific situations. I wish to avoid where possible referring to white or Black people as if they constitute any sort of clearly defined, monolithic grouping. "White" in white supremacy may seem less contestable, but actually there are wide variations in how white supremacy is manifested in discrete contexts. One of the difficulties of writing about these subjects is the ease with which one can reinscribe meanings while trying to resist them.

7. Paul Kivel, *Uprooting Racism: How White People Can Work for Racial Justice* (Philadelphia: New Society Publishers, 1996), 160–62.

8. Simone claims that even the growth of a Black middle class "provides a representative and safe sample of blackness for white consumption" by assuring "whites that the significance of race is not really about race, but rather individual effort and determination." See Timothy Maliqalim Simone, *About Face: Race in Postmodern America* (Brooklyn, N.Y.: Autonomedia, 1989), 89.

9. Kimberlé Crenshaw and Gary Peller observe "the symmetry of the idea of 'racism' in mainstream American culture: once race is divorced from its social meaning in schools, workplaces, streets, homes, prisons, and paychecks and from its historic meaning in terms of the repeated American embrace of white privilege, then all that's left, really, is a hollow, analytic norm of 'color blind' — an image of racial power as embodied in abstract classifications by race that could run either way, against whites as easily as against blacks." See "Reel Time/Real Justice," in *Reading Rodney King: Reading Urban Uprising,* ed. Robert Gooding-Williams (New York: Routledge, 1993), 63.

10. Cornel West, *Prophesy Deliverance: An Afro-American Revolutionary Christianity* (Philadelphia: Westminster, 1982), 53–54.

11. David Theo Goldberg, *Racist Culture: Philosophy and the Politics of Meaning* (Cambridge, Mass.: Blackwell Publishers, 1993), 119.

12. Ibid., 149.

13. Ruth Frankenberg, *White Women, Race Matters: The Social Construction of Whiteness* (Minneapolis: University of Minnesota Press, 1993), 238.

14. Ibid., 197–204.

15. Reinhold Niebuhr, *Moral Man and Immoral Society* (New York: Charles Scribner's Sons, 1960 [1932]), 253.

16. George D. Kelsey, *Racism and the Christian Understanding of Man* (New York: Charles Scribner's Sons, 1965), 9.

17. William Stringfellow, *My People Is the Enemy: An Autobiographical Polemic* (New York: Holt, Rinehart & Winston, 1964), 127.

18. Ibid., 142–43.

19. Barbara Hilkert Andolsen, *"Daughters of Jefferson, Daughters of Bootblacks": Racism and American Feminism* (Macon, Ga.: Mercer University Press, 1986), 108–9. Andolsen cites Ruether as her source for the concept of "interstructured oppressions," as outlined in Rosemary Radford Ruether's *New Woman, New Earth* (Boston: Beacon, 1995 [1975]), 116. It should be noted that Third World feminists, particularly among African Americans, had been living and exploring this concept for many years.

20. Susan Brooks Thistlethwaite, *Sex, Race, and God: Christian Feminism in Black and White* (New York: Crossroad, 1991), 2.

21. Sharon D. Welch, *A Feminist Ethic of Risk,* rev. ed. (Minneapolis: Fortress Press, 2000 [1989]).

22. Sharon D. Welch, *Sweet Dreams in America: Making Ethics and Spirituality Work* (New York: Routledge, 1999).

23. Hobgood, *Dismantling,* 152.

24. Ruether, *New Woman, New Earth.*

25. Ellen T. Armour, *Deconstruction, Feminist Theology, and the Problem of Difference: Subverting the Race/Gender Divide* (Chicago: University of Chicago Press, 1999), 11–16.

26. Stringfellow, *My People,* 133–34.

27. Jeffrey Gros, "A Sharing of Gifts and Struggles in God's Will and Our Unity," in *Ending Racism in the Church,* ed. Susan E. Davies and Sister Paul Teresa Hennessee, S.A. (Cleveland: United Church Press, 1998), 121–27.

28. For example, the Anti-Racism Committee is a subcommittee of the Executive Council of the Episcopal Church in the United States. The group works on a number of fronts, including training local trainers. Presbyterian Women in the Presbyterian Church (U.S.A.) have declared themselves to be an anti-racism organization and reaffirmed their 1997 commitment to strive to eradicate racism.

29. Louis Schoen, "Case Study: Minnesota Churches Anti-Racism Initiative," in *Ending Racism in the Church,* ed. Susan E. Davies and Sister Paul Teresa Hennessee, S.A. (Cleveland: United Church Press, 1998), 7–14, describes the Minnesota project well.

30. Joseph Barndt, *Dismantling Racism: The Continuing Challenge to White America* (Minneapolis: Augsburg, 1991).

31. See also Becky Thompson, *A Promise and a Way of Life: White Antiracist Activism* (Minneapolis: University of Minnesota Press, 2001), for an excellent history of white anti-racist activism in the past fifty years, including that among religious people.

32. Cornel West recounts just such an instance in the preface to *Race Matters* (Boston: Beacon, 1993), x–xi.

33. Frankenberg, *White Women,* 197–204. Frankenberg is not speaking of theology or theologians. Still, her construct is a useful way to understand the normative power of theology written by white people standing in the center of the theological world.

34. Robin Hawley Gorsline, "A Queer Church, Open to All," *Union Seminary Quarterly Review,* in press. Marvin Ellison first suggested this idea in "The NCC on the Hook," *Christian Century* 100 (November 2, 1983): 982.

35. Raymond Blanks, "Conversion, Covenant, Commitment, and Change," in *Ending Racism in the Church,* ed. Susan E. Davies and Sister Paul Teresa Hennessee, S.A. (Cleveland: United Church Press, 1998), 101–9, makes this point well.

36. Cone, *A Black Theology of Liberation,* 7.

37. Robin Hawley Gorsline, "Bearing Witness to the Dark: Resources for Anti-White-Supremacist, Pro-Same-Sex(es), Pro-Feminist Theologizing in Queer Modes," Ph.D. diss., Union Theological Seminary in the City of New York, 1999. Also, "James Baldwin and Audre Lorde as Theological Resources for the Celebration of Darkness," *Theology and Sexuality* 10 (2003): 1, 58–72.

38. Beverly Wildung Harrison, "The Power of Anger in the Work of Love: Christian Ethics for Women and Other Strangers," in *Making the Connections: Essays in Feminist Social Ethics,* ed. Carol S. Robb (Boston: Beacon Press, 1985), 7.

39. Hobgood, *Dismantling,* 34.

40. James A. Baldwin, "The Fire Next Time," in *The Price of the Ticket: Collected Nonfiction, 1948–1985* (New York: St. Martin's/Marek, 1985), 335–36.

Two

CLAIMING WHITE SOCIAL LOCATION AS A SITE OF RESISTANCE TO WHITE SUPREMACY

KARIN A. CASE

O N AN APRIL AFTERNOON in 1992 I attended a rally on the campus of Columbia University in New York. The acquittal of four white Los Angeles Police Department officers,[1] who had been video-recorded beating African American motorist Rodney King, had triggered waves of rage, violence, and protest across the nation. The violence was felt most intensely in Black neighborhoods of major cities across the nation, and particularly in Los Angeles, where fifty-five people were killed and more than one thousand were injured in three days of rioting. Many white U.S.-Americans were profoundly disturbed by the brutality of the four officers that was so graphic in the videotaped beating, which was being played and replayed by the broadcast media.[2] Many were stunned by the acquittal since excessive use of force had seemed so clearly in evidence. The acquittal of the white officers was widely recognized as a prominent public case of racial bias in the U.S. judicial system. It served as a wake-up call for many white U.S.-Americans who had not comprehended that racism of that nature persisted.

The week of the L.A. rebellion I went to the protest rally at Columbia to express outrage at the verdict. I needed to give voice to my distress, to be connected with others who shared my concern over issues of racism, and to identify constructive avenues to work for change. I acted out of the conviction that it was important for U.S.-Americans to fill the streets in public witness to our nation's ongoing crisis over race.[3] The rally at Columbia was attended by a large and diverse group of students, concerned citizens, activists, elected officials, and civic leaders. I was, indeed, surrounded by people who shared my outrage and many who shared a similar critique of white supremacy in American society. I was glad to be able to add my voice and presence.

The thing I remember most vividly about that day, however, was not a sense of empowerment or connection with anti-racist activism, but a profound sense of isolation and incoherence. At that historic moment, in the midst of nationwide turmoil, I felt a keen desire to act incisively, to be on the side of racial justice.[4] I felt urgency and passion about the injustice of the acquittal and the entrenched institutional racism that made it possible, yet, I felt mute and inert. *I did not know what to do.*

This was more than a little ironic, since I am trained as a social ethicist, adept at analyzing social problems, experienced as an activist in the antinuclear movement. Moreover, I had begun to be active in anti-racism work on campus. I had even uprooted my family from the West Coast (leaving behind my husband's secure job — our only source of income) and moved to New York to do doctoral studies at an institution renowned for its Black and womanist theologians.[5] I was eager to learn and willing (at least to some extent) to order my life so that I could more deeply engage issues of racism. Certainly my training, life experience, and commitment should supply me with adequate vision.[6] That moment at the Columbia rally was painful. I had stumbled — for all the right reasons — onto the recognition that my whiteness and the deep ways in which my life was structured by white supremacy kept me from seeing clearly what to do. I was reminded of the old organizing slogan: "If you're not part of the solution, you are part of the problem." It seemed to me that I was part of the problem. I recognized that despite my express commitment to anti-racism, most aspects of my life — my friendships, professional

relationships, church and community life, and my own consciousness — remained deeply conditioned by the social arrangements of a
white supremacist culture. Little in my experience or education had
led me to understand my own whiteness as an issue or prepared me
to make significant, enduring alliances with peoples of all colors to
challenge white supremacy. I realized — with considerable anguish —
how little I really understood about the dynamics of white supremacy.

This essay emerges out of the conviction that I am not alone. While
it is true that many white people are invested (consciously and unconsciously) in holding onto white advantage,[7] it is my experience that
there are also *many* of us who are actively struggling with our racism,
trying to remedy damage that has been done to peoples of colors, to
ourselves and our society; aching to know how to act effectively;
seeking genuine and meaningful interracial relationships; and desir-
ing to take part in coalitions for change. I believe there are many
justice-minded white people who are perplexed about how we —
as white people — can work against racial injustice, ignorant about
the precise dynamics and effects of white supremacy, and lacking
the personal and organizational connections with peoples of colors
necessary for meaningful relationship and strategic coalition building. We see throughout U.S. history examples of white individuals
and movements that have been passionately engaged in anti-racist
activism. Yet, white people who are truly on the side of racial justice
remain exemplary rather than normative.

I cannot state strongly enough that *these dynamics are the result
of the system of white supremacy.* Our ignorance and sense of being
perplexed are not the result of personal inadequacies, but rather
a collective condition — the result of powerful socialization into a
dominant social location. White people have an urgent moral responsibility to recognize that the system of white supremacy limits
our consciousness, restricts our vision, and structures social relations
so that all too frequently we remain silent and inert in the face of
injustice. The culture of white supremacy keeps many white people

silent, unaware, and disengaged from issues of racial justice. Our socialization into a dominant location encourages erasure, amnesia, and
denial of the harms of racism. Because these dynamics are endemic,
the work to develop understanding of them is itself a morally imperative task as well as the necessary route for moving into anti-racist
practice.

Although we are conditioned to remain mute and passive, we need
not accept our role as acquiescent accomplices to injustice. As our
nation's long history of white anti-racist activism demonstrates, having white skin does not automatically determine our consciousness,
our politics, or our actions. It is our moral and ethical responsibility
as human beings and as Christians to oppose white supremacy. The
stakes are high. Quite obviously, the stakes include the well-being of
peoples of colors: sometimes life itself is at stake. Also at issue are
the deep structures of our collective life in U.S.-American society. To
what extent will our society be able to reflect the democratic principles of justice, equality, and fairness? And finally, the *souls of white
folk* are at stake (to invert W. E. B. Du Bois's famous title,[8]) for when
we remain passive accomplices to violence and injustice our souls are
at peril.

The persistence of white supremacy relies not only on deliberate
perpetrators — those who intentionally discriminate, subjugate, or
abuse others — but also on the aloofness and detachment of a large
percentage of the white population in the face of injustice. Most of
us feel distant and disconnected from the relatively small percentage of white people who actively cultivate racial hatred, and likewise
from the relatively few who have been in a position to exercise great
power over others — through land seizure, enslavement, forced labor,
sweatshop labor, and the like. It is hard for us to see how our lives
are implicated in racist practices. Most of us are not intentional perpetrators of racial injustice, yet our lack of awareness, the absence of
a sense of pain or outrage, our silence, our indifference to the injuries
of racism, and our failure to actively intervene may make us accomplices in the system. This essay is directed to those white people who

strive to be anti-racist and are looking for some clarity and direction in the struggle.

White people can and must take action against white supremacy. We must speak and act — out of the lived complexity of our own lives: as recipients of unearned advantage and conferred dominance, and as justice-seeking people, who hold a disproportionate amount of social power by virtue of our skin color, and who have customarily been taught to disregard the evils inherent in the social arrangements of white supremacy. The ambiguities of our social location, as *white* anti-racist people, often create complexities that impede ethical clarity and decisive, liberative action. We must speak about our experience of this complexity, and we must give and receive the help we need to become clear and to act. The color of our skin is something we cannot change, but we *can* work to change our *consciousness* and our *actions* and we can join with people of every race to create a better future. Our resistance may create vital opportunities for social transformation, and it can move us collectively and personally toward greater integrity and wholeness.

This essay focuses on how the dynamics of white supremacy — specifically, socialization into white social location — operate to shape our consciousness and actions and to forestall active resistance. Why are basically well-intentioned, justice-minded white people so affected by the system of white supremacy that sustained anti-racist action is the *exception* rather than the norm? Of course, a simple argument can be made that white supremacy is in the interest of most white people and therefore we do not challenge the system that advantages us.[9] It is absolutely true that we receive innumerable *advantages* by virtue of being white. It is also true, although seldom acknowledged, that the *costs* for white people are extremely high — injuries to our psyches, spirits, relationships, communities, and to the fabric of U.S.-American society. While its most direct negative impact is clearly to individuals and communities of colors, all of us who live in U.S. society are profoundly affected by white supremacy. It is a

destructive and grossly unjust system that breaches human relationships and causes psychological and spiritual damage to everyone as
well as causing the more obvious socioeconomic injuries to peoples
of colors. White supremacy is a violation of persons, an abrogation
of justice, and an affront to humanity. It is so destructive as to be
morally intolerable.

In the pages that follow, I invite you to reflect with me on the
ethical and spiritual issues we face as white people, by virtue of our
social location. What does it mean to assert our moral agency *as
white persons* in a system that gives us so much advantage? What are
our particular obligations and responsibilities? How can we equip
ourselves to understand the dynamics of white supremacy so that we
can actively work to undermine it? What is at stake in our choice
between passivity and resistance? What is involved in developing an
actively anti-racist white identity?

The perceptions and observations I develop in these pages have
emerged not only out of academic study, but also as I have sought to
be attentive to the particularity of my own life situation as a white
person. My perceptions are undoubtedly filtered through the particularity of my experience as an upper-middle-class, educated white
woman. I do not presume that what I say in these pages pertains to
all white people in precisely the same way, for the experience of being
white is refracted through many lenses. I have read and listened carefully and sought also to learn from what peoples of colors have to
say about race and whiteness, and what it means to be white in the
U.S. context. I hope the reader finds some essential truth in the pages
that follow.

WHITE SKIN, WHITE SOCIAL LOCATION, AND WHITE IDENTITY IN THE CONTEXT OF WHITE SUPREMACY

In order to be effective agents for racial justice, white people must
undergo *conscientization* — a coming to awareness — of the mechanisms of white supremacy. This includes awareness of the specific

ways our own moral agency is co-opted by the system of domination. Only when we understand how the system operates and how we are implicated and caught in it can we engage in informed praxis to disrupt it. For white Christians this means we must develop our own form of *emancipatory praxis* as white people opposed to white supremacy. Emancipatory praxis is a cycle of action and critical reflection that helps illuminate the system of domination, so that our own consciousness and actions are transformed. Our praxis may have concrete effects in terms of social change as we begin to act decisively to disrupt the system of domination. Emancipatory praxis can also have profound effects on us personally as our lives and spirits are opened to new consciousness, new ways of being, and the in-breaking of God's realm.

Before moving into a more substantive discussion of emancipatory praxis, I wish to sort through distinctions between white skin, white social location, white racial identity, and the system of white supremacy. Under white supremacy these aspects of whiteness are woven together in complex ways that frequently foster incoherence and inaction on the part of white people. It is often confusing, perplexing, and even painful to be a white-skinned person committed to opposing white supremacy. The pain is a result of our (willing or unwilling) involvement in injustice, our complicity in something that is both harmful and wrong. Those of us with *white skin advantage* occupy positions of unearned advantage in a system that is grossly unjust. Our families, ancestors, many of the social institutions in which we participate, and we ourselves have benefited from white advantage and will continue to do so until and unless the system is disrupted and dismantled. These realities often result in white guilt, shame, confusion, incoherence, and inaction that, in turn, keep white supremacy in place. It is helpful, therefore, to understand how our white skin, social location, and racial identity connect to aspects of the domination system, so that we can break free from subservience to white supremacy.

On the most basic level, light skin is a physical characteristic — a biological trait, just as hair color or eye color. Of course, no one (even the palest albino) actually has *white* skin (or red or yellow or black, for that matter). Obviously the primary aim of racial classification is not to describe skin pigment, but rather to create social stratification. Although the names of racial categories sometimes refer to skin color, in racial classification systems skin color gets bundled with other physical characteristics — such as hair color, eye color, body shape, facial features — and social traits — such as ethnicity, place of origin, and native language. These together are labeled as "race."

When we look cross-culturally, or transhistorically, it becomes apparent that "white" is a socially constructed and historically conditioned category that is permeable and changing. What it means to be "white" (and *who belongs to that category*) is different in South Africa than it is in the United States; and what it meant to be "white" in North Carolina in 1690 was different from what it meant to be "white" in L.A. in 2003. What counts as "white" is constructed by concrete and specific political, economic, sociocultural, and legal mechanisms, as Jennifer Harvey argues in her essay in this volume.[10] So, although the color of our skin may relegate us to a particular racial category, it does so only in combination with a host of other physical and social characteristics and only in a social context in which racial categorization is charged with significance.

In the United States, "white" is a dominant social location within the system of white supremacy, commonly assigned to those with light skin. *Social location* refers to any personal, familial, or cultural characteristic, or any aspect of social identity that locates us in a particular place with regard to systems of privilege and exclusion, such as (but not limited to) patriarchy, capitalism, and white supremacy. These systems shape our life chances by offering greater resources, liberties, and protections to persons with certain advantaged characteristics. Some aspects of social location are an integral and chosen part of our self-identity; other aspects have been assigned to us by others in society; some are a consequence of birth; others are the result of social arrangements. In each case, aspects of social location have concrete and specific social, political, and economic consequences.

Social location is a complex phenomenon because it combines aspects of self-identity, material reality, and others' perceptions of us within socially constructed, hierarchical systems in which these characteristics have positive and negative valences. Because we live within the context of multiple systems of domination, there are multiple axes to our social location that have bearing on our identity, the way we are perceived, labeled, and treated by others. White social location is one of these. I often visualize social location as a three-dimensional matrix in which we might locate ourselves with regard to multiple characteristics such as gender, race, class, sexual orientation, able-bodied-ness, etc.[11] Each of our characteristics affects our lives, sometimes compounding privileges or exclusions, and sometimes mitigating them.

Our white racialization is a salient feature of the experience of all white persons, yet whiteness is not a monolithic, singular entity. Not all persons with light skin are conferred the same advantages, because the kind and degree of benefit varies with other aspects of social location, such as religion, immigration status, native language, degree of English fluency, or level of educational attainment. While our experience of whiteness may be nuanced by our location within the matrix of privileges and exclusions, those of us who are white are nonetheless automatic recipients of white skin advantage. If we are walking on the street at night, passing through U.S. customs, or applying for a bank loan, we receive privileges and protections according to our skin color and perceived "race." Other facets of our location may give us greater or lesser advantage in combination with white advantage, but our white advantage remains. It is a mistake to read the complexity of social location as mitigating the effects of white privilege itself.

Given that white people automatically accrue undue advantages within an unjust system, we may well ask whether it is possible to have any positive identity *as white people*. Social psychologists in the field of racial identity development theory have demonstrated that constructing a racial identity is a significant part of our formation as human beings.[12] Yet, insofar as we identify with and desire superiority and dominance based on our race, aspects of white socialization are clearly harmful and dehumanizing. Beverly Daniel Tatum and Janet Helms argue that because of this significant obstacle, it is possible for white people to develop as psychologically and socially healthy persons only if two conditions are satisfied. First, we must be aware of our identity *as racialized*. Second, we must *take an active stand against racism*.[13] Both of these conditions, necessary for healthy white racial identity, are also fundamental to white anti-racist practice.

Although light-skinned people do experience them simultaneously, our biological features and our social identity are not identical to the system of white supremacy that reproduces and promotes white dominance. It is possible and necessary to distinguish between, on one hand, our physiological traits, social identity, and social location within the system of domination, and, on the other hand, our stance toward that system. Socialization into being white encourages us to conflate these: to assume that having white skin equals the right to dominance, a desire for unearned advantage, and the desire to benefit from the system of racial domination. In opposition to this, we must insist that having light skin does not automatically signify our wholesale acceptance of the system of white supremacy. Each person living under a system of domination must decide where she or he stands. As recipients of white skin advantage it is morally incumbent on us to take an active stand against white supremacy.

THE WAY OF EMANCIPATORY PRAXIS

It is possible for white people — those of us who have been socialized to identify with white advantage — to develop an actively anti-racist identity and to engage in the difficult work of disrupting white supremacy from within. *Emancipatory praxis* — the process of action, critical reflection, and learning — makes it possible for us to loosen the clutches of white supremacy and to become part of the movement for social transformation. The conversion of white social location from a site of collusion and acquiescence to a site of active resistance is possible *only* insofar as we undertake certain crucial tasks. The steps of emancipatory praxis enable us to understand the mechanisms of white supremacy, perceive the injuries it inflicts, scrutinize our own participation, and make strategic choices to disrupt it.

These steps need to include:

- breaking our silence on issues of race and racism;
- recovering memory;
- confessing the limits of our understanding;
- opening ourselves to being changed;
- seeking accurate information about the mechanisms and harms of white supremacy;
- listening respectfully and humbly to the voices of those who are harmed by white supremacy, receiving and integrating new information on both cognitive and emotional levels;
- analyzing and confessing our own participation in the system of white supremacy;
- and taking action against white supremacy.

Beyond these initial tasks, of course, there are many additional steps needed for establishing relationships of genuine mutuality with peoples of colors and building strategic coalitions to disrupt white supremacy in all its manifestations.

Breaking Our Silence

Among white people there is relatively little open and honest dialogue about race or the devastating effects of racism. Silence about such a profound and pervasive reality conveys the message that racism is not significant or worthy of attention; not substantive or serious; or conversely, that racism is too shameful to speak about openly.[14] As

Toni Morrison observes with regard to literature, "In matters of race, silence and evasion have historically ruled literary discourse. Evasion has fostered another substitute language in which the issues are encoded, foreclosing open debate."[15] As in literature, so in life: our silence plays a role in maintaining white supremacy. Soul-searching dialogue and open public debate can help break the shackles of racism. Peoples of colors have carried not only the burden of white supremacy itself, but also the burden of articulating over and over the moral urgency of disrupting white supremacy. White people must speak, for white supremacy requires our silence.

It may be that the first thing white people can do to break our complicity with the system of white supremacy is to speak candidly about our experience, including our confusion, pain, and the fact that we simultaneously desire justice and receive unfair advantages from societal and institutional racism. White people need to talk with each other about the challenges of being white and anti-racist. Just as urgently, we need to talk with people of different races. Breaking our silence can open the way to sharing information, experiences, and strategies with a wide variety of people from diverse perspectives.

Recovering Memory

James Cone writes, "There can be no justice without memory — without remembering the horrible crimes committed against humanity and the great human struggles for justice. But oppressors always try to erase the history of their crimes and often portray themselves as the innocent ones."[16] Indeed, the recovery of memory and critical interrogation of memory are matters of some urgency where erasure and denial are manifest. Locating the memories of our forbears; our own personal memories; and broader social memories of pain, struggle, and resistance is a vital link to emancipatory praxis in the present. Yet there is seldom a simple path to memory of those painful things that have been suppressed and denied. We must delve into forbidden territory, into the dangerous memories of our personal and collective histories to learn — perhaps for the first time — about the injuries of racism.

Often the "master narrative" of history, told from the vantage point of white dominance, omits not only our role as oppressors, but also *any* mention of our own racialization, or racism as an explanatory framework for historical dynamics. As we unearth collective memory we reconstruct a picture of the salient racial dynamics that have seemed to us sketchy at best. We may uncover family secrets — for example, our own mixed-racial ancestry or hidden histories of violence. Many white families are connected with the institution of slavery; possibly we may even learn stories of resistance. Recovering these memories can be painful, yet for committed, justice-minded white folks it is the only path open to us. Justice cannot be built on lies and half-truths.

Womanist ethicist Katie Geneva Cannon uses the phrase "remembering what we never knew" to refer both to the marks that have been pressed inchoately on the bodies and souls of African Americans, and to memory as a deep source of collective wisdom. For Cannon, "remembering what we never knew" entails recalling the particular ways in which African Americans have been wounded, but also recovering the "sources and resources to resist domination."[17] For white folks, "remembering what we never knew" may entail, in part, recovering stories of our own brokenness. But the more urgent moral task is to recount the ways we are implicated in the wounding of others. Facing our personal and collective racialized histories, in all their ugliness and complexity, is our only route to emancipatory praxis.

Confessing the Limits of Our Understanding

One of the most potent mechanisms of white supremacy is the way it becomes invisible to those in a dominant social location. The norms and practices of the dominant white culture come to be seen as natural or inevitable. This occurs at societal, institutional, and civilizational levels,[18] so that it may become (for white people) extremely difficult to see our own racialization, and the fact that our taken-for-granted assumptions and standard institutional practices are specific and contingent. The molding of our consciousness in this way is especially potent because the ideology of white supremacy tells us that "our" view of the world is entirely sufficient. An absolutely critical step for white people is admitting, or confessing (to use Christian theological language), that our view of reality is limited and partial and that we need to look outside ourselves, beyond customary white perceptions, for a fuller and more accurate view of reality. There is a humility in this, which is uncharacteristic of white consciousness, for we have been socialized to believe that our view of the world is correct. Like the recovery of memory, confessing the limits of our understanding opens the way to acknowledging the particularity and distortions of our perspectives (as white people), and to recognizing our dependence on persons of different "races," whose perceptions may be far more accurate than our own. It also opens the way to seeking more accurate information.

The consciousness and perceptions of white people are commonly distorted in a number of important ways. In her essay *"Hablando Cara a Cara,"* philosopher María Lugones identifies these key aspects of racism:

> one's affirmation of or acquiescence to or lack of recognition of the structures and mechanisms of the racial state; one's lack of awareness or blindness or indifference to one's being racialized; one's affirmation of, indifference or blindness to the harm that the racial state inflicts on some of its members.[19]

Lugones cogently articulates several key features of the consciousness of those who are socialized into positions of dominance within white supremacy. These include erasure and denial, ignorance, indifference, and acquiescence. In addition to these features identified by Lugones, I would name amnesia, silence, incoherence,[20] and passivity. These are fundamental mechanisms of white supremacy that function to obscure serious injustices, thus permitting them. These dynamics are reproduced in white-dominated institutions, but also rooted in the psyches of individual persons, particularly white persons as a result of socialization, but also, to some extent, *any* person who uncritically internalizes the norms of white supremacy.

White People's Ignorance of Our Own Racialization

Let me be very specific about erasure, amnesia, and denial. Precisely what is it that white people may fail to perceive? First, for many, our own race is invisible to us. We may perceive *others* in racial terms, yet be unable to conceptualize *ourselves* in this way. The fact that we are racialized (ironically) escapes our perception. Whiteness thus functions as an invisible and unspoken norm and maintains its power through its very invisibility. Psychologist Robert T. Carter remarks:

> The predominant comment of Whites is that they are not aware of themselves as White. This is interesting when one considers the fact that Whites, specifically Europeans and Americans, essentially created racial classification and the ideological and sociopolitical meanings associated with race. Moreover, Whites, through various mechanisms, continue to this day to maintain racial divisions in the society.[21]

We fail to note our own racialization in part because the dominant culture sees white as normative. Psychologist Beverly Daniel Tatum describes a classroom exercise she conducts regularly with her students:

> I ask my students to complete the sentence, "I am _____," using as many descriptions as they can think of in sixty seconds.... Students of color usually mention their racial or ethnic group: for instance, I am Black, Puerto Rican, Korean American. White students who have grown up in strong ethnic enclaves occasionally mention being Irish or Italian. But in general, White students rarely mention being White.... Common across these examples is that in the areas where a person is a member of the

dominant or advantaged social group, the category is usually not mentioned. That element of their identity is so taken for granted by them that it goes without comment. It is taken for granted by them because it is taken for granted by the dominant culture.[22]

Power Evasion

What is invisible to white people is not literally our (white) skin color, but rather (white) power. Ruth Frankenberg describes this form of perception as *power evasion* or *power blindness*. Frankenberg conducted extensive interviews with white women and notes that some of the women she interviewed found "the naming of inequality, power imbalance, hatred, or fear"[23] to be uncomfortable. Rather than face these uncomfortable issues directly, these women tended "to evade by means of partial description, euphemism, and self-contradiction those [subjects or issues] that [made] the speaker feel bad."[24]

White people's lack of conscious awareness of our own racialization may seem like stunning obliviousness, willful ignorance, or sheer stupidity to those for whom racialized existence is painfully evident. One reason white ignorance can be so vexing and anger producing is that it is a form of consciousness unthinkable to anyone who is a member of a target group — those who experience racial discrimination daily. It is all the more enraging because of the social function it performs: it is a way of rendering power less visible so as to maintain dominance.

Concomitant with a lack of awareness of our own racialization is white people's failure to perceive the ways the system of white supremacy advantages us. Peggy McIntosh observes that many white people acknowledge that racism adversely disadvantages peoples of colors, but are still unable to perceive the corollary: that *white people are the recipients of unfair advantage.* Many of the social benefits that seem to come to us "naturally" or as the result of merit are actually functions of unearned advantage.[25]

Seeking New Information

Once we admit that our view of reality is limited and partial by virtue of having been taught to identify with white dominance and power, it is appropriate to seek additional information about the mechanisms and harms of white supremacy. As we make visible these past and present dynamics we may gain perspective on both our own complicity with white supremacy and potential sites of resistance. Only then can we work honestly and effectively toward social transformation.

It is safe to assume that most white people do not understand the precise racialized dynamics that are in effect in our society. We have not been taught to take racism seriously as something we need to address. This lesson is most often communicated to us as children through the silence and inaction of white adults who remain passive in the face of injustice. Because white culture is seen as normative, we are not taught to know and value the richness of other cultures. Finally, many white people simply do not have intimate connections — family relationships, friendships, or collegial relations — with people of color, and we lack intimate knowledge of what it feels like to be a target of racism. The "information" white people must search out is first and foremost a more balanced view of history and present-day social arrangements, especially from the vantage points of peoples of colors — those whose lives are most profoundly affected by racial injustice. But what white people may lack is not merely cognitive; it is not just "factual" information. As recipients of unfair advantage, we have often been shielded from the harshest effects of white supremacy. We, thus, may lack emotional and spiritual understanding of the devastation of racism — both to ourselves and to peoples of colors. Part of the work that white people need to do to get our house in order is to open ourselves to emotional knowledge of the harms of racism.

Ignorance of Our Nation's Racialized Histories

White U.S.-Americans may be unaware of the substantial role race has played in the historical development of the United States, when in fact the geographical boundaries and political economy of the United States were established through land seizure, enslavement, and forced labor. Likewise, white people may forget or deny that hegemony is established through violence, terror, and intimidation. We celebrate Columbus Day as a national holiday, despite the fact that with the arrival of Europeans on the North American continent commenced land seizure, wholesale destruction of Native American cultures, and the near genocide of Native peoples. Our most prevalent historical narratives are invested in white power and do not fairly and accurately represent the experiences of those whose lives, land, and labor were seized.

Sometimes white folks are aware of racial injustice in a general way. We know, for example, that Japanese Americans were interned during World War II. Yet we minimize the severity of this injustice, not seeking out detailed information about how that affected Japanese American lives. We excuse it as an isolated event, failing to see historical patterns of discrimination and abuse. Or we imagine it as an aberration, rather than the result of U.S. governmental policy. We may relegate racist abuses to the distant past, failing to see — for example, in the case of internment — that Japanese Americans are affected for generations to come.

James Baldwin wrote:

> People who imagine that history flatters them (as it does, indeed, since they wrote it) are impaled on their history like a butterfly on a pin and become incapable of seeing or changing themselves, or the world.
>
> This is the place in which it seems to me most white Americans find themselves. Impaled. They are dimly, or vividly, aware that the history they have fed themselves is mainly a lie, but they do not know how to release themselves from it, and they suffer enormously from the resulting personal incoherence.[26]

Baldwin's words should be for us a mandate to subject our historical narratives to critical scrutiny, and to open ourselves to being changed by what we discover.

Ironically perhaps, not only histories that tell of white complicity are erased, but also the histories of our resistance, as Sally Mac Nichol writes elsewhere in this volume. When we fail to talk openly about our histories of complicity, we also risk losing our stories of resistance. There have been many white people willing to engage and risk themselves in anti-racist resistance. These are a vital part of our legacy: crucial resources in our effort to disrupt white domination.[27]

Ignorance of Other Cultures

Concomitant with our ignorance of the dynamics of white supremacy, white people may be profoundly ignorant of cultures other than our own. Because we hold a disproportionate amount of power, white persons can afford to be almost completely ignorant of the lives, customs, culture, literature, music, arts, theoretical work, scientific and technical achievements, and political and economic achievements of peoples of colors within the United States and around the world. Customarily, it has not been necessary to have functional knowledge of these things in order to be rewarded according to the standards of the dominant culture. This is one of the manifestations of white privilege. Civilizational racism functions at the level of our most taken-for-granted assumptions, shaping what counts as "real," significant, or worthy of attention. Thus, white people often see those things associated with our own cultures and ways of doing things as normative and superior, while we dismiss as less significant those things associated with peoples of colors. Because our socialization into being white predisposes us to see this way of operating as "normal," it is difficult to recognize how our own perceptions are conditioned by our particular experiences and vested interests and the social structures that support them. If white normativity is to be decentered, we need to be far more educated, aware, and respectful of cultures other than our own.

Listening to the Voices of Peoples of Colors

Listening attentively to the voices and perspectives of peoples of colors — those who are most directly harmed by white supremacy — is a necessary step for white people. It helps us obtain a fuller and more accurate picture of the machinations of white supremacy; opens the way to establishing relationships of mutuality and respect; and opens the way to multiracial strategizing and coalition building. *How* we listen, especially in face-to-face situations, is a matter that requires considerable attention. At a minimum white people need to listen with respect and the expectation that we will learn something vitally important from peoples of colors. This does not mean that we listen uncritically, but that we come to the encounter aware that our perspective is limited and partial, and open to being changed by what we hear.

It must be stated emphatically that it is not the responsibility of peoples of colors to educate white people about the effects of racism. But it is the responsibility of white people to listen carefully to what peoples of colors have to say. Face-to-face conversations and collaborative work with peoples of colors are obvious opportunities for intentional listening. For white people seeking deeper and more accurate understanding, a huge volume of material in the public domain offers excellent sources of information. We can pick up a Chinese newspaper, listen to a Black radio station, visit a Native American museum, and read extensively — journal articles, scholarly works, and works of fiction by peoples of colors. If we avail ourselves of these resources in the public domain, our perceptions of white supremacy and our place in it will be more fully informed.[28]

Analyzing Our Location as White People

All of the tasks discussed above — from breaking our silence, to confessing the limits of our understanding, to seeking new information — lead us to a critical stage in white emancipatory praxis. We must attend specifically to our location *as white people* and engage in critical interrogation of our social location. Justice-minded people of every race need to be engaged in anti-racist struggle. But for white people, as beneficiaries and recipients of unfair advantage, the struggle is different because of our social location than it is for those who are oppressed under the system of white supremacy. White people need to understand precisely how racism functions at the societal level and to make the connection between this systemic evil and our own personal lives. We must take full personal and collective responsibility for our role(s) in perpetuating this evil. Unless and until we do, not only are we on the side of injustice, but also we are a broken people — in James Baldwin's words — in need of "help and healing."[29]

The system of white supremacy is created and sustained (not exclusively, but primarily) by white people, and as such it is our responsibility — not ours alone, but clearly ours — to challenge and dismantle it. The effects of racism and our complicity in it are realities white people may deny, in part, because they are so painful. But perpetual denial is a meager and wholly inadequate response to systemic injustice. Evasion imperils our moral agency and helps keep white supremacy in place. It makes us useless as agents of change and instruments of justice.

This liberation framework shares in common with other liberation methodologies the insistence that lived experience must be the starting point of ethical reflection. I insist, however, that it is not solely the experience of oppression and subjugation that constitutes an acceptable starting point for ethical reflection, but rather *any critically examined experience* of living under the system of domination. White people can — in fact, *must* — begin our ethics with the ambiguities, contradictions, privileges, pain, guilt, and even shame of our own experience *as white people* in a white supremacist society. We must begin, in the words of ethicist Jennifer Harvey, with "how we are shaped by our history, roles and practices."[30]

One piece of our work as white people, then, is to turn critical scrutiny on ourselves. We can ask questions that begin to get at the dynamics of race and racism in our lives. We might ask, for example: How is my own (white) race constructed and co-constructed with other races under the system of white supremacy? What is the significance of being white in the family, class, ethnic, and cultural tradition from which I come? How did being white impact my ancestors? What are the narratives about race that have been handed down in my family, class, or ethnic group? Are there hidden histories in my family of interracial relations (either positive or negative)? How does being white influence what is possible for me and what I hope for in life? How does it shape my perceptions and awareness? How does it influence my friendships, workplace relationships, and church affiliation? Does my identification with or desire for white power and privilege inhibit me from speaking and acting against racial injustice? Answering these questions is never an end in itself, for the objective is always to engage in concrete and specific actions to undermine white supremacy. Critical scrutiny helps us get at the complex truths of our lives so we may more honestly and freely engage in liberative action.

Taking Action against White Supremacy

Although it is urgent that we come to a greater understanding of white supremacy and our role in it, *awareness alone* is not our aim. Our goal is transformative action. Louise Derman-Sparks and Carol Brunson Phillips observe:

> Anti-racism education is not an end in itself but rather the beginning of a new approach to thinking, feeling, and acting. Anti-racist consciousness and behavior means having the self-awareness, knowledge, and skills — as well as the confidence, patience, and persistence — to challenge, interrupt, modify, erode, and eliminate any and all manifestations of racism within one's own spheres of influence. It requires vision and will, an analysis of racism's complexities and changing forms, and an understanding of how it affects people socially and psychologically.[31]

The purpose of the above enumerated steps of emancipatory praxis is to gain the clarity and conviction needed for effective, sustained anti-racist action. The more real understanding and knowledge we have, the more we are able to participate in coalitions for change.

At the same time, we must take action even before we have all the information we need, and before we feel "ready."

White persons will be engaged in concrete specific anti-racist actions — teaching, protesting, organizing — and what takes place in these arenas is *the main point.* Concrete work, whether teaching or organizing, is also a chief source of information (for white people) about race and racism. What we learn in the context of anti-racist action is the grist for our reflection. It should be emphasized that, in practice, the steps of emancipatory praxis do not proceed in a linear progression. It is possible to enter in at any point. The insights we gain in one area illumine other aspects of the struggle. The steps work together and reinforce each other. Likewise, these tasks are never truly completed, for white supremacy is endlessly complex, and being actively anti-racist is a lifelong commitment to action and reflection.

CONCLUSION

White Social Location as a Site of Resistance to White Supremacy

Can white social location be a site of resistance to white supremacy? Yes! History is full of examples of white folks who have joined with peoples of colors in the struggle to end white dominance. Examples include John Brown's organizing armed resistance, Lillian Smith's outspoken critique of Christianity and southern white culture in her writings from the 1930s, the Freedom Riders — northern white folks who literally gave their lives in the Civil Rights Movement of the 1960s, contemporary white theorists such as Ruth Frankenberg who have focused their academic work on analysis of the dynamics of white supremacy, and countless white people who have been involved in anti-racism movements at every level from neighborhood to international. Each of us is responsible for exercising anti-racist moral agency within our own spheres of influence.

Still, being white and committed to anti-racist practice poses a particular set of challenges. How do we maintain our identities as white persons, while actively opposing white supremacy? Is it necessary to reject who we are? To the extent that we have embraced things that are life-denying in the course of forming our white identity, the answer is yes. We need to reject our identification with white power privilege. Many white people are not aware of how deeply we identify with white power until we begin to work consciously at relinquishing it. The good news is that we can also let go of the many ways white supremacy has deformed us. Most of us have been taught to numb our feelings, to disregard our sense of injustice, to remain silent in the face of terrible agony and suffering, and to limit our intimacy and our friendships to a racially circumscribed group. We have been taught to be suspicious, untrusting, fearful, judgmental, and even hateful toward persons of different races. When we explicitly reject this socialization, we may find ourselves more free to form relationships of genuine respect and mutuality across race.

Even as we reject those aspects of white socialization that encourage us to identify with white power and dominance, there are many distinctive aspects of our identities we may wish to celebrate. We can take pride in and enjoy many aspects of our family, ethnic, and cultural heritages.

For white people, anti-racism requires an active choice because it is inherently nonconformist and counter-(white)culture. It requires intentionality, reflection, and commitment; it elicits and engages our moral agency. In the process of forming an active anti-racist identity, we choose for ourselves those values by which we will live, critically evaluating what we have been taught and rejecting some of it. We may choose to uphold values such as justice, equality, solidarity, resistance, and struggle, over and against values of conformity, "fitting in," or perceived loyalty to other white people. We may choose to speak out, act out, and to disrupt white supremacy. Opposing racism obviously gives priority to certain social values, but it can also be a conscious means of attending to spiritual and moral dimensions of our lives.

The Promises of Anti-Racist Praxis

Anti-racist practice takes us directly into the messiness, imperfection, and social-embeddedness of our lives. We encounter pressures to conform to white supremacist ways of being and doing. And even after years of conscientization and activism, we find in ourselves pockets of ignorance, prejudice, and unwillingness to change. The grist for our learning is the stuff of relationships. The cross-racial friendships we form in school, neighborhood, church, and workplace may offer the unique gifts of interracial understanding. But they also serve as the place of our hardest learnings — where we may discover the hurts and limitations racism has inflicted on all of us. This knowledge is close to the surface and familiar in its dailiness for many people of color. For white people it is frequently buried and suppressed, and the process of bringing it into our awareness can be both painful and liberating.

As with other forms of liberationist struggle there are some risks involved in anti-racist practice, but the promises are great. The promise is no less than liberation from white supremacy — that demonic system that has all of us in its grip. We may see, at last, the extent to which we as white people are caught in its clutches. Our liberation is intimately connected with the liberation of peoples of colors, for until all of us are free, none of us is truly free.

There is a kind of basic honesty entailed in white emancipatory praxis — an honesty before God and one another when we acknowledge the extent of our brokenness and inability to save ourselves. Anti-racist praxis may help us acknowledge our humanness: the ways we are stuck and unable to free ourselves, the ways our psyches and spirits are damaged, our limitations, and our dependence on others. We may reclaim our compassion, our capacity for relationship, and our creativity, flexibility, and humility. We may deepen our moral and spiritual capabilities. At the same time anti-racist praxis can equip us to be fierce and determined in the fight for justice. All of this is good and necessary, for there is much work to be done in society as a whole and in white churches so they become sites of liberation and change, places where the realm of God breaks into our human arrangements and something new transpires.

NOTES

1. Four officers — Laurence Powell, Stacey Koon, Theodore Briseno, and Timothy Wind — were accused of beating motorist Rodney King on March 3, 1991. The case, *California v. Powell, et al.*, was tried in courtroom in Simi Valley, a suburb of Los Angeles. The four officers were acquitted on April 29, 1992. In a subsequent case, the four officers were arraigned on federal charges of violating Mr. King's civil rights. In April 1993, Sgt. Stacey Koon and Ofc. Laurence Powell were found guilty. Officers Briseno and Wind were acquitted.

2. A man named George Holliday videotaped the incident from the balcony of a nearby building. Holliday released his videotape to a Los Angeles television station the following day.

3. I felt this was a particularly important moment for white people to speak up, since the burden of protest against racial injustice is so frequently borne by peoples of colors.

4. The expectation that I might "have a sense of efficacy" in the face of injustice is itself an expectation born of my white privilege and class privilege. It is interesting that the failure of my own efficacy was a signal for me that something larger was at play.

5. Dr. James H. Cone and Dr. Delores Williams were teaching at Union Theological Seminary at that time. dr. emilie m. townes subsequently joined the faculty and later served as my dissertation advisor.

6. Adequate vision is rarely something possessed by an individual, but rather something that is won collectively by diverse people working together and sharing their multiple vantage points. I suspect the assumption that my personal vision should be adequate was a result not only of individualism, but also of my class and educational privilege.

7. I prefer the terms "unearned advantage" and "conferred dominance" to the more commonly used term "privilege." For an article that makes a case for this preference, see Peggy McIntosh, "White Privilege and Male Privilege: A Personal Account of Coming to See the Correspondences Through Work in Women's Studies," in *Race, Class, and Gender: An Anthology,* ed. Margaret L. Andersen and Patricia Hill Collins (Belmont, Calif.: Wadsworth Publishing Company, 1992), 77.

8. W. E. B. Du Bois, *The Souls of Black Folk* (Chicago: A. C. McClurg & Company, 1903; reprint, New York: Penguin, 1996).

9. The dynamics that keep white supremacy in place are complex issues of socialization, ideology, and the interplay of several systems of domination. Thus, it is insufficient to dismiss white passivity as merely a product of self-interest. See, for

example, Mary Elizabeth Hobgood, *Dismantling Privilege: An Ethics of Accountability* (Cleveland: Pilgrim Press, 2000). Hobgood argues that white people buy into the ideology of white supremacy because of the influence of capitalist ideology.

10. See also legal scholar Ian F. Haney López's book *White by Law: The Legal Construction of Race* (New York: New York University Press, 1996); and Winthrop D. Jordan's monumental historical work *White over Black: American Attitudes toward the Negro, 1550–1812* (Chapel Hill: University of North Carolina Press, 1968).

11. For foundational theorizing on the interstructuring of oppressions, see, for example: Angela Y. Davis, *Women, Race, and Class* (New York: Random House, 1981); Rosemary Radford Ruether, *New Woman, New Earth: Sexist Ideologies and Human Liberation,* 20th anniversary ed. (Boston: Beacon, 1995 [1975]); Patricia Hill Collins, *Black Feminist Thought: Knowledge, Consciousness, and the Politics of Empowerment,* vol. 2, *Perspectives on Gender* (New York: Routledge, 1991).

12. See, for example, Robert T. Carter, "Is White a Race? Expressions of White Racial Identity," in *Off White: Readings on Race, Power, and Society,* ed. Michelle Fine, Lois Weis, Linda C. Powell, and L. Mun Wong (New York: Routledge, 1997), 198–209; Janet E. Helms, ed. *Black and White Racial Identity: Theory, Research, and Practice* (Westport, Conn.: Praeger, 1990).

13. Janet E. Helms, *A Race Is a Nice Thing to Have: A Guide to Being a White Person or Understanding the White Persons in Your Life* (Topeka, Kans.: Content Communications, 1992); Beverly Daniel Tatum, "Talking about Race, Learning about Racism: The Application of Racial Identity Development Theory in the Classroom," *Harvard Educational Review* 62, no. 1 (1992): 1–24; and Beverly Daniel Tatum, *"Why Are All the Black Kids Sitting Together in the Cafeteria?" and Other Conversations about Race* (New York: Basic Books, 1997).

14. Thandeka argues persuasively that white people's shame is a primary dynamic in our failure to address racism. Thandeka, *Learning to Be White: Money, Race and God in America* (New York: Continuum, 1999).

15. Toni Morrison, *Playing in the Dark: Whiteness and the Literary Imagination* (New York: Random House, Vintage Books, 1992), 9.

16. James H. Cone, "White Theology Revisited, 1998," in *Risks of Faith: The Emergence of a Black Theology of Liberation, 1968–1998* (Boston: Beacon Press, 1999).

17. Katie G. Cannon, "Remembering What We Never Knew," *Journal of Women and Religion* 16 (1998): 172.

18. The introduction in this volume describes five levels on which white supremacy operates. This framework is borrowed from James Joseph Scheurich and Michelle D. Young, "Coloring Epistemologies: Are Our Research Epistemologies Racially Biased?" *Educational Researcher* 26, no. 3 (1997): 4–16.

19. María Lugones, *"Hablando Cara a Cara/*Speaking Face to Face: An Exploration of Ethnocentric Racism," in *Making Face, Making Soul: Haciendo Caras: Creative and Critical Perspectives by Feminists of Color,* ed. Gloria Anzaldúa (San Francisco: Aunt Lute Books, 1990), 48–49. Lugones's definition of racism is only one of the approaches I explore. It is helpful because it gets so incisively at one of the central issues of white privilege.

20. Ethicist Jennifer Harvey initially pointed out the connection between white normativity and incoherence and urged me to develop this theme.

21. Carter, "Is White a Race?" 198–99.

22. Tatum, *Why Are All the Black Kids Sitting Together in the Cafeteria?"* 20–21.

23. Ruth Frankenberg, *White Women, Race Matters: The Social Construction of Race* (Minneapolis: University of Minnesota Press, 1993), 156–57.

24. Ibid.

25. McIntosh, "White Privilege and Male Privilege."

26. James Baldwin, "White Man's Guilt," in *Black on White: Black Writers on What It Means to Be White,* ed. and with an introduction by David R. Roediger (New York: Schocken Books, 1998), 321.

27. An excellent account of white anti-racist activism can be found in Becky Thompson's book *A Promise and a Way of Life: White Antiracist Activism* (Minneapolis: University of Minnesota Press, 2001).

28. An exceptionally helpful resource is a David Roediger's edited collection of essays, poetry, and articles by African American authors: David R. Roediger, ed., *Black on White: Black Writers on What It Means to Be White* (New York: Schocken Books, 1998).

29. Baldwin writes, "The history of white people has led them to a fearful and baffling place where they have begun to lose touch with reality — to lose touch, that is, with themselves — and where they certainly are not truly happy for they know they are not truly safe. They do not know how this came about; they do not dare examine how this came about. On the one hand they can scarcely dare to open a dialogue which must, if it is honest, become a personal confession — a cry for help and healing which is, really, I think, the basis of all dialogues and, on the other hand, the black man can scarcely dare to open a dialogue which must, if it is honest, become a personal confession which fatally contains an accusation. And yet if neither of us can do this each of us will perish in those traps in which we have been struggling for so long." Baldwin, "White Man's Guilt," 323.

30. Jennifer Harvey, "White Racism: An Ethic of Responsibility" (M.Div. thesis, Union Theological Seminary, New York, 1997), 36.

31. Louise Derman-Sparks and Carol Brunson Phillips, *Teaching/Learning Anti-Racism: A Developmental Approach* (New York: Teachers College Press, 1997), 3.

Three

RACE AND REPARATIONS

The Material Logics of White Supremacy

JENNIFER HARVEY

I N 1903 W. E. B. Du Bois penned his clairvoyant (and oft quoted) claim that "the problem of the twentieth century is the problem of the color-line."[1] As he assessed the centrality of race in U.S. society, Du Bois also articulated the peculiar understanding white people manifested in relation to it. He wrote of his encounters with white folk, "Between me and the other world there is ever an unasked question: ... How does it feel to be a problem?"[2]

Du Bois's depiction invokes the alienating experience of the scrutinizing gaze with which his white peers interrogated him as a Black man and reduced his being to the status of "problem." It also indicts a faulty and oppressive perception of race among white folk. Although *The Souls of Black Folk* was written in the specific context of the crisis of African American life in a post-Reconstruction United States, a similar faulty and oppressive perception remains prevalent one hundred years later. Those of us who are white tend to assume that the pervasive problem of the color-line is a problem about Black people, Native American people, Latino/a people, Chinese American people, or other peoples of colors. " 'Race,' " writes Kathleen Neal Cleaver, "usually makes one think of blacks. ... As a rule, white Americans no longer see race in relation to their own identity, and genuinely believe that racism poses a problem for 'others.' "[3]

The indictment in Du Bois's depiction is that the problem of the color-line — or white supremacy and racism — is and has always been a white problem.[4] White people created white supremacy, and people who are white sustain it. Our actions, attitudes, and ways of being subvert justice, cross-racial solidarity, and reconciliation. We benefit profusely from the prevalence of racial injustice, even as we are spiritually, psychologically, and morally malformed by it.

It is out of the perception of these truths that this volume and the field of "critical studies of whiteness" as a whole have emerged.[5] Perceiving racism as a white problem invites a lens through which the scrutinizing gaze is turned upon white people; whiteness becomes subject to interrogation in relation to the seemingly intractable problem of white supremacy. When this turn takes place, various lines of theoretical inquiry and pragmatic responses are made available.

Two such lines of inquiry pertain directly to my consideration of reparations in this chapter: the vexing question of who we are as white racial selves and the insistence that concrete disruptions of white supremacy are a white responsibility. In fact, these two lines of inquiry are deeply intertwined. Who we *are* as white people cannot be answered apart from the question of what we *do* in relationship to white supremacy. I want to demonstrate in this chapter that, in the matter of white supremacy in the United States, the interrelationship of being (who we are racially) and doing (what we do) brings reparations to the forefront as an urgent justice issue about which white Christians should be deeply concerned.

This chapter focuses specifically on reparations to African American people. It does not engage the experiences of the many other communities to whom reparations might be due in the United States. More significantly still, it does not explore the relationship between African enslavement and Native American genocide and land theft, which is a major limitation. The work in this chapter is, however, potentially relevant to other racial communities in the United States, as the theoretical frameworks articulated in the first half of the chapter do not rely on a binary (white/Black) logic. Moreover, the articulation of the materiality of race and white supremacy is directly relevant to all communities negatively impacted by white supremacy. Such frameworks might be usefully employed (perhaps requiring expansion to account for imperialism, nationhood, citizenship, etc.), for example, to undertake historical analyses of the experience of Chinese immigrants who built the U.S. rails, Puerto Ricans' experience of colonization and the atrocities resulting from the U.S. military presence at Vieques, and other historical and contemporary experiences.

REPARATIONS: RACE AND RACIAL OPPRESSION

Social movements for reparations for the enslavement of people of African descent in the United States have acquired increasing strength and visibility in recent years. So much has this been the case that New York City Councilman Charles Baron, in terms that echo Du Bois, has insisted, "Reparations is the defining issue of the 21st century."[6] These movements are not new. Calls for reparations began before the abolition of slavery and have continued ever since. The reparative concept of "forty acres and a mule" emerged in 1865 from a field order given by General Sherman — a concept that has had a larger place in national mythology than it had in historical fact.[7]

Most often the call for reparations is made through the struggle, resistance, and advocacy of people of African descent. In 1963, for example, Queen Mother Audley E. Moore submitted a petition calling for reparations to President John F. Kennedy that had over one million signatures. Every year since 1989, Representative John Conyers (D-MI) has introduced House Bill HR-40, which calls for congressional hearings on the nature and impact of slavery and postslavery discrimination. Local legislative bodies in some cities, as a result of the hard work of individual legislators and grassroots activists, have passed resolutions calling upon the federal government to pass Conyers's bill.[8] Presently, organizations like the National Coalition of Blacks for Reparations in America (N'Cobra) and the National Reparations Convention Committee (NRCC) are pursuing litigation and legislation in order to put the issue on the national radar screen, and ultimately secure reparations.[9] Many legal steps have been taken since the abolition of slavery to address persistent racial injustice in the United States. None of these has manifested in so much as a national apology for slavery, however, let alone in reparations.[10] For as long as African Americans have resisted white supremacy and for as long as they have engaged in the struggle for reparations, the U.S. government has refused to hear and respond to such demands.

The refusal to engage seriously the issue of reparations has been not only a political refusal. It also has been, and remains, a social refusal evident in white attitudes toward reparations. Some surveys have suggested that up to 67 percent of whites acknowledge that discrimination against Blacks continues, yet 62 percent polled in New York say that not even an apology for slavery is due.[11] I would venture to guess that this percentage would be as high or higher in other parts of the nation. Meanwhile, an equal percentage of African Americans (62 percent) believe that Blacks are owed reparations.[12]

There are many things worth noting in the face of such figures. The disparity of these figures indicates widely divergent understandings of the legacy of slavery among white and African American racial groups. This divergence poses significant obstacles to the cross-racial reconciliation about which many mainline Protestant Christians, churches, and denominations express concern. My more immediate concern here, however, is with questions these figures raise about white understanding of our relationships to race and racial oppression. In what follows, I engage the issue of reparations only after substantive theoretical and historical analysis of these relationships.

The very genesis of race lies within a genocidal history. Thus, adequate understanding of race itself is necessary in order to understand racial oppression sufficiently. After exploring the question "what is race?" I offer the response that "race is a social construction." This theoretical work is intended to demonstrate how constructionism makes visible the ways race functions in white supremacist systems, the meanings it has been given, and the human agencies at work in its creation. I further demonstrate that these visibilities can be leveraged to pose questions about the meaning of "white" as a racial category and the agency of white people in giving race meaning. To explore these questions the chapter turns from theory to historical analysis. I use the methodologies of a constructionist approach to argue that white U.S.-Americans became white through the institutionalization of lifelong chattel slavery of African peoples and their descendants. The chapter closes by making explicit how the implications of this history bear on the matter of reparations and its implicit themes of repentance, repair, and reconciliation.

The thrust of my argument is this: If, with an eye toward racial justice, we dig deeply enough and with sufficient theoretical clarity into the issue of who white people are, as our racial being emerges from what we do in relationship to white supremacy, reparations becomes an unavoidable moral imperative. The very processes of history that have constituted "white," the legacies of which remain present in the present,[13] are the same processes we must actively alter, address, and redress if we wish to journey toward moral reformation and transformation.

SO, WHAT IS RACE?

Race in U.S.-American life is at once so self-evident and so complex that it is important to be as clear as possible about what it is. When we recognize race in the United States we typically do so by noticing skin "color." We might notice other bodily features or other personal characteristics — a name or an accent — that seem to indicate race. From here, we might make assumptions about cultural traditions, geographical origins, economic status, or any number of things. Conversely, awareness of culture, geography, or economics might prompt recognition of race. Whether or not our assumptions are correct, these various indicators come together loosely to suggest how someone might be racially categorized.

Still, what is race? Recognizing it is not the same as defining it. Nor is race reducible to any of the infinite varieties of human features I take in when I observe my own or another person's physical being. Race does not, for example, equal skin color.

Because we can, or think we can, recognize race by such visible indications, it is a short, and often unconscious, step to assume that race simply *is:* that race exists on its own, an autonomous, self-evident category. Indeed, common wisdom long held that race was a fact of nature, a scientific or biological category that distinguishes groups of people. Yet, as is noted throughout this volume, science has increasingly admitted that it will not find between one white person and every other white person any biological similarity greater than the potential similarity between that white person and a Latino/a, Chinese, or African American person. Despite the "common sense" of race into which most of us have been socialized in the United States, race is not something that just *is.*[14]

To say that race is not a biological or natural category is not to say that it is not real. Rather than offering a definition of race at this point, however, let me provide an example of it. Say that same person whom a scientist cannot identify as having a biological race walks down the street very late one night. If that person has physical features generally recognized as "white," a passing police officer might slow down to make sure that person is not lost. If that same person has features recognized as "Latino/a" or "Black," he might find this same officer slows down and asks him for identification, or interrogates her based on the assumption that, out alone at night, she must be engaged in illicit activity.[15]

Race is very real. It is just that the physical characteristics by which we tend to recognize it are not significant in and of themselves. Instead, these characteristics *become* significant as they are given meanings in the social realm. In the above example, race is *created* at the juncture between certain bodily features and the activity of racial profiling: profiling one person for protection, another for harassment. In theoretical terms, it is less the case that particular physical attributes mean one *is* white — a preexisting, essential racial category. It is more the case that repeated and institutionally supported police responses to certain physical characteristics invest those physical attributes with significance and particular meanings. In the dynamic convergences of various systems, activities, beliefs, and behaviors — undergirded with power — white, as a racial category, is created, or comes to be.

Race is, thus, a social-political reality that comes to be, over and over again, through laws, economic practices, the education and criminal justice systems, and an infinite number of other social phenomena. It is created through corporate and individual human activities and behaviors. It is produced through "social relations [among groups] over time."[16]

CONSTRUCTIONIST IMPLICATIONS: THE MEANINGS OF RACE AND HUMAN AGENCY

The contrast I am mapping here is roughly the contrast between essentialist notions of race and notions of race as a social construction. Michael Omi and Howard Winant define essentialism as follows: "Essentialism . . . is understood as belief in real, true human essences, existing outside or impervious to social and historical context."[17] Essentialism would understand race to be something inherent to one's being — for example, a biological attribute. In theological terms, essentialism might understand race to be an ontological category — a reality created by God, or a "natural" attribute of humanity. In contrast, a constructionist view, and the definition I use in the remainder of this chapter, would identify race as follows:

> . . . [R]ace [is] an unstable and "decentered" complex of social meanings constantly being transformed by political struggle. . . . *[R]ace is a concept which signifies and symbolizes social conflicts and interests by referring to different types of human bodies* [emphasis in the original]. Although the concept of race invokes biologically based human characteristics (so-called

"phenotypes"), selection of these particular human features for purposes of racial signification is always and necessarily a social historical process.[18]

To state that race is socially constructed does not constitute a unique claim. This is a prevalent theoretical articulation at this juncture in scholarship, but there is less consensus as to how the significance of this claim is to be assessed. Claiming that race is not essential does not make self-evident what to do about concrete realities of racial oppression. The question must therefore be asked: What are the implications of such a theory for the pragmatic goal of undermining or disrupting white supremacy? There is a great deal at stake in how this question is answered. So, before I turn to it, I want to address a few conclusions often drawn from the claim "race is a social construction" that need to be assiduously avoided.

Among those of us who find ourselves morally imperiled by how race comes to be (namely, among those of us who are white in a white supremacist social order), there might exist the temptation to say something like this: "Phew, if race is not essence or biology, then it is less real." This response assesses the significance of a constructionist paradigm by wrongly concluding that race is more illusion than reality. This response is unacceptable because it evades the challenge of justice. To understand that race is socially constructed does not make white supremacy evaporate, nor does it cause my white skin to cease having real meaning in my social worlds. Moreover, such a response threatens to erase the agencies of communities of color who have given meaning to racial identity in political and cultural resistances and creativities.[19]

Some scholarship assesses the significance of constructionist views as primarily indicating the need to rid ourselves of essentialist notions of race. This assessment correctly notes that essentialist projects are responsible for virulent and damaging manifestations of white supremacy. Essentialism, for example, ascribes certain (superior/inferior) characteristics, behaviors, or qualities to particular racial groups, which then become the basis for all kinds of social atrocities. Essentialism is also used to sustain white supremacy by explaining realities that exist as a result of unjust social structures and historical legacies — for example, the disparity in wealth among Native Americans and whites — in terms of natural differences — for example, "Native Americans are not fit for modern society," while "white Americans are industrious and motivated."

However, to take as the *primary* learning of constructionism that essentialism is to be denounced is to slip into making racial essentialism, rather than white supremacy, the problem.[20] Such slippage equates the end of racial essentialism with the end of white supremacy. Such an equation misses the extent to which unjust material realities underlie essentialist ideologies, realities that could easily remain even if essentialism were thoroughly banished.[21] Such an equation also risks devolving into fixations on mere theoretical abstractions that will, ultimately, do little to further the concrete project of dismantling racism. Philosopher Naomi Zack states it well: "the social reality of race is often physical in a way that overpowers the lack of biological foundation, which renders the lack of a scientific foundation for the concept of race a mere theoretical truth."[22] The mistake, here, is taking an essentialist understanding of race as the *cause* of white supremacy, rather than recognizing it as one mechanism of it.

Another tendency, when the entire freight of white supremacy is laid onto essentialism, is for scholarship to conclude that any use of race as a category of analysis is, therefore, inherently problematic. This claim precludes the necessary and strategic use of race in disrupting white supremacy and ameliorating the effects of racial injustice — for example, affirmative action. Or, similar to the above example, this claim can be used to erase or dismiss the use of race in resistance projects among communities of colors — for example, the political tactic of strategic essentialism, the use of race in Black nationalism, or the invaluable role of identity politics.

Despite these dangers, claiming that race is socially constructed is a significant theoretical claim. Constructionist theories do not lead to easy solutions to white supremacy, but they do make it possible to identify the ever-changing ideological and material processes — economic, political, religious, legal, cultural — through which race comes to be. They specifically enable us to point to the ways white supremacy is enforced through such processes. They also make it more possible to understand how white supremacy is structured in relationship to the bodies we inhabit and the behaviors we enact.

The possibilities raised by constructionist theories have major implications. First, once it is recognized that race is not a fixed or static fact of nature, but a contested and changing social-political reality, it becomes possible to interrogate the *meanings* it has been given. The meanings of race — what Zack calls "pragmatic meanings" — are a more appropriate focus for theories about race than are abstractions about racial categories. Second, constructionist theories enable more sufficient understanding of how racial oppression actually works. Understanding how race *functions* in processes of white supremacy can lead to pragmatic thinking toward resistance. Third, recognizing race as constructed makes visible the human agency involved in constructing it, one of the most important insights to leverage in understanding racism as a white problem.

Zack cites one example of a moment in which race was given meaning: as the importation of slaves into the United States was made illegal, legal proscriptions gave "race" meaning by designating children of enslaved women "black."[23] Certainly there were (negative) essentialist notions ascribed to "black" in this moment to justify this legal proscription. But, recognizing race as socially constructed is best used here to bring into focus the *meaning* of "race." The meaning of race in that historical moment, if one was socially identified as "black," was the experience of inherited lifelong enslavement. It is this meaning — namely, the experience of racial oppression and the material realities that accompanied it — with which we must be primarily concerned if white supremacy is to be challenged and changed.

Zack's example also demonstrates perfectly how race *functions* in terms of our working definition of race: "*race* [here, the category 'black'] *is a concept which signifies and symbolizes social conflicts* [conflicts: the various social relations and subordinations between elites and the nonelite masses over whom elites wanted to maintain control, one manifestation of which was the decision to make enslavement a permanent caste in the social strata by making it inheritable] *and interests* [European colonial landholders' desire to maximize economic profits] *by referring to different types of human bodies* [those which had dark skin or who could be identified genealogically as being of African descent]."[24] If the meaning of the racial category "black" in this example was enslavement, we can see that race functioned for oppressive ends by way of legal discourse linking particular social and material realities to particular physical attributes (a process I described in the preceding section). This clarity is important as it enables a better sense of the kinds of activities required to disrupt white supremacy. Specifically, it makes obvious that it is the linkages between oppressive material realities and particular physical attributes that must be targeted and ruptured.

So, on the most obvious level, in this case, such clarity would mean targeting for disruption the law that linked enslavement to dark-skinned bodies. But it opens onto more complex strategies and insights as well, as it reveals how white supremacy is structured in relationship to bodies and behaviors, and reveals the social relations on which it relies. A myriad of social mechanisms are necessary to sustain the unstable and constructed linkages between material realities and particular physical attributes; a legal ruling on its own could not have enforced and sustained enslavement.

An unspoken side of race's function in this historical moment was that *other* physical attributes (e.g., light skin) were linked to social and material realities of *non*-enslavement: legal proscriptions gave "race" meaning by designating those who were not eligible to be enslaved as "white." Enforcing enslavement required widespread and various forms of human collusion, and a particularly acute reliance on the behaviors of these light-skinned bodies: from their service as overseers to enforce captivity, to not harboring those called "black" when they ran away, to importing or buying cotton produced by slave labor. In other words, links were made between bodily attributes and expected behaviors — in this case, behaviors that lent support to institutionalized slavery. In terms of strategic thinking, therefore, if bodily attributes were invoked to enact such behaviors, undermining the behaviors presumed to flow from such physical indications has the potential to rupture the linkages. For example, in this case, if people with light-skinned bodies cannot be relied upon to return to the so-called owners those people whose darker-skinned bodies make them recognizable as legally "enslaved/able," the way race is supposed to function is potentially derailed.

The possibility of recognizing how race functions leads to the third implication of a constructionist understanding of race. Throughout U.S. history, race's meanings and how it has functioned have varied. This is largely because of implications Zack's example does not convey overtly: the role of human agency. The processes by which race is given meaning is never omnidirectional: supremacist processes do not simply act on human lives. Nor do the ideological and material processes that constitute race function without human input. Individual, corporate, and institutional human activities are also always at work creating race, altering the manner in which it functions and participating in giving it meaning.

Activities of communities of colors have given race meaning in the process of creating unique and rich cultural traditions and forging communities of political resistance. Even though race is bound up with white supremacy, supremacist ideologies and practices have never been the final arbiters of the meaning of race. White supremacy has never fully circumscribed or controlled the agency of those whose lives it seeks to use as commodity. This is one primary reason that ridding ourselves of the notion of race, for fear of essentialism or because it has been used to enact social atrocities, is not a viable, nor a desirable, option.

"'Race' must be retained as an analytic category," writes Paul Gilroy, "... because it refers investigation to the power that collective identities acquire by means of their roots in tradition."[25] In *"There Ain't No Black in the Union Jack"* Gilroy documents agencies of diasporic Black communities and demonstrates race to be a site of cultural and political productivity. Gilroy describes this productivity as emerging out of human agency interacting with social structures that create race: "Racial meanings are ... a salient feature in a general process whereby culture mediates the world of agents and the structures which are created by their social praxis."[26] Race has been, and remains, an ever-changing but always live site of human meaning-making and moral, political, and cultural agencies.

As a heuristic strategy, we might turn back to Zack's example at this point. If the pragmatic meaning of "black" (as a racial category) came to be in this historical moment so described, perhaps the meaning-making human agency that constituted Black (as a resistant racial identity) might be recognized as emerging in the subversive activities of Harriet Tubman, the composition of the spirituals, and the infinite ways in which peoples of African descent survived and resisted the deadly legal enforcements of a white world. These activities turned white notions of "black" in on themselves to forge Black identities, giving race different meanings than a white supremacist world would give it.

At this point I want to turn more explicitly back to the nonslave or to the owner who was (or became) called "white" in this moment. If the material meanings and experiences of the creation of "black" as a racial category constitute racial oppression, they also constitute racial domination and represent pragmatic meanings of "white" race. Moreover, white supremacist processes rely heavily on the consent and collusion of those called white if the mechanisms securing the dominative meanings of white are to operate smoothly. Here, then, the question of *white* agency begins to haunt, as the behavior of the nonslave or slave owner is cast in sharp relief in the process of race's creation and in the meaning of being white in such a violent and unjust system. For, here, it begins to become most clear how inextricable is the question of who we are as white people to that of what it is we do in relationship to white supremacy.

The particular justice questions that beg to be asked at this point emerge from having made it possible to recognize the function and material meanings of race and the human agency lived at the site of race. What have been and what are the meanings of race in relationship to white people? What has been and what is white moral agency in the process of racial meaning-making activity? How do answers to these questions help articulate the responsibility of white people in a white supremacist society?

These questions are ethical, but they are also deeply historical. The problem of the color-line is utterly rooted in U.S.-American history. Thus, I now turn to engage white people's relationship to white supremacy by going back to the genesis of race in this land, using the theoretical framework from the first half of this chapter. How race first came to be, what meanings it was given, and how it functioned are at the crux of the matter in thinking about how we became white, what the meaning of white was and is, and what implications this has for white relationships to race and racial oppression today.

A HISTORICAL LOOK AT BECOMING WHITE

In 1984, James Baldwin wrote in *Essence* magazine:

America became white — the people who, as they claim, "settled" the country became white — because of the necessity of denying the Black presence and justifying the Black subjugation. ... White men — from Norway, for example, where they were

Norwegians — became white by slaughtering the cattle, poisoning the wells, torching the houses, massacring Native Americans, raping Black women.[27]

Baldwin's words are not to be taken figuratively. His charge is not merely that white people have committed atrocious crimes in U.S.-American history. It is, quite literally, that people who arrived in this land, nationalities intact, *became white* colonists and, later, *white* U.S.-Americans through engagement in particular kinds of behaviors and practices.

The social category of race did not exist when those who colonized this land now known as the United States first encountered the Indigenous peoples who lived here.[28] Visible differences — whether in dress, bodily attributes, skin pigmentation, cultural expressions — were remarked upon heavily in European accounts of these encounters, but these differences were given religious meanings. The primary category through which Europeans understood such differences became Christian, or heathen: "Christian" meant, of course, "God-ordained beneficiary of this land"; "heathen" meant "evil and worthy of genocide" (at worst), and "object for conversion and removal from land" (at best).

This encounter was, however, part of the process of race's emergence in what later became the United States. Omi and Winant write, "When European explorers reached the Western Hemisphere,... the distinctions and categorizations fundamental to a racialized social structure, and a discourse of race, began to appear."[29] Europeans were obsessed with differences during these imperialistic ventures. Their obsession was intrinsic to deliberations over whether or not all peoples were part of "the human family," part of a larger debate over "the extent to which native peoples could be exploited and enslaved." The ideological result of these deliberations, manifesting into devastating and genocidal results, was the "ferocious division of society into Europeans and 'Others.'"[30]

When Africans were first wrenched from their homelands and brought here to be enslaved, race as we know it in the United States today still did not exist. "European" and "Other" were certainly at work in both the ideologies of Europeans and the social relations between the English and African peoples.[31] As with Indigenous peoples this division had imperialistic, cultural, and economic meanings that turned on European obsessions with differences. However, in the context of early-1600s colonial America and internal to the colonies, the primary difference of significance was that between owner and servant. For several decades this category might invoke the difference between a European owner and a European indentured servant, or a European owner and an African indentured servant.

Up until the 1640s, people from different geographic regions with different skin tones might occupy the same servant category. One should not draw the conclusion that the experience of Africans and Europeans was, thus, the same. Historian Winthrop D. Jordan makes a convincing case that English obsession with "blackness" renders the likelihood that Africans and Europeans ever had the same experience very slim indeed.[32] "Negro," a word taken from the Spanish, had been used by the English even prior to English participation in the slave trade. Its use suggests significance being attached to visible difference — significance that pertained directly to exploitative relations established between English and African peoples. For example, while there was a period in which some English citizens were brought to the colonies against their will, the entire history of African relocation is a history of violent coercion.[33] But, as was the case with Indigenous peoples, differences were not first refracted through racial categorizations, nor was race the reified social category — defined by law and pseudo-science — that it would become.

The first colonial settlers in Jamestown, Virginia (1607), were primarily aristocrats who arrived not expecting to work. Instead, they expected to find gold and become quickly rich.[34] In time, however, the fantasy of gold was replaced by cognizance that tobacco would be their source of wealth.[35] Meanwhile, back in England, there existed a surplus population of impoverished citizenry. English elites began to recognize in the colonial situation the opportunity to relieve population pressures at home, while addressing the colonial problem of labor, which had become acute in the transition to tobacco farming. In the earliest years of colonial America (approximately 1610–18), therefore, English plantation workers were the primary source of labor as tenant farmers.[36]

In less than a decade, capitalist visions — which rely on masses of "unattached labor-power" — of colonial landholders propelled a ruthless drive to lower labor costs.[37] Indentured servitude became the answer, historian Theodore Allen argues, to colonial Virginia's lack of such an unemployed labor reserve. The earliest historical records of indentured servitude replacing tenantry are from 1619. Servants were to be held for a period of seven years.[38] Over the course of the century, the experiences of European servitude varied: indenture time increased with the ongoing drive for profit, and voluntary emigration gave way to people brought against their will and sold (into indenture, not lifelong slavery) upon arrival.[39]

During this same period, the English began to participate in the African slave trade. In time, Africans were brought to the colonies to labor. The first documentation of permanent African settlers is in 1619.[40] For the next twenty years little is known about their status (by 1649, 2 percent of the people in Virginia were African or of African descent) — except that it was in servitude of some sort and the result of forced relocation.[41] There does exist, from this period, evidence of impulses — expressed during the "crisis" of labor costs that underlay the transition from tenantry to indenture for European laborers — to add unpaid labor time to the economy by making African servitude lifelong, hereditary bond-labor.[42]

By the mid-1600s, race as a social category had unequivocally begun to emerge. In 1640, the word "negro" appears in a court document, specifically in order to demarcate, for the first time, the difference in status between a person of African descent and two persons of European descent. Three indentured servants stood accused of the same crime: running away from their owner. As punishments were meted out the Europeans were sentenced to four extra years of servitude. The person of African descent was made a slave for life. From the ruling: "The third being *a negro* named John Punch shall serve his said master of his assigns *for the time of his natural Life.*"[43] There exist no historical records of a European servant ever receiving such a sentence.[44]

What I am highlighting here is not that this was the first time physical difference was recognized. Rather, what I underscore is the moment in which the difference was invoked formally to assign Africans a different status vis-à-vis their European laborer counterparts. From this point, lifelong enslavement came to be the norm for people of African descent and freedom the norm for people of European descent. Indentured servitude was phased out in deference to the benefits of holding a lifelong (African) slave versus a temporary (European) servant.[45] The owner/servant difference that indicated a status defined in legal terms became the difference between free/slave — now a legal definition that relied upon and referenced bodies. The definition began to name skin color as that which demarcated "kinds" of people. Race, as a reified social category of meaning, thus came to be.

The social significance attributed to bodies, pigmentation, genealogies — the color-line — became more deeply entrenched as chattel slavery became more institutionalized. In 1641, Massachusetts became the first colony to pass a statute legalizing lifelong bondage for people of African descent. Connecticut and Virginia followed suit in 1650. Race cohered as institutionalization progressed.

Despite regional differences, race's emergence as unequivocally bound with slavery is core to the entire nation. Slavery was more prominent and lasting in the South for many reasons, but the North was no less implicated. Slavery had been abolished or was on its way to being abolished in most northern colonies by 1800. Because all

northern states pursued abolition under conditions of gradual emancipation, however, it was a full fifty years post–Revolutionary War
before all northern Blacks were free.[46]

Moreover, the national economy was built through this institution. While the labor of four million Africans and their descendants
generated southern wealth, it fueled the shipping yards and factories
of the North. Slavery was at the heart of the New England textile
industry: from the raw material (cotton), which was imported from
the South, to the finished product (textiles), which was exported to
the South and also into the world market.[47] By the 1830s cotton
textiles constituted two-thirds of the value of large-scale New England manufacturing, and by 1860 cotton was the leading industry in
the United States.[48] Ronald Bailey writes, "The Industrial Revolution
served to fasten even more tightly the dying and anachronistic institution of U.S. slavery to the chariot of fast-paced national progress
for the next fifty years."[49]

The legacies of the colonial America and U.S. relationships to Indigenous peoples is also deeply intertwined in this economic and
social history. There were cases in which Indigenous peoples were
enslaved. But the greater force and impact of the historical trajec-
tory lay in the fact that the land of Native people, which the labor
of African peoples made "productive," was foundational to securing
wealth for white America and white Americans. Related to this land
theft was the genocidal violence through which colonists and white
U.S. citizens secured access to it. The relationship between the United
States and Native Americans may be better understood through
imperialism, colonization, and nationhood, rather than through dif-
ferentiations along racial lines. Nonetheless, this aspect of this history
also points toward issues of reparative measures. For Native peoples,
however, responses to the legacies of genocide and imperialism are
more frequently articulated through the struggle for sovereignty and
self-determination.

In terms of the enslavement of Africans and peoples of African
descent, the unpaid labor that poured into this nation's economy

through it is only one aspect of what was a vast and horrific experience. Still, that figure alone is staggering in its estimation: Sam Anderson, co-chair of the New York Metro Chapter of the Black Radical Congress, puts a low estimate of these wages at 97.1 trillion dollars.

The racial category of "white" and the ascription of persons with light skin to this category, the meaning of which was *free,* took place through the processes that constitute this devastating history. In this context I want to locate the issue of reparations. Becoming white in this racial system meant directly and concretely benefiting from the enslavement of those who became and were Black, rendering being white nothing less than a moral crisis. The very humanity of white people was eviscerated as we became white through processes that attempted to dehumanize people of African descent. This historical truth is key to understanding white relationships to race as a social construction and to racial oppression.

Not all whites benefited in the same way, and an important history of capitalism can be told here, one that details race's function in the lives of impoverished and working-class whites. Setting moral implications aside for a moment, in the South, slavery as an institution worked against the interests of all but the wealthy landholding elites — who were a significant minority. One effect of the coerced, unpaid labor of Blacks was to suppress severely the wages of those whites who were in the lowest economic tiers (the majority).[50] Why poor southern whites ultimately allied with white elites when their economic interests lay with Blacks merits, and has received, its own inquiry.[51]

Though it is beyond the scope of this chapter, such inquiry has much to reveal about the power of white supremacist ideologies and their complex role in sustaining social inequities. Here, however, I simply want to flag that different groups of people who became white benefited differently. This remains true, as racial privileges vary in strength and kind depending on other issues, from class to gender to sexual orientation (see Elizabeth Bounds and Laurel Schneider in this volume). This recognition not only helps name differences in benefits, but, perhaps more importantly, demonstrates the real costs that white supremacy exacts upon many of us, even as we benefit in our social location vis-à-vis others.

Despite ways in which the institution of slavery functioned to the overall detriment of many, all of those who became white received some direct benefits, privileges, and/or protections in relation to those who became Black. For some, this benefit came through owning slaves. For others, it was a stake in corporations that insured slaves or earned interest on slave owners' assets. For some it was access to a job as a wage laborer in an industry sustained by the unpaid labor of Blacks, and for others the chance to eke out a living on a small farm — impoverished, but guaranteed never to be shackled and bound to the land of another. For a number of whites in the South it was employment in a middle-tier group — as overseers or slave catchers — charged with maintaining the social control needed to ensure slavery's function. For all of those who became white the benefit was insulation from the systemic terrors legally inflicted upon Black people.

A multitude of concrete legal and economic benefits was acquired by those who became white through these historic processes. These processes not only impacted individual people; they spawned legacies of familial, corporate, and national wealth in the United States. The legacies have conferred on whites accumulated benefits in education, health, land, housing, and virtually any other aspect of life in which public/social institutions impact human well-being. To the extent that the color-line has remained an organizing principle of U.S.-American life, even as how it functions has changed (for example, slavery became "separate but equal," which now has become color-blindness), these benefits have been passed down from generation to generation. They continue to accrue to those of us who occupy the social category "white." Reparations activists call this phenomenon "unjust enrichment," and it is this phenomenon that gives currency to calls for reparations for an evil that legally ended in 1863.

REPARATIONS:
REPENTANCE, REPAIR, AND TRANSFORMATION

To the extent that such unjust material realities have remained un-redressed, the legacies of slavery remain with us in the present. Racism and white supremacy are not just attitudes of the mind and heart; they have a solid texture, touch, and feel. They are part of the social landscape in which we live and the air we all breathe; our lives are embodied in them every day.

Theoretical clarity about what race is, contextualized by the historical realities of how it originated, brings us to a crucial point in ethical analysis. The mass horrors of racial atrocities in U.S. history can never be undone, but what is clear is that attempts at true racial justice and disruptions of white supremacy must take place through material, not abstract, processes. Moreover, such attempts must come by way of interventions in the very relations of production and social processes which created and continue to create race — especially those which created and continue to create whiteness.[52] This theoretical clarity, brought to the history of race's genesis in the United States, brings to the surface the imperative of reparations, which assumes economic, social, and political response, redress, and repair.

The analysis here pulls, in a particular way, on those of us who are white in the national landscape. Realities of unredressed racial injustice — and their effects in the present — have resounding moral implications that go to the core of who we are as white racial selves. If we employ a constructionist framework of race, we can recognize that the *meaning* of race implicates the atrocities of racial oppression into our very being as white people. White is a category constituted by oppression. It came to be through the history of slavery. The decades (we cannot even say centuries!) since this institution came to an end have seen the meanings of "white" continue to pertain, mostly, to unjust enrichments of myriad kinds.

The *co-production* of oppression and our whiteness is one reason that, early in this chapter, I described as vexing the question of who we are as white selves. If you were to ask a group of white people to make a list of five characteristics unique to our racial identity that do not result from power and privilege, we, unlike our sisters and brothers of colors, will have little or nothing to offer.[53] The question of our agency at the site of race is, therefore, relentless for those of us who are white. Just as communities of colors have lived political, moral agency at the site of race in ways that have given race meanings other than what white supremacy conferred, those of us who are white must do the same. Only to the extent that we live concrete responses — *what we do* — that refuse and disrupt the material meanings of white can *who we are as racial selves* come to be something other than the relations of subordination, violence, and unjust benefits that have, to this point, overwhelmingly constituted what it means to be white in the United States.

Reparations is, thus, a moral imperative. First, for justice: to ameliorate the effects and vestiges of slavery that remain at work in the lives of African American communities. Second, for transformation: to beckon white people to the starting point of living our agency in ways that might alter the meanings of "white" — in both economic-material *and* spiritual-moral terms. Ethicist emilie m. townes writes:

> reparations talk, to my mind, is not ultimately about black
> folks
>
>> it is about white power and privilege sashaying around
>> with forgottenness
>>
>> that translates directly into forms of social organization
>> that shape daily life...
>
> in this country, when it comes to black folks
>
>> i believe reparations are about the ability or inability
>> of whites and their kin
>>
>> to recognize they have attained their power and privilege

on the backs of

>   the poor

>   the darker skinned

>   the feminine

and it just might be the time to have an honest conversation
about this

>   deal with the denial and guilt it is sure to spark....[54]

In short, white responsibility for racial oppression requires active and
concrete participation in processes that disrupt the material meanings
of what it has been, and is, to become, and to be, white. We must use
our bodies and lives to interrupt the mechanisms that link dominative material meanings of race to our particular physical attributes —
mechanisms whose functions have depended and continue to depend
on our collusion and consent. There are many fronts in our society in
which such a process is necessary and urgent. I do not pretend that
creating strategies for such is an easy or obvious task, but I do believe
that understanding how race functions is a crucial starting point. We
have much political strategizing to do.

On May 4, 1969, James Forman interrupted worship at the Riverside Church in New York City and presented *The Black Manifesto,*
which had been conceived and written at the National Black Economic Development Conference a month before. At the center of
The Manifesto was a demand for reparations.[55] Many denominations responded with programs to address racial disparities. They
did so with vehement insistence, however, that their responses *not* be
called reparations.[56] Amid this fracas, William Stringfellow, a white
Episcopalian, wrote of the predominant white responses to Forman,

>   Meanwhile, it does not take a psychiatrist to discern that the
>   denial of inherited, corporate guilt is a symptom of it. That, of
>   course, points further still to the fact that corporate guilt is a

pathological state, a condition of profound disorientation, and even a kind of moral insanity.[57]

Stringfellow's words touch the deeply moral and spiritual call to white folks that reparations embodies. Any and all benefits — even those that should be rights granted to all peoples — which have come and continue to come to us through racial history and current practices have led to white dehumanization and moral malformation. The moral and spiritual implications of the genesis of race will continue to bear down on the lives of those of us who are white until we make a choice to turn and face our history.

By casting the issue of reparations in deeply theological terms — discerning corporate guilt — Stringfellow summons the possibility of repentance. In theo-ethical terms, reparations is nothing less than the possibility, for white people, of teleological movement from the brutal inhumanity and moral malformation inherent to an existence dependent upon the subjugation of others to the possibility of a fundamental reconstitution of who we are as racial selves as we attempt to re-form our relations — material and otherwise — to history and to other peoples.[58]

This perspective enables a return to consider the disparate statistics I noted at the beginning of this chapter, in which white and African American people manifest widely divergent understandings of the legacy of slavery and because of which white Christians' interest in reconciliation is a fraught proposition. The theo-ethical learning from a critical analysis of race and race's history is that repentance and concrete repair remain prior conditions for reconciliation and solidarity between white people and African American people. Racial reconciliation is not an abstract problem that has to do with race. It is fundamentally rooted in the *white* problem of white supremacy. It is subverted and denied through white failure to come to terms — morally, spiritually, and materially — with realities that have had lasting effects on our sisters and brothers of colors, and different, but equally lasting, effects on ourselves. Reparations, emerging as a necessary response to the insidious nature of white relationships to race and racial oppression, sets out the conditions, work, and responsibilities for white Christians if we are sincere about reconciliation. In this view, burgeoning movements for reparations represent an invitation for white Christians to take first steps into a long and hard, truth-requiring, and material/human relation–altering journey toward reconciliation.

Some Christian denominations have begun to manifest impulses toward repentance and repair in terms that differ greatly from those which were put forward by denominational responses to *The Black Manifesto* nearly four decades ago. As of the end of 2002 the Disciples of Christ, the United Church of Christ, and the Episcopal Church had all passed resolutions or had resolutions under consideration calling on individual churches to educate themselves about the historical evils of the slave trade and its legacy, calling on the national government to issue an apology to African Americans for slavery, and/or reviewing the issues of reparations itself. In 2001, the Unitarian Universalist Association contributed twenty thousand dollars toward reparations payments to 131 survivors of deadly racial violence against African Americans in the Greenwood neighborhood of Tulsa, Oklahoma, in 1921.[59]

The theoretical frameworks and historical analysis I have articulated here suggest how morally and politically appropriate such impulses are, as is the heightened advocacy of movements of reparations for the enslavement of African peoples and their descendants. White U.S.-Americans are fortunate that movements for reparations are becoming so visible on the social and national scene. These give us an opportunity to engage in much needed, honest, and painful conversation, repentance, and, if we have the will, repair. At the same time, my analysis does not suggest what reparations should look like. Though my experience is that one of the first responses of those of us who are white to the word "reparations" is an angst-filled "what should it look like?" I am going to forego, unapologetically, such discussion here. My reason for so doing is twofold: first, because a white-led discussion on what reparations *should* look like misses the point of what it means to be among the party charged with the wrong (moreover, African American communities, within the church and outside the church, are already leading the way in terms of helping us to understand what our responses, corporately and as a nation, need to be[60]); second, because the first, fundamental step for those of us who are white is to orient ourselves in this landscape at all. For many of us, the understanding that our very being as racial selves is inextricably bound with the material realities that began with slavery and continue to accrue today is a radically new perspective.

Reparations is nothing less than an ethical imperative. What I am interested in here is leaving the reader with a framework for thinking about reparations as an urgent social, political, and moral issue that fundamentally calls into question the relationship of white people to race and racial oppression. For white readers, I am interested, further, in destabilizing the tendency among those of us who are white to perceive reparations as the threat white U.S.-Americans and the U.S. government usually experience them to be. Reparations, instead, are and should be understood as a call of hope. They are an imperative that offers those of us who are white a response *other than* the paralysis and guilt that often accompanies our recognition that we are white in a social system of white supremacy. As we increasingly come to understand what race is, how it is given meaning, and what its meaning has been, those of us who are white can increasingly recognize the choices we face about whether and for how long we will allow the history that has heretofore defined the meaning of race in our lives to continue to do so.

Given the realities of race in the United States, the choice for moral and spiritual transformation requires nothing less than going back to our racial beginnings. The continuing emergence of reparations movements should be deeply engaged by those of us who are white, for as white communities take up the work of repairing the actual harm done, we participate in helping to create a different present and future.

Metanoia — repentance — means to change direction, to turn from the brokenness of sin and evil, and to choose a radically different life way. It is in the context of the life-giving call of repentance that movements for reparations invite those of us who are white to journey into moral sanity and re-formation. Reparations calls us to choose to be human and to be made whole: first, by issuing the challenge to stalwartly face the history we have inherited and in which our racial lives are embedded; then, by offering tools with which to refuse the malforming ease of perpetuating those legacies that have come to us from the past. Reparations invites us to change directions by repairing the harm that has been done and in the process create a different present and future. This invitation is not an easy one. It is an invitation, however, into the hard, but life-giving journey of moral and spiritual transformation: a call to white people — as Baldwin would put it — "to do our first works over."[61]

NOTES

1. W. E. B. Du Bois, *The Souls of Black Folk,* unabridged (New York: Dover Publications, 1994; first published by A. C. McClurg and Co., Chicago, 1903), 9.

2. Ibid., 1.

3. Kathleen Neal Cleaver, "The Antidemocratic Power of Whiteness," in *Critical White Studies: Looking Behind the Mirror,* ed. Richard Delgado and Jean Stefancic (Philadelphia: Temple University Press, 1997), 157. Cleaver's use of "black" is, unfortunately, representative of the ongoing tendency for analyses of race to pull toward a Black/white dualism.

4. A truth peoples of colors have always known. Indeed, in 1860, Brooklyn schoolteacher William J. Wilson wrote a piece entitled "What Shall We Do with the White People?" See David R. Roediger, *Colored White: Transcending the Racial Past* (Berkeley: University of California Press, 2002), 21.

5. Roediger writes that naming this field is important as it needs to reflect that it is an overtly political and scholarly perspective seeking ways to disrupt white supremacy. He emphasizes that intellectuals of colors constructed this lens — a select few of whom include, along with Du Bois, Ralph Ellison, James Baldwin, and Toni Morrison. At their best critical studies of whiteness are heirs to this scholarship. Roediger, *Colored White,* 21.

6. Adamma Ince, "Getting Back on the Bus," *Village Voice,* August 14–20, 2002, 49.

7. In historical fact a mule was never promised, and the land was in a highly circumscribed area. "Congress never fully supported it and president johnson began

dismantling it just 1 year later," writes emilie m. townes. See emilie m. townes, "empire and forgottenness: abysmal sylphs in the reparations debate for black folks in the united states," *Union Seminary Quarterly Review* 56, no. 1–2 (2002): 99–101, 107, 108.

8. In 2000, the Chicago City Council passed such an ordinance, making Chicago the fifth city to do so. In 2002 the council passed legislation that requires all corporations doing business with the city of Chicago to research and disclose information on involvement of their predecessor companies in the slave industry. See Dorothy J. Tillman, "Slavery, Reparations, and the Role of the Churches," *Union Seminary Quarterly Review* 56, no. 1–2 (2002): 215–19.

9. See online: www.ncobra.com. The NRCC has initiated lawsuits against Aetna, Fleet Boston, and CSX Railroads, all corporations that profited from slavery and/or the slave trade. Other corporations have been identified and legal action is anticipated.

10. The closest to thing to an apology was President Bill Clinton's statement in April 1998: "Going back, to the time before we were even a nation, European Americans received the fruits of the slave trade. And we were wrong in that." Clinton's remarks were carefully worded to avoid actually apologizing. They were made in Uganda, not in the United States, and the White House specifically dismissed the possibility of a direct apology to African Americans because it would "touch off a demand for reparations." Online: www.pub.umich.edu/daily/1997/set/09-30-97/news/news13.html.

11. Ince, "Getting Back on the Bus," 49.

12. Ibid.

13. "White man, hear me! History...does not refer merely, or even principally, to the past. On the contrary, the great force of history comes from the fact that we carry it within us, are unconsciously controlled by it in many ways, and history is literally *present* in all that we do." James Baldwin, "White Man's Guilt," in *The Price of the Ticket: Collected Nonfiction, 1948–1985* (New York: St. Martin's/Marek, 1985), 409.

14. "Common sense" is Michael Omi and Howard Winant's language. They write: "In each epoch of U.S. history, a certain school of racial theory has been dominant, serving as the racial 'common sense' of its age." Michael Omi and Howard Winant, *Racial Formation in the United States: From the 1960s to the 1990s,* 2nd ed. (New York: Routledge, 1994), 4.

15. Latino/a is also an ethnic category, and the distinctions and overlap between ethnicity and race are important — though beyond the purpose of this chapter. Similarly those who identify as Black might also include various nationalities and ethnicities: Afro-Caribbean, Haitian American, Black Latino/a, etc.

16. Roediger, *Colored White,* 15, 16.

17. See footnote 57 in Omi and Winant, *Racial Formation in the United States,* 187.

18. Ibid., 55.

19. As bell hooks writes in her critique of white feminist Diana Fuss's work on essentialism, "a totalizing critique of 'subjectivity, essence, identity' can seem very threatening to marginalized groups, for whom it has been an active gesture of

political resistance to name one's identity as part of a struggle to challenge domination." bell hooks, *Teaching to Transgress* (New York and London: Routledge, 1994), 78.

20. Roediger writes, "The central political implication arising from the insight that race is socially constructed is the specific need to attack *whiteness* as a destructive ideology rather than to attack the concept of race abstractly." David R. Roediger, *Towards the Abolition of Whiteness* (London and New York: Verso Books, 1994), 3.

21. Omi and Winant, for example, who offer an otherwise excellent analysis of race in the United States, write the following: "A racial project can be defined as racist if and only if it *creates or reproduces structures of domination based on essentialist categories of race* [emphasis in the original]." Omi and Winant, *Racial Formation in the United States,* 71. While the overall thrust of their analysis does not lead in this direction, this definition points toward conclusions that colorblind approaches to race would be legitimate, as would a constructionist approach that named race as illusion. Either of these would reproduce white supremacist social realities, just as structures of domination can result with no overt reference being made to race. Omi and Winant would reject naming race as illusion, but their definition of racism in this regard is insufficient.

22. Naomi Zack, "Introduction: Aim, Questions, and Overview," in *Race/Sex: Their Sameness, Difference, and Interplay,* ed. Naomi Zack (New York and London: Routledge, 1997), 2.

23. Naomi Zack, "Race and Philosophic Meaning," *Race/Sex: Their Sameness, Difference, and Interplay,* ed. Naomi Zack (New York and London: Routledge, 1997), 39.

24. Omi and Winant, *Racial Formation in the United States,* 55.

25. Paul Gilroy, *"There Ain't No Black in the Union Jack": The Cultural Politics of Race and Nation* (Chicago: University of Chicago Press, 1991), 5.

26. Ibid., 17.

27. James Baldwin, "On Being White and Other Lies," *Essence* (April 1984): 90–92.

28. Omi and Winant, *Racial Formation in the United States,* 62.

29. Ibid., 61.

30. Ibid., 62.

31. See the exhaustive treatment of English attitudes toward blackness in chapter 1 of Winthrop D. Jordan, *White over Black: American Attitudes Toward the Negro, 1550–1812* (Chapel Hill: University of North Carolina Press, 1968), 3–25.

32. Ibid., 41.

33. Theodore Allen, *The Invention of the White Race,* vol. 2, *The Origin of Racial Oppression in Anglo-America* (London and New York: Verso, 1997), 123.

34. Ibid., 30.

35. Ibid., 53.

36. Questions exist about the exact arrangement, but it is clear tenants were to "have possession" of the allotted land and had "future prospects of becoming independent landowners." Ibid., 54.

37. Ibid., 97.

38. Ibid., 99. Some variance of length was in place in later years and depending on the reasons for indenture.

39. Ibid., 125, 126. In 1637, on a ship with seventy-six English passengers, all but two were bond-laborers to be offered for sale. Ibid., 109.

40. Charles Johnson, Patricia Smith, and the WGBH Series Research Team, *Africans in America: America's Journey through Slavery* (San Diego: Harcourt Brace, 1998), 36, 37.

41. Jordan, *White over Black*, 26, 27.

42. Allen, *The Invention of the White Race*, 123. This impulse demonstrates both early impulses to make Africans into slaves and suggests that the first Africans in the colonies were most likely existing in some form of indenture.

43. Johnson and Smith, *Africans in America*, 41.

44. Jordan, *White over Black*, 42.

45. Historians disagree over the "cause" of this shift. See Allen, *The Invention of the White Race*, 123, and Jordan, *White over Black*, 43.

46. Robert L. Hall, "An Introduction," in *The Meaning of Slavery in the North*, ed. David Roediger and Martin H. Blatt (New York and London: Garland, 1998), xvii.

47. Ronald Bailey, " 'Those Valuable People, the Africans': The Economic Impact of the Slave(ry) Trade on Textile Industrialization in New England," in *The Meaning of Slavery in the North*, ed. David Roediger and Martin H. Blatt (New York and London: Garland, 1998), 20, 21.

48. Ibid., 13, 18.

49. Beginning in approximately 1810. Ibid., 3.

50. The economic interest of white workers was at the heart of northern concern to prevent westward expansion of slavery. Many northern antislavery positions insisted they were as, if not more, concerned about white workers than about enslaved Blacks. See Eric Foner, *Free Soil, Free Labor, Free Men: The Ideology of the Republican Party Before the Civil War* (London, Oxford, and New York: Oxford University Press, 1970), esp. chaps. 2 and 4.

51. Ethicist Mary E. Hobgood has explored this to some extent. See *Dismantling Privilege: An Ethics of Accountability* (Cleveland: Pilgrim Press, 2000). See also Theodore Allen, *The Invention of the White Race*; Noel Ignatiev, *How the Irish Became White* (New York: Routledge, 1995); and David R. Roediger, *The Wages of Whiteness: Race and the Making of the American Working Class*, rev. ed. (New York: Verso, 1999).

52. "Relations of production" is the phrase Janet Jakobsen employs to note that diversity strategies for dealing with racism are insufficient because they do not articulate the relations of production that produce difference. Janet Jakobsen, *Working Alliances and the Politics of Difference: Diversity and Feminist Ethics* (Bloomington and Indianapolis: Indiana University Press, 1998), 5.

53. This is a common exercise done in anti-racist education workshops. Its purpose is to begin to get white people to think critically about and to interrogate their racial identity.

54. townes, "empire and forgottenness," 113, 114.

55. *The Manifesto* began: "We the black people assembled in Detroit, Michigan, for the National Black Economic Development Conference are fully aware that we have been forced to come together because racist white America has exploited our resources, our minds, our bodies, our labor." The demand was for $500 million for initiatives including a land bank, publishing and audiovisual industries, and a Black university. James Forman, "The Black Manifesto," in *Black Manifesto: Religion, Racism and Reparations,* ed. Robert S. Lecky and H. Elliot Wright (New York: Sheed and Ward, 1969), 114, 120–22.

56. This history reveals white supremacy's ahistoricity. Denominations expressed a desire to ameliorate the conditions under which Black Americans lived, but never named causes of such disparity.

57. William Stringfellow, "Reparations: Repentance as a Necessity to Reconciliation," in *Black Manifesto: Religion, Racism and Reparations,* ed. Robert S. Lecky and H. Elliot Wright (New York: Sheed and Ward, 1969), 59.

58. See Baldwin, "White Man's Guilt."

59. See "The Movement for Reparations," compiled by Jennifer Harvey and Ethan Flad, *Witness Magazine* 85, no. 12 (December 2002): 25.

60. A statement from N'Cobra reads, "In order for reparations to make us whole, it must remove blacks from dependence on others (the government, and the descendants of slave owners and colonizers), to create our jobs, manufacture the goods we consume, feed, clothe, and shelter us, build our institutions, and oversee our money.... A good academic exercise would be to develop a plan for how reparations could be used collectively to enable the African community to become independent from racist institutions and economically self-sufficient for at least seven generations." n.p. Online: www.ncobra.com.

61. James A. Baldwin, "Introduction," in *The Price of the Ticket: Collected Nonfiction, 1948–1985* (New York: St. Martin's/Marek, 1985), xix.

Four

GAPS AND FLASHPOINTS

Untangling Race and Class

ELIZABETH M. BOUNDS

SOME YEARS AGO, I decided to put together a panel on race for the state women's studies conference to be hosted that year by my institution. I wanted not a set of formal academic papers, but some sort of direct dialogue across racial differences that would, I thought, be more urgent and more compelling. I sent out a message on the women's email list at my school, a large state university in the Appalachian region of southwest Virginia, asking anyone to contact me who was interested in discussing "whiteness" and "blackness" as part of preparing a presentation on race for the conference.[1]

We first met just as the summer began. There were seven of us: four white women and three African American women. Six of us were professors and/or administrators at our school, while one white woman was a secretary. As we talked about our interest in such a conversation, it was clear that the black women had been attracted by the idea of working with a group of white women who were willing to talk about being white. As for the white women, I discerned a general interest in racial dialogue, along with — for some of us — a commitment to anti-racist work. After our initial discussion, I wrote an abstract for the fall conference program that described our process for the next few months. We would start with white women asking about what it means to be white and how we could attend to "the power dynamics that occur in the most ordinary meetings among different races." This conversation would be paralleled by an all-black conversation about the experience of being black women. Then we planned to meet for common discussion, with co-facilitation by one black and one white woman, asking how "the acknowledged and unacknowledged privilege of 'whiteness' is consciously and unconsciously used by white women and how that privilege often alienates black women and limits honest communication" (quotations from original proposal).

From the beginning of the process, there were "problems" with Martha, the white woman on the support staff. Martha simply did not talk about race the way we other white women did. A single mother who had been in an abusive marriage, Martha was involved with various women's groups on campus and had read many white feminist works. When I had noted her words in an early email exchange among the white women about "whiteness," I wondered why she wanted to be in this group: "I can truly say that being white NEVER helped or hindered me... establishing myself as a single woman with children... was much more difficult. As far as the GOOD OLD BOY system of justice I felt discrimination [emphasis in the original]." When the rest of us started by talking about our most immediate experiences with black women, with some of us talking about having black cleaning women, she talked about being in welfare offices. One of the other white women was from a similar working-class background, but was now a full professor. Well-versed in issues of race, gender, and sexuality, she never mentioned class.[2] As I look back at my notes of our conversations, I can track Martha's discomfort. At one point, clearly feeling our disagreement/disapproval, she wrote in an email, "I think I will be much more careful and much more reserved — which makes me not me anymore — in some ways."

When we came together as a group for cross-racial discussion, Martha managed to offend the black women through comments about her poor black neighbors ("they really didn't take care of their stuff"), and about black women on welfare ("why [do black women] feel that they should NOT get off welfare after a certain period of time and work. This bothers me since I had to get off my butt and work not just one job but several to raise my kids and put them through college") that were seen by all of the rest of us as "racist." I do not remember any angry confrontations, but I do remember a constant sense that Martha was on "another page." I knew, from some comments by the African American women, that her contributions had been talked about privately among themselves. By the end of the summer, I wrote to the group noting that Martha had withdrawn. As commentary I added, "On the one hand we were discussing some important ways black and white women experience things in profoundly different ways. Yet, simultaneously, since we kept class/status as an invisible category in our conversation, there was little space for Martha's class-different experience." I have no memory of our group ever following up on my comments.[3]

One of the white women, a playwright, wrote up our various conversations as a play, *Color Conversations,* which we performed to great acclaim at the women's studies meeting. As I read through the script again, I note with pride the ways we talked about trust and privilege that went beyond some of the usual limits of white/black conversation. We named very clearly the crippling nature of white guilt, black anger at "performing" for whites, subtle exclusions of black perspectives in academic meetings, (im)possibilities of black/white friendship, white anger at being blamed for unearned privileges. Certain commonalities or crosscutting differences around sexism and relations with men were put out in the open. (White woman: "Can't we as women come together around the issue of sexism?" Black woman: "Sexism in our world is not as much of a threat as racism.") Some part of the kind of anti-racist conversations I had always hoped for had occurred. These went beyond the ritual condemnations and affirmations that I had listened to in so many other academic conferences. I felt we had spoken personally and experientially while always pointing to the powerful structures of racism. We had taken the time to get to know each other, to move beyond initial stereotypes and assumptions, to build some relations among women that might serve us well when we tried to work together for attention to sexism and racism within our university. There was a beginning sense that we might, indeed, have each other's backs, which I knew was (and is) still a rare enough occurrence between white and black women in academic circles.

Nevertheless, I also notice, as I now read the script, how our awkward grappling with class was rendered invisible. In our opening affirmations of commonalities and differences, we said "we are well educated ... although we have many class experiences as a group, we are all now academic middle class." Martha's presence and the questions I had raised after her departure had disappeared, except for one statement I made, "Understanding ANYTHING about white racism is hard work." We represented whiteness — and we understood that in new ways at each meeting. And yet I still am troubled by the fact we never addressed the ways that we all shared the privilege of being professionals. Throughout this process, even after Martha's departure, I was acutely uncomfortable. I tried to mediate between Martha and the others, having at least one private conversation with Martha. I knew that I did not want her to leave. Even after our successful final presentation/performance, I felt we had failed in some way. While there was much painful difference evident in our discussion of race, I felt we had made good efforts at unpacking some of the lived complexities of race and gender. But any possibility of discussing class as part of these complexities had been simply negated. I knew the issue was structural, rather than personal. Even though Martha was, in many ways, a difficult person, one of the other white women in the group was, in my view, an equally difficult person. Yet, there had been no sense of her as "different" in the way there had been in the interactions with Martha. While we had laid bare many of the ways race and racism structured our personal interactions, we had been unable to talk about ways class might also affect these interactions.

The most obvious reading of this experience was that Martha was not willing to acknowledge her racism and to engage in critical self-scrutiny and transformation of her own white-skin privileges.[4]

Indeed, as I have said, she generally insisted that being white had offered her no privilege in life. For her, the group had not been about acknowledging the dominating power of whiteness, but about overcoming what she saw as unnecessary barriers and misunderstandings; finding a place where we could, in her words, "see past an issue, a color, a race, a choice of any kind." She had ended up being tacitly labeled as "more racist" than the rest of us white middle-class women. But was this fair? Did we other white women distance ourselves from her in order to see ourselves as "better" (i.e., less racist)? Were the black women not willing to engage in discussion around any class privilege they might have?

When I step back and look at the situation, I find tangles I cannot easily unravel. We were located in a large state university in a small town on the edge of Appalachia, where the traditional population had been poor whites. This history was reflected in the support structure of the school where all the office and grounds staff persons were, like Martha, white. Virtually all African Americans at our school were "imports," brought in as students, upper-level administrators, and/or faculty. I knew well that when African Americans ventured beyond the confines of the university and its town in which a culture of affirmative action ruled out overt racism, there was no prediction about what they could experience. One of my African American colleagues, for example, out for a walk, had nearly been run over by a truck full of young white men, all of whom were screaming "N_____ B_____!"

Yet I also knew how the power of status and class structured the lives of the white support staff. All of the women in our group, both white and African American, had far more power than Martha over our immediate work conditions. At the most simple level, for example, we could leave our offices for meetings when we wished, without worrying about being responsible for keeping an office "open" or fulfilling our thirty-five-hour workweek. Many women on the support staff knew, either personally or through family, Martha's

experience of being on welfare. I was aware I had no real understanding of the humiliations surrounding working with the welfare
system, so, I wondered how I could have responded to Martha's
strong sense that black women "played" the welfare system in ways
white women such as her did not. From my own experience with my
white working-class relatives (who could go bankrupt or take un-
employment, but would *never* go on welfare), I knew that this attitude
toward welfare recipients was not simply Martha's personal view, but
a view pervasive among white working-class people, which rendered
them vulnerable to the appeal of the racially shaped "welfare queen"
language pervasive in debates over welfare.[5]

When I think back on the conversations, race and class elided in
different configurations for the black women participating. Some of
their greatest anger was directed at the way businesses in the town
often tacitly assumed that if they were black, they would surely be
poor. One woman spoke of how, whenever she went into one of
the better clothing stores in town, she would be directed to the sale
rack.[6] Here I can see the flip side of Martha's insistence that not all
white women were economically privileged. Loaded into the dominant understandings of what it meant to be black or white were clear
class distinctions — to be black was to be poor and to be white was
to be, at the very least, middle-class. What would have happened if
our group had been able to talk about this paired assumption? Did
we need to talk not only about how to name racism/white privilege,
but also classism/class privilege? Was it possible to talk substantively
about the one without addressing the other? In the play, after we
said, "We are now all academic middle-class," we went on to say,
"We are also white and black. That is what we came together to talk
about. Everything we are has been affected by that." In other words,
we could not talk about class and race together; one had to trump
the other. This was made easy for us with Martha's departure.

The experience of this "tangle" is what I want to address in the
remainder of this essay. I want to try to sort out some of the complex intersections of race and class experienced in this one effort to

address, through alliance and solidarity, whiteness and racism. I do so with great caution, as the places where race and class intersect are complex, overdetermined flashpoints, which arouse emotions on all sides.[7] In discussing the ways sexuality and race intersect in the experience of black women, Hortense Spillers speaks of interstices, or gaps, where experiences exceed and contradict the trajectories of the intersecting categories.[8] While we have language to discuss the experience of each social category, we do not have language that easily expresses what happens in the *lived experience* of the categories as they always overflow analytic boundaries.[9]

Why do our analyses of social problems (and "our" here means those groups of people who try to build a more just society and, in the case of this essay, particularly white people serious about racism and oppression) so quickly rest on one analytic dimension? Part of the reason, I think, rests in the nature of theory. I understand theory pragmatically — as a reflexive hermeneutical tool enabling exploration of experience, in which we are constantly reconstructing the theory in light of practice, watchful for the ways our own theoretical assumptions and social locations preselect what we see and how we understand.[10] Theory, however, easily hardens into fixed claims about the way the world is. In the case of progressive discussions, this leads to endless struggles over whose oppression is primary.

Yet, why should not black people focus on racial explanations or white women on gender explanations? These are places where we experience the greatest suffering caused by exploitation, discrimination, and oppression. And, to give credence to another, entwined explanation can seem like a betrayal of this suffering.[11] We fear that plunging into a thicket of qualifiers will weaken the clarity of a univocal call for justice, decreasing its attraction to those in our community and decreasing the possibilities of any strategic successes.[12] Also we may fear that to insist upon attention to different dimensions of a problem is to retreat from responsibility for one's own structural privilege. Progressive politics becomes a zero-sum game; if I insist upon gender,

I negate race and class; if I insist upon class, I negate gender and race, and on and on.

All of these inherent tendencies have been evident in the kinds of identity politics practiced in the 1980s and into the '90s, in which a focus on identity tended to eliminate attention to differences within identities. More recent theoretical work has corrected this tendency, insisting upon differences, fractures, intersections, interstices, and multiplicities. These are welcome developments, enabling theory to probe more deeply into the complexity of our actual lives. This corrective stress on multiplicity, however, can also neglect to attend to patterned continuities in the ways race and class interact. I find myself wanting to press class here because, at this point, in works produced by progressive academic theorists, it seems more easily dropped from view.[13] Often I read a ritual invocation to "race, class, gender" and, if the writer is at some level of awareness, "sexuality." But when I go through the actual analysis carefully, I often cannot discover where class operates. Let me take as an example an excellent book, *Beyond the Pale: White Women, Racism and History* by Vron Ware, which explores the construction of white womanhood as a category defined by race and gender. Ware does a careful reconstruction of the idea of white womanhood as intertwined with the structures of slavery and imperialism, and with attention to the ways early feminist struggles and early racial struggles overlapped and often clashed. Her purpose is to help build a contemporary feminism that "has a future as a radical movement that can unite women across existing divisions of class, race and culture."[14] But as I read through her insightful analysis of the racialization of white women's movements, I am struck by how, in spite of the deeply *classed* notions of white womanhood she has described, Ware never goes beyond a cursory invocation of class. At the end of the book, as she is building her constructive vision, she says, "I want to look first at common ground shared by some Black people and some women.... Although class is an essential factor in all these equations, for the sake of clarity I shall concentrate on race and gender for this part of my argument."[15]

Ware's diminution of class is easier to understand in her own context, Great Britain, where there exists a strong sense of class stratification and a history of class-based working-class movements. She is reacting against the heritage of a conversation within the Left where gender and race were pitted against the dominant Marxist class analysis.[16] However, her work is read here through rather different lenses. The ongoing sense of class in the United States is much more complicated, because we have long lived with an image of ourselves as a classless society in which value rests in the individual. Class has been more fluid here than it has been in European countries. In Europe one could identify far more easily working-class cultures against a background of greater cultural homogeneity. But, strong anti-Bolshevik/Communist sentiment here in the United States, since the Russian Revolution, prevented the development of a strong Marxist left. This sentiment also contributed to the relative weakness of class as a mobilizing language in this country. In the decades since World War II, economic trends in "developed" countries, such as the decline in large-scale heavy industry, the growth of a differentiated service economy, and broadly diffused increases in consumption, further reduced the existence of easily differentiated classes. While this trend is evident throughout both Europe and the United States, its impact has been, I would argue, more pronounced here.

Yet, class does still exist in the United States, and not least in the eyes of those who are less privileged. I need to make some distinction here between different forms of stratification involved in a concept of class. On the one hand, there are empirically evident patterns of income stratification. Using these as guides to class distinctions, one could argue that class differences have been increasing in recent decades. Since the 1970s, income gaps, which narrowed in the decades after World War II, have been steadily widening, leading economist Paul Krugman to write that the United States is entering a second "gilded age."[17] While the median overall wage has dropped by 10 percent since 1979, this loss has been not been evenly distributed. From 1983 to 1998, the bottom 40 percent of the U.S. population lost

76 percent of income while the top 1 percent gained 42 percent. As of 1998, the richest 5 percent of U.S. households held more than 59 percent of the nation's private wealth, while the top 1 percent of households held 38 percent of the wealth.[18] Class location is not only a matter of income, but of the type of job, the degree of supervisory status, the amount of education, the place of residence, and family identification. In the United States, education has been and continues to be a particularly important factor. Great differentiation between middle- and working-class people can be seen in the statistic that males with only high school degrees and some work experience have lost about 30 percent in real wages since 1979 while earnings for college graduates, on the other hand, went from being 20 percent higher than high school graduates in the '60s to 83 percent higher in 1992.[19]

On the other hand, class existence is not only determinable by statistics and data. To try to sort out the relations of race and class requires looking at the complex ways these social formations are lived out, through the ways we understand our world, and through the actions we take on the basis of these understandings. While class may be able to be separated out from race at a level of abstract theory and quantifiable data, when we try to look at class identity as it is lived in daily life or in history, it is impossible to completely disentangle them. "Race is the modality," Stuart Hall wrote, "in which class is lived."[20] To explore the tangle I experienced requires considering the complex ways class distinctions have been racialized and race distinctions have been "classed" as they have developed throughout U.S. social history. I focus in this discussion on racialization as black and white persons, not only because those are the relations in my story, but also because I believe that this formation has been the dominant pattern for living as racialized persons in this country and, consequently, these relations bear the most psychosocial intensity.[21]

The European immigrants who founded the first colonies were founding societies without the settled class structures of their home countries. Yet forms of division soon emerged. Drawing on the work of Edmond Morgan, Thandeka describes the ways in which structures of white racial exclusion emerged in seventeenth-century colonial Virginia. Creating a widening gap between poor white indentured servants and enslaved blacks protected the power of the white elites.[22] Distinctions were based not on whether a person was indentured/enslaved or free, but whether they were white or black. Yet this gap between blacks and whites was intimately connected to gaps among whites, policed by notions of class and culture. Thandeka argues that poor whites became psychologically allied with white elites through a sense of race superiority that, however, was always tied to a sense of class and cultural inferiority.[23] But white racism enabled poorer white people to ignore the restrictions (or, in Thandeka's language, "injury"[24]) of class through the sense of superiority on the basis of their race.

Becoming white was not a simple matter of having white skin, but a process of induction into the class and race assumptions structuring what it meant to be "American." In the nineteenth century the United States came to be recognized as the land so many generations of immigrants sought because it promised opportunities not available to their class in the "old" country. Here, they believed, you were not pegged into a particular lot in life in which you could never escape poverty because of your class or your religion. Yet, what these immigrants found were new structures of ranking and exclusion that continued to reproduce the complicated intersection of class and race through assignation of black and white. The confrontation with these structures was especially evident among the groups of immigrants not considered part of white, Anglo-Saxon Protestant culture, including Middle European Jews, Italians, and Irish. Writing about immigrants from Naples and Sicily, a white Protestant minister, H. H. Boyesen, reflected in 1887,

> I have, during the past year, again and again seen the Battery Park black with these creatures (in fact, preternaturally black), and the odors which surrounded them turned the milk of human

kindness within me, and made me marvel at the heedless hospi-
tality of the American nation, which was willing to mingle this
coarse and brutal strain in their own fresh and vigorous blood.[25]

The cultural connection of blackness with "inferior" cultural qualities
makes clear that success in the United States would require the shed-
ding of these qualities. Thandeka speaks of "the process of forgetting
of prewhited selves" undergone by generations of workers, along
with the process of acquiring new white racial and class identities.[26]

There was, of course, a reward for forgetting — greater economic
security and opportunity to be realized by children and grandchil-
dren, particularly in times of economic expansion. This security was
understood as white entitlement. W. E. B. Du Bois wrote that even
when white workers "received a low wage [they were] compensated
in part by a ... public and psychological wage." He continues, "They
were given public deference ... because they were white.... Their
votes selected public officials and while this had small effect upon
the economic situation, it had great effect upon their personal treatment."[27] Both Thandeka and David Roediger argue that these wages
came with both internal and external costs for white identity, which
were inextricably entangled with the construction of black identity.
White workers projected notions of sexuality, dependency, and lack
of discipline on black people as a way of repressing their desire for
these experiences, while at the same time living with an internal sense
of loss and shame.[28]

The link I want to stress here is between whiteness and upward
mobility — to participate in U.S.-American society required being or
becoming white. And since there was no actual skin color change
among Irish or Italians, clearly becoming white meant adopting a certain set of cultural and class behaviors that were Anglo-Saxon and
middle-class. These behaviors were even more important for women
than men to become "American" since they were responsible for the
nurture of children and shaping the culture of the home, which involved both moral and material practices. The way a woman kept her

home was not a matter of taste but a matter of morality. Thus, for example, Jane Addams saw her settlement house as enabling assimilation of immigrants whose "ideas and resources are cramped." "[A]n Italian girl," she wrote, "who had had lessons in cooking...will help her mother to connect the entire family with American food and household habits."[29]

Racialized class formation has been central to the construction of U.S. citizenship and culture. It is true that dominant discourses (such as mainstream media) generally no longer use the blatant kinds of language used by the Rev. Boyesen. Such language and imagery may appear in newspaper "Letters to the Editor," but even then, it is evident that the authors have some self-consciousness about possible problems with its usage (signaled generally by irritated references to "political correctness") that would not have been present in previous generations. Nevertheless, these accrued understandings are still present in our social repertoire, able to be accessed under certain circumstances.

Such circumstances, I would argue, are often class-dependent. In *Racial Situations: Class Predicaments of Whiteness in Detroit,* John Hartigan studies three economically distinct white communities. He concludes that "white racialness varies by class position."[30] During his year of living in an extremely poor white neighborhood, he found complex and shifting close relationships between blacks and whites (most of whom claimed a marginalized white identity as "hillbillies"). Significantly, in this community it was only those whites seeking some kind of upward mobility who tried to avoid blacks. A different form of distancing also occurred among the gentrifying whites he studied in another neighborhood, who, unlike the poorer whites, had the economic means to keep their lives at some physical distance from blacks. These whites tended to downplay or ignore race as a factor in the issues of their community, maintaining, as Hartigan puts it, "a conviction of racelessness, the race of no race."[31] The third community Hartigan studied was a neighborhood of working-class whites who had protested when their local public school was closed and reopened as the Malcolm X Academy. The conflict between these working-class whites and the black professional school leadership quickly become racialized, not least through media portrayal. In Hartigan's reading, the emphasis on race erased the simultaneous presence of class, a process which was intensified by the ways that professionals in the city and the media read the class-based emotionalism of many of the whites (who had started the protest out of a sense they had no control over their neighborhood school) as particular evidence of racism.

While Hartigan's work shows the interactive construction of whiteness, Michèle Lamont's interviews in *The Dignity of Working Men: Morality and the Boundaries of Race, Class and Immigration* reveal the ways individual constructions of identity are shaped through race and class. Her work contrasts the ways white and black male workers in the United States make sense of their selves and their surroundings.[32] Lamont argues that an emphasis on morality enables working-class men to make sense of their world while maintaining a sense of personal dignity. Yet the moral sense of white and black workers is not the same. The white working-class men interviewed "repeatedly and spontaneously referred to blacks when drawing moral boundaries . . . [criticizing] blacks for not stressing the disciplined self they value."[33] Comparisons of themselves to blacks were central to their self-understanding as morally worthy persons. Lamont remarks that "whiteness continues to stand for what these workers cherish and value."[34] Their moral framework also has class boundaries as white workers stress their own straightforwardness and integrity as contrasting to the shallow moral nature of managers and professionals ("Ken and Barbie people") and the laziness of the poor.[35] Moral worth tended to be separated from socioeconomic status when white workers talked about themselves and those above them. But morality and resources tended to be combined when they talked about the poor, assumed generally to be black. Black workers, by contrast, based their sense of moral worth on a caring and resilient self, and saw the disciplined selves of whites, almost always assumed to be middle class, as domineering and manipulative.[36]

Lamont found that while the white middle class also emphasized a disciplined, self-reliant self, their sense of their moral worth did not rest on a black/white comparison, but on their own and their children's financial, educational, and occupational success. Race played almost no role in the moral maps they constructed.[37]

These studies by Hartigan and Lamont, along with the racialized history of class formation, enable me to go back to my initial tangle. We need to understand "whiteness" (and "blackness") not as a static category but instead as a relational constructive process shaped by history and by immediate context. Race and class are boundary markers, defining not only physical communities but also particular identities. Martha's pride in her life as an independent working-class woman was inevitably a racial pride, partially determined by the ways she could contrast herself from the black women on welfare. By contrast, the identities of the professional white women were not racialized in the same way. And, if we had pursued the conversation on class, we would have doubtless found that the black professional women understood and lived "middle class" in ways different than any of the white women.

How does this kind of historical and cultural understanding help the work of anti-racism? On one level, I think it confirms something we already know: working for solidarity requires a process that includes addressing injury, loss, and fear, along with recognizing the multiple forms of oppression and domination in which we live. More specifically, this understanding shows why we need to be cautious about any wholesale usage of terms such as "white privilege," or at least aware of the potentially different impact on white persons. White U.S. upper- and middle-class persons can more easily view themselves as privileged, and then often move to a stage of guilt that needs to be worked through before they can enter into real engagement with black U.S. persons.[38] However, white working-class persons generally do not experience themselves as privileged, and are likely to feel that this idea adds insult to class injury. Some of the features attributed to whiteness and white privilege, such as rational knowledge, are features of *elite* white culture. Further, Lamont's study suggests that for white working-class persons to engage with the idea of white privilege can be extremely psychologically disturbing, since such a core part of a working-class person's sense of self-worth, unlike that of middle-class persons, is racialized.

This discussion also, I believe, suggests that we need to do cultural and racial work with our eye always on economic issues. We live in a society that struggles not only with racism but also with the reality of an economic system that extends the greatest benefits and privileges to a very small group of people, most of whom are white, while disempowering the rest in a myriad of differing ways. Sorting out these often mystified and overwhelming complexities is hard work, but, as bell hooks puts it, "To work for change we need to know where we stand."[39] We can only survive as a human race if we can figure out how, in spite of — or perhaps because of — terrible histories of violence and oppression, we can stand together.

NOTES

1. I consciously limited the racial conversation to black and white because this relation was the flashpoint in our university. There was no history of Asian or Hispanic presence in this area and only a handful of Asian and Hispanic students at the school, mostly overseas students. Although there was a historical Native presence in the region, there was no Native American group in the area or on campus. Also, the campus was at that time struggling over a controversial situation where a white female student had accused two black students, both football players, of rape — while the players argued the sex was consensual. Race and gender were very much at odds in the ways groups at the university were trying to deal with this situation.

2. This silence about class was prevalent in the Women Studies program in which all of the three white professors in this group taught. In one retreat where we had named our priorities for the program, I had found myself the only one interested in working with questions of poverty and class.

3. I should add that my notes and emails are mostly records of the white women's conversations, which I was facilitating. I, of course, have no notes of the black women's separate conversations and rather thin notes of the black/white conversations, which were held just as the fall semester began leaving all of us less time for reflective emails and careful notes.

4. I am using "privilege" in the sense developed by Peggy McIntosh in her classic article about the subtle and blatant ways white people can live more easily in society.

Peggy McIntosh, "White Privilege: Unpacking the Invisible Knapsack," *Peace & Freedom* (July–August 1989): 10–12 (also reprinted in innumerable anthologies for Women's Studies classes).

5. It was significant that we were conducting our conversation during the summer of 1996, a year marked by protracted use of racially loaded language over the passage of the 1996 welfare reform act or PWRORA. Studies by researchers such as Kathryn Edin have shown that racial differences among women on welfare do not affect reported work participation, although African American women were less likely to receive cash assistance from family and from fathers/boyfriends, a finding linked to overall racial differences in job access (including likelihood of finding work, type of work available, and wages given). See Kathryn Edin and Laura Lein, *Making Ends Meet: How Single Mothers Survive Welfare and Low-Wage Work* (New York: Russell Sage Foundation, 1997), 211–17. For a good discussion of the use of racist language in the welfare legislation debate, see Traci West, "Agenda for the Churches: Uprooting a National Policy of Morally Stigmatizing Poor Single Black Moms," in *Welfare Policy: Feminist Critiques,* ed. Elizabeth M. Bounds et al. (Cleveland: Pilgrim Press, 1999), 133–53. All of my intuitive observations about white working-class attitudes about welfare and poverty have been confirmed by Michèle Lamont's interviews with U.S. white working-class males, which I will discuss below.

6. See Joe Feagin and Melvin Sykes, *Living With Racism: the Black Middle-Class Experience* (Boston: Beacon Press, 1994), viii; Feagin and Sykes present powerful interviews of middle-class blacks to demonstrate the ongoing pernicious nature of white racism as experienced even by those who have achieved some level of class privilege. Their interviews connect with other studies of middle-class African Americans to make a compelling case that blacks cannot be middle-class in the same way as whites. They offer a critical challenge to what they see as the dangerous "white illusion" of "untrammeled Black middle-class prosperity" with painful accounts of the depth of often unconscious white racism and the ongoing "energy-consuming, life-consuming experience" of discrimination by black middle-class persons in the United States.

7. One obvious flashpoint is that I am limiting my reflection here to black and white relations. While this is partially because, as I have said, my story involves black and white women, it is also because of my conviction that race issues in this country are shaped by a "black/white" template. All issues of plurality, such as the presence of Asian or Latino persons in this country, run through the powerful history of U.S. black/white relations.

8. Hortense Spillers, "Interstices: A Small Drama of Words," in *Pleasure and Danger: Exploring Female Sexuality,* 3rd ed., ed. Carole Vance (London: Pandora Press, 1992).

9. The language often used in contemporary postmodern approaches, influenced by Freud, is "excess" or "gap." I often find that less theoretically laden terms such as "tangle" and "confusion" better convey the actual experience of these crosscutting and contradictory structures.

10. I draw here on Bent Flyvbjerg's work on the nature of social inquiry, *Making Social Science Matter* (New York: Cambridge University Press, 2001).

11. This single-note focus is especially important in the early stages of a movement where people are working to valorize identities crushed by centuries of exploitation and domination.

12. I choose "community" here as the word generally used by activists, but I use it with caution as this word often does exactly what I am worrying about here: reducing identity to one factor.

13. While such theorists work in and across a variety of disciplines, many work within a cultural studies/humanities framework. Attention to class is more apparent in the work of those trained in the social sciences.

14. Vron Ware, *Beyond the Pale: White Women, Racism and History* (New York: Verso, 1992), xvii.

15. Ibid., 235–36.

16. For a good summary of these debates through the early 1980s, see Arthur Brittan and Mary Maynard, *Sexism, Racism and Oppression* (New York: Basil Blackwell, 1984), 35–70.

17. Paul Krugman, "For Richer," *New York Times Magazine,* October 20, 2002.

18. The Economic Policy Institute, *The State of Working America 2002–03,* available at www.inequality.org/factsfr.html.

19. William Julius Wilson, *The Bridge over the Racial Divide: Rising Inequality and Coalition Politics* (Berkeley: University of California Press, 1999), 11–43.

20. Stuart Hall et al., *Policing the Crisis: Mugging, the State, and Law and Order* (London: Macmillan, 1978), 394.

21. I do not seek in any way to diminish the reality of other racial oppressions. For example, the reason there is less intensity in the way white persons relate to Native Americans lies in the historical reality that Native Americans were simply eliminated — through slaughter, disease, and displacement onto reservations where there were not the same intimate relations with white persons as were experienced by African Americans.

22. Thandeka, *Learning to Be White: Money, Race, and God in America* (New York: Continuum, 1999), 47.

23. Ibid., 51.

24. I find Thandeka's work extremely helpful in discussing the damages inflicted by the formation of whiteness. But I am cautious about relying as exclusively on psychological models as she does, which I think can freeze or reify what are far more fluid processes.

25. Quoted in Robert L. Handy, *A Christian American: Protestant Hopes and Historical Realities* (New York: Oxford University Press, 1971), 75.

26. Thandeka, *Learning to Be White,* 69.

27. W. E. B. Du Bois, *Black Reconstruction in the United States 1860–1880* (1935) as cited in David R. Roediger, *The Wages of Whiteness: Race and the Making of the American Working Class* (New York: Verso, 1991), 12.

28. Roediger describes how white workers dealt with the restrictive disciplining of industrial life through such things as blackface minstrelsy which allowed "respectable rowdiness and safe rebellion" and through the terrified fantasies of "miscegenation" which helped to justify violence against black persons, as in the 1863 Draft Riots in

New York. These collective experiences embodied both opposition and repression, resistance and racism. Roediger, *The Wages of Whiteness,* 115–63.

29. Quoted in Gwendolyn Mink, "The Lady and the Tramp: Gender, Race, and the Origins of the American Welfare State," in *Women, the State, and Welfare,* ed. Linda Gordon (Madison: University of Wisconsin Press, 1990), 103.

30. John Hartigan, *Racial Situations: Class Predicaments of Whiteness in Detroit* (Princeton, N.J.: Princeton University Press, 1999), 279.

31. Ibid., 205.

32. See Michèle Lamont, *The Dignity of Working Men: Morality and the Boundaries of Race, Class and Immigration* (New York: Russell Sage Foundation, and Cambridge, Mass.: Harvard University Press, 2000). Lamont compares her U.S interviews with similar interviews conducted with white and black (North African) workers in France. Her comparisons support some of my earlier observations about the particular history of U.S. class formation. For example, unlike their U.S. counterparts, French workers use concepts of solidarity and demonstrate suspicion of market forces that are part of a socialist heritage not available in the United States. This volume follows an earlier interview study by Lamont of the U.S. and French upper-middle classes, *Money, Morals, and Manners: The French and American Upper-Middle Class* (Chicago: University of Chicago Press, 1992).

33. Lamont, *The Dignity of Working Men,* 57.

34. Ibid., 64.

35. Ibid., 100, 101, 148.

36. Ibid., 80, 101.

37. Ibid., 57, 73.

38. For good accounts of this process, see the autobiographical narratives in Becky Thompson and Sangeeta Tyagi, eds., *Names We Call Home: Autobiography on Racial Identity* (New York: Routledge, 1996), especially those by Ruth Frankenberg and Becky Thompson.

39. bell hooks, *Where We Stand: Class Matters* (New York: Routledge, 2000), 9.

*Five*_____

WHAT RACE IS YOUR SEX?

LAUREL C. SCHNEIDER _____

T HE QUESTION "What race is your sex?" or its corollary "what
sex is your race?" may seem nonsensical at first, particularly
to white people. When I pose it to students, regardless of race or
ethnicity their faces tend to go to a startled blank. The question
seems unanswerable to many of them, like a Zen koan. Common
use separates the etiology of "race" and "sex," assuming the factors
that determine "race" to be independent of the factors that determine "sex" or "gender." As African Americans and other peoples
of colors particularly know, race affects one's experience and even
embodiment of one's gender, and gender affects one's experience and
even embodiment of race. But it is difficult for everyone fully to digest the co-constitutive qualities of race, sex, and gender, or the utter
dependence of one upon the others for meaning and existence. It is
this co-constitutive quality of race, sex, and gender that I am interested in, primarily because of the support each construction gives in
the modern West to the tenacity of white supremacy.

To make the claim that sex, gender, and race all constitute each
other (suggesting, for example, that whiteness itself has a gender) sup-
poses an unseemly or even grotesque conflation of "natures." In fact,
correlating race and sex or gender brings into question the natural
status of all three categories, implying that they could be otherwise,
unmooring them from nature and thereby disrupting just about everything taken for granted in modernity. To make such a sweeping claim
means that simplistic biological definitions of race, sex, and gender

142

cannot apply. However, given the ambiguity of race, gender and sexuality on scientific or genetic grounds, I believe that we are justified in assuming all three to be largely other than biology.[1]

But saying that race is largely other than skin color, facial features, and hair texture; that sex is largely other than genital and libidinal formation; and that gender is largely other than hormonal deployment does not mean that the categories of race, sex, and gender become meaningless or ungrounded. Anne McClintock points out, for example, that to "dispute the notion that race is a fixed and transcendent essence, unchanged through the ages, does not mean that 'all talk of race must cease,' nor does it mean that the baroque inventions of racial difference 'had no tangible or terrible effects.' " On the contrary, she argues, "it is precisely the inventedness of historical hierarchies that renders attention to social power and violence so much more urgent."[2] The very same point can be made when disputing the notion that sex and gender are fixed and transcendent essences.

It is difficult to think around the corners of the world one inhabits, or to glimpse the limits and gaps in one's own inherited view. While specific modern theorizations of racial, sexual, and gender difference began in the late eighteenth century, were cast increasingly into scientific terms in the nineteenth, and only began to disintegrate late in the twentieth century,[3] biologistic and reductive assumptions about race, sex, and gender as divinely ordained, physically based distinctions between humans remain common. This means that in modern conceptualizations, race, sex, and gender function as more or less benign signifiers of "natural" (and so immutable) human difference. From this viewpoint, it is what people *do* with the "natural differences" of race, sex or gender that may not be so benign, but that is not the fault of "nature" (or God). Lately, however, as modernity shows more and more cracks, Western conceptions of reality and particularly of race, sex, and gender become increasingly brittle, exposing their relatively recent invention and their enmeshment in Western colonial enterprises. The idea of race, sex, and gender as meaningful signifiers of so-called natural difference is less and less persuasive, and certainly less and less benign.

I am in fact convinced that race, sex, and gender are not only constructed for particular purposes of social order but that to contemplate them in isolation from each other is to perpetuate their more insidious social and political effects and to ignore their more profound theological implications. Evelyn Brooks Higgenbotham's notion of race as a "metalanguage" rather than a stable identifier rooted in biology is helpful here in contemplating race, sex, and gender together.[4] Since the start of European colonial expansion which, as Robert Young says so vividly, "ended in the Western occupation of nine tenths of the surface territory of the globe,"[5] Higgenbotham argues that race has served as a "global sign" or "ultimate trope of difference, arbitrarily contrived to produce and maintain relations of power and subordination."[6] Taken together, I argue that race and sex co-constitute a corporate merging of meanings located in human and divine hierarchies that solidify the power and make resilient the supremacy of white people, exemplified in the white male from which, in this view, all others differentiate in useful degrees of degenerate separation.

In each case, modern concepts of race, sex, and gender extrapolate an immutable nature from a few "arbitrarily contrived" features and each, ironically, requires constant reiteration and enforcement to remain constant or immutable. "Race" extrapolates nature and behavioral norms (who one is and how one should behave) from the color of skin and other geographically based, hereditary characteristics of appearance that apply regardless of other hereditary contradictions or changes. "Sex" extrapolates nature and behavioral norms from a few selected genetic features focused on the genitals that apply regardless of other genetic features, contradictions, or changes. And "gender" extrapolates nature and behavioral norms from social claims about "the nature of sex" and selected behavioral patterns nominally identified as masculine or feminine regardless of other behavioral patterns, contradictions, or changes. The result of this is not a reliable and consistent explanation of human difference but a set of *ideologies* of race, sex, and gender — ideologies that serve to keep individual persons in place. This dynamic might not be so troubling if the "places" assigned to different groups of persons based on race, sex, and gender did not blatantly serve larger systems of privilege and power. How ideologies of race, sex, and gender intersect and produce each other and thereby resist change is what interests me in my own work as a white woman committed to the dogged, daily, and sometimes intimate task of subverting white supremacy.

The issue that I plan to raise here is neither small nor is it smooth. A great deal of white evasion from our complicity in white supremacy is accomplished by efforts to "complicate the issue" with other, attendant concerns (like sexism, heterosexism, or classism). It is not my intention to evade white complicity here, but rather to search out some of the many ways that white supremacy eludes even the most seasoned, committed, and trustworthy anti-racist whites when it goes incognito in the guise of unexamined sex, gender, or class ideology. While it may be clear to most that the "isms" are linked in theory, deep understandings of the ways in which modern concepts of race, sex, and gender are *co-constitutive,* meaning that they cannot meaningfully be separated *except* in support of racist and sexist goals, is much more difficult to grasp and even more difficult to practice, particularly for white people, whom the separation most effectively serves.

McClintock makes this very point when she argues that "race, gender and class are not distinct realms of experience, existing in splendid isolation from each other; nor can they be simply yoked together retrospectively like armatures of Lego. Rather, they come into existence *in and through* relation to each other — if in contradictory and conflictual ways."[7] Lorraine O'Grady puts a finer point on the inseparability and co-constitutive quality of race, sex, and gender in a quote that Evelynn Hammonds uses to begin her essay entitled "Black (W)holes and the Geometry of Black Female Sexuality":

The female body in the West is not a unitary sign. Rather, like a coin, it has an obverse and a reverse: on the one side, it is white; on the other, not-white or, prototypically, black. The two bodies cannot be separated, nor can one body be understood in isolation from the other in the West's metaphoric construction of "woman." *White is what woman is; not-white (and the stereotypes not-white gathers in) is what she had better not be* [emphasis added].[8]

If "white is what woman is," then the co-constitutive qualities of race, sex, and gender are such that each becomes nonsensical apart from the others. This becomes especially clear when the gendering of race, or what Abdul JanMohamed calls "racialized sexuality," is more vividly limned.[9] Furthermore, one of the consequences of eighteenth- and nineteenth-century European expansion and the Atlantic slave industry is that race and gender constitute each other in such powerful and necessary ways that separating them from each other serves to mask the naturalizing functions of colonialism and so masks the pervasive tenacity of white supremacy. White supremacy, in service first to European colonial expansion and then in service to global capitalism, lies at the heart of the race/sex co-constitution, a co-constitution that ultimately functions to preserve the power and privilege of white males in a symbolic and very material economy of human diversity, positioned for the maintenance of its own order and the benefit of a few.

Modernity, a period beginning roughly with the scientific revolution and the emergence of European competition for colonial power and wealth (at the cost of millions of African and Native American lives), denotes the rise of global industrial capitalism and its attendant obsessions with property and individualism. To say that race, sex, and gender are inventions of modernity does not mean that prior to this period meaningful concepts of race, sex, or gender did not exist. Certainly people in every culture have always found ways to distinguish between themselves in terms of sexual and reproductive practices, familial allegiances, and affectional behavior. Among others, for example, Helen Scott has argued that prior to colonial expansion, race was understood generally by Europeans to refer to familial lineages rather than to whole classes of nations and tribes. This earlier understanding materially served a feudal system of indentured servitude and class division based flexibly on individual families in ways that a modern conceptualization of race would not have done. It is only with the rise of labor-ravenous industries and agricultures in England and the Americas that a conceptualization of race based on entire nations and continents served and took hold.[10]

Likewise, sex and gender conceptualizations follow more or less economic trajectories that, enmeshed with emergent concepts of race, morphed into categories of difference that primarily served European and American colonial capitalism. While the labor of reproduction falls most heavily on females in most cultures of the world, in the European colonial enterprise gender became racialized and classed specifically in service of creating an endless labor pool for the growing industries of the North and the growing plantations of the American South on the one hand, and in service of perpetuating and maintaining a class of white capitalist beneficiaries on the other.

SEX AND GENDER CO-CONSTITUTED FOR SUPREMACY

Long before the first colonial armada left port, the naturalization of gender difference and of sex had taken place in European thought, firmly establishing the legitimacy of human hierarchies in the absolute position of the male over the female in body, mind, law, and right. In the thirteenth century, Thomas Aquinas had harnessed Aristotle to consolidate and systematize a "natural" (meaning God-given and established) Christian hierarchy of males over females. This resulted in what appears as a divinely naturalized set of gendered sexual norms in which maleness is conceived as active and dominant, while femaleness is conceived as passive and subservient. "Natural" gender placements thus determined "natural" sex and sexual practices as well. This

gender and sex hierarchy was not new to the thirteenth century by
any means, but Thomas's *Summa Theologica* and *Contra Gentiles*
helped further to solidify and legitimize it, making masculinity and
dominance co-constitutive terms that began even more explicitly to
shape the meaning of "Christian civilization." By the time John Milton wrote the hugely popular *Paradise Lost* in the late seventeenth
century, the idea that humans are naturally and perfectly ordered in
superior and inferior categories made common sense and was understood to be divinely ordained, European in origin, and absolutely
sexualized in character. All this is present in Milton's imagining of
Adam and Eve before Satan has approached them:

> Whence true authority in men, though both
> Not equal, as their sex not equal seem'd;
> For contemplation hee and valour form'd,
> For softness shee and sweet attractive Grace,
> Hee for God only, shee for God in him:
> His fair large Front and Eye sublime declar'd
> Absolute rule; and Hyacinthine Locks
> Round from his parted forelock manly hung
> Clust'ring, but not beneath his shoulders broad:
> Shee as a veil down to the slender waist
> Her unadorned golden tresses wore
> Dishevell'd, but in wanton ringlets wav'd
> As the Vine curls her tendrils, which impli'd
> Subjection, but requir'd with gentle sway,
> And by her yielded, by him best receiv'd,
> Yielded with shy submission, modest pride,
> And sweet reluctant amorous delay.[11]

Here the appearance of the perfect male and perfect female are
"gendered" into dominance and submission, codified by sex and
ultimately by race. How Adam and Eve's hair look, for example,
determines her wanton and subject nature on the one hand, and his
"true authority" on the other. Her perfect femaleness is made evident

by her appearance, an appearance codified in both sexual and racial terms familiar to any reader.

The result of such imagistic sex-gender-race conflation in the story of divine creation was deeply insidious in real life, contributing to an emergent economic and social structure based on "biology." First of all, by making passivity a sign of true womanhood, no working-class or slave female could measure up to the basic definition of being a woman and survive by virtue of her class position and its requirement that she labor, although she could still submit to men. Likewise, by making dominance a sign of true manhood, no working-class or slave male could measure up to the basic definition of being a man and survive by virtue of his class position and its requirement that he submit to authority, although he could still dominate some women. In a curious and sometimes homoerotic twist, this co-constitution of gender with class and eventually with race meant (and continues to mean) that manhood is limited but not destroyed by submission to other, more powerful men. From the poorest day laborer to the archbishop of Canterbury, submitting to more dominant males (from boss to God) is preferable to the alternative of submitting to females and so losing all claim to manhood. M. Shawn Copeland has observed, for example, that even in the extremes of slavery European gender hierarchies made their mark as black men were rewarded for dominating black women. Slavery, she argues, not only exploited black women's bodies and sex for labor and reproduction of labor but undermined relationships between black women and black men. "So it was that colonization and slavery, as both ideology and practice, not only sustained patriarchy but also initiated black men into, and rewarded them for, brutalizing *mimesis*."[12]

THE INVENTION OF RACE FOR COLONIAL DOMINATION

If *Paradise Lost* was the Hollywood-style image-maker of eighteenth-century England, then the divinely ordained true woman, spread across the globe through colonial expansion, was subservient, passive, soft, blonde, and slightly wanton (in need of direction and sexual supervision). Because it is this image of white femininity that defines womanhood in the colonial enterprise, both race and gender are intersecting here in a racialized sexuality. The link of sex and gender to whiteness here lies at the crux of the matter, for, to echo O'Grady, "white is what woman is; not-white (and the stereotypes not-white gathers in) is what she had better not be." The only way that a statement like this makes sense is through the lens of colonialism and its attendant conflation of sex and race.

In the early and mid-nineteenth century, racial theory was a popular enterprise of European academics and politicians interested in confirming both the superiority of Europeans and the legitimacy of colonial expansion and domination over the rest of the world. The major disagreement among these theorists had to do with whether the different human "races" could be traced to a single source (monogenesis) or to multiple sources (polygenesis). Young points out that polygenesis had the advantage of accounting for differences between human groups on the basis of different origins, allowing Europeans to continue to affirm Enlightenment ideals of equality among "men" by limiting the category of "man" more explicitly and exclusively to those of European descent. But monogenesis had the advantage of squaring with the biblical story of Eden in Genesis 2 and tended to find more adherents despite requiring one more step to solidify white supremacy. From a monogenetic perspective, differences between human groups could be accounted for through theories of degeneration. "This meant that the pure origin of man [sic] was the white male — that universal mean and measure of all things — and that all other forms were a deterioration from this ideal, as a result of gender or geography or both."[13] The theory of degeneration also fit nicely with the European take on the biblical story of the fall from paradise. Eve, the paradigm of white womanhood, is not male and so represents already a slippage from the ideal, or at least a slippage from the universal mean and measure of all things. Her difference from

Adam serves to highlight the contours of white masculinity through her deficiencies. It is to her that Satan makes his move, ensuring the further degeneration of this ideal of whiteness into the various races.

Because the modern concept of race as biology had to be invented — meaning that prior to the modern slave trade and European colonial expansion there was little or no need for anyone to have a refined theory of biological or scientific differences between people — I am persuaded by the arguments that place economics at the heart of the matter. The significant fact is that American slavery itself did not begin as a race-based institution but rather evolved out of class-based indentured servitude that failed when the demand for labor in Europe and in the Americas far exceeded both the criminal and working classes of those populations.[14] At just the historical moment when Enlightenment ideals about liberty as an endowment of humanity began to be adopted and fought for in both Europe and colonial North America, the cotton and sugar economy of the American South and the concomitant textile factories of the North yawned wide for cheap, permanent labor that indentured servitude could no longer satisfy both because of the changing political idealism of democracy and the savage brutality of the work itself.

At the same time, Europeans vied for control of the world in pursuit of greater economic gain and dominance over trade. The emergence of colonial capitalism with its emphasis on private property also fueled the search for a rationale for acquiring cheaper and cheaper labor, with outright ownership of labor being the ideal. Scientific theories of race served both acquisitive goals, for the most part "substantiating convictions that preceded scientific enquiry,"[15] legitimizing and institutionalizing the already growing practice of complete ownership of human beings, their children, and the products of their labor. Doing so served the twofold purpose of making available to white colonial property owners all non-white peoples for exploitation, without contravening Enlightenment ideals, while simultaneously funneling all of the resulting wealth to themselves.

As a case in point, historians of race point to the story of legal development in the early United States to trace the evolution of theories
that sought to associate all blacks incontrovertibly with slavery. To
achieve this result, Scott argues:

> Whites had to be taught to be white and blacks taught to be
> black, and the two groups separated.... Laws against misce-
> genation, intermarriage and association were passed throughout
> the colonies in the last decade of the seventeenth and first of
> the eighteenth centuries [and the] former interracial coexistence
> among laborers was ruthlessly dismantled.[16]

The invention of race as an absolute signifier of difference — a
"global sign" — was codified in pseudo-scientific theories about biology and evolution that rested on the primacy of whiteness as the
standard against which all differences were cited as degeneration and
lack. Consequently, race emerged as a theory primarily of whiteness,
a condition that is contradictorily evidenced in "nature" and necessarily achieved and maintained through practice. Facial features, skin
color, bone structure, and so forth all formed a catalogue of "race"
that, while officially disavowed by member nations after 1945 with
the UNESCO statements on race, remain a part of common association and even official census and political identification throughout
the world today. More subtle and so perhaps at a more powerful and
tenacious level, the practices of race evidence the resilience of white
supremacy, particularly through race's co-constituting connections to
sex and gender.

THE CO-CONSTITUTION OF SEX, RACE,
AND GENDER IN CLASS

Because the issue of the co-constitutive quality of modern concepts
of race, sex, and gender begins in colonialism, it makes sense to focus
briefly on how race was gendered and sexed in support of colonial
expansion and of white supremacy in particular. The evolution and

naturalization of gender hierarchies parallels the evolution and naturalization of race hierarchies, but parallelism does not necessarily imply co-constitution. The fact is that "race scientists" made sex and gender foundational to a racial theory of white supremacy. The link was not accidental. Gendering race gave further legitimacy to both hierarchies, more firmly grounding both sex and race differentials in divinely ordained nature in such a way that the colonial enterprise could progress apace secure in the rightness of white domination of non-white, through the divinely preordained domination of females by males. The legitimacy for both hierarchies came from a theory of natural endowment in which the superior qualities of one group could, through a kind of trickle-down effect, improve the overall position of everyone while further cementing its own dominant position.

For example, many slave traders and investors sought to legitimate their own practices through the notion that slavery in the land of white people was in effect an act of charity, improving the lot of otherwise free African peoples mired in unhappy degeneracy. This same logic became foundational to later capitalist theory, in which the superior endowments of the wealthy would establish an unequal field of competition but insist that free mobility and deployment of these dominant resources improve the overall economic position of all players while further cementing the dominant position of the wealthy. In both equations, the contradictory and misleading motto is "everyone wins."

The gendering of whiteness as dominant, as global sign of civilization, and therefore as male (and blackness or yellowness or brownness or redness as subordinate, as global sign of "wantonness" and therefore as female) has its roots deep in ancient genderings of reality. The explicit gendering of race, however, could only emerge with the invention of race as a universal concept that occurred in the pseudo-science of race theories of the mid-nineteenth century. The degeneration of the races from original and ideal whiteness could be rationalized through the lens of sex and gender in self-referencing logic. Just as Adam needed companionship and the opportunity to fully express his perfect manhood through dominance and wise governance, making necessary the emergence of a lesser being from his own body, differentiation in the races ultimately serves to provide the white race with its fullest potential for improvement through exercise of heroic dominance and wise governance over the world.

The white race is thus gendered male by virtue of its dominance, and the non-white races are gendered female, indicating their need for supervision. No other but gender ideology could so neatly turn a differentiation of the races into a normative hierarchy that justifies white supremacy on the one hand, and consolidates the position of upper-class males at the same time. As Robert Young observes:

> The "natural" gender relations of European society are once again used to establish the authority of the natural laws that determine the relations between the races. Just as the white male rules at home, so he also lords it abroad. The orthodox hierarchy of gender is confirmed and reaffirmed at the level of race, which then in turn feminizes males and females alike in the black and yellow races. All hierarchies, together with their cultural values, can, it seems, be assimilated, so long as the white male remains on top.[17]

Nineteenth-century racial theorists made explicit the association between the gender dominance of males and the claims that they were attempting to establish scientifically about whiteness. This association served to bolster and clarify the dominance of the upper class within Europe by associating color and sex more and more with class position, and so bolstered whiteness as a signifier of rule throughout the world, further legitimating colonial expansion in general. Gender and race both became instruments of class by mirroring the priorities of those already in positions of power. McClintock points out, for example, that preeminent German race theorist Carl Vogt "saw similarities between the skulls of white male infants and those of the white female working class, while noticing that a mature black male shared his 'pendulous belly' with a white woman who had had many children."[18] The notoriously pendulous bellies of upper-class German males aside (and that is precisely a filter Vogt is attempting to install), these associations served the curious task of masculinizing nondominant females and of feminizing nondominant males to the same end: solidifying the "natural" superiority of the dominant (white) male. The co-constitutive qualities of race, sex, and gender thus conceived allow them to function as stand-ins for one another, making them much more effective and, ultimately, more resilient.

The ideal of womanhood in colonial Europe (soft, subservient, passive, and preferably blonde) clarifies this point. She is also upper-class because all of these qualities cannot be attained by working women. Labor invalidates passivity and softness. This means that subservience alone did not suffice to establish ideal womanhood. Indeed, the most dominated of women were also the least feminized by virtue of enforced labor (through slavery or economic necessity) and the most dominated of men were, contradictorily, the most feminized by virtue of limited power (through slavery or economic necessity). McClintock has documented the dubious gender *and race* of charwomen in Victorian England as an illustration of the gendering and racializing of class that put most women in a conflicted relationship to both womanhood and to whiteness.[19]

Despite the dubious gender and race of women who were unable economically to achieve womanhood because it depended on the labor of others, marriage became an important marker of gender *and* race accomplishment, and served the progressive ideal of colonial powers. Through "marriage" a woman can effectively change race by improving her class position. Nineteenth-century French race theorist Joseph Gobineau strove to develop a rationale for colonial expansion through this metaphor of sex and marriage. Since the non-white races were female to the white race's masculinity, the white race harbors a deep attraction for the black and yellow races, literally aching for union and therefore improvement of the issue through marriage. The resistance of the black and yellow races to "marriage" through colonial domination is to be understood as natural, just as females tend to resist the advances of males.[20]

Gobineau's pseudo-rape fantasy of white colonial "intercourse" with black and yellow cultures reiterates the creed of white upper-class supremacy, on the one hand, and addresses the growing perception of many Europeans that the upper class was becoming insipid, ingrown, and weak, on the other. The legitimation of colonial expansion through theories of racialized gender/sex and sexualized race/gender was standard intellectual practice. "Virgin" lands and "wanton" peoples were powerful sexual projections that made the fantasy of male satisfaction a metonymic for colonial expansion (or perhaps we should call it enlargement). And as Kadiatu Kanneh points out, the "feminizing of colonized territory is, of course, a trope in colonial thought."[21]

While some nineteenth-century race theorists may have worried about sexualizing race along accepted European gender hierarchies, doing so had multiple benefits for male European property owners. The gender hierarchy was a well-established feature of Christian civilization, but it required reiteration and constant vigilance lest women forget their natural place. Therefore, not only did notions of sexualized race naturalize the inferiority of non-whites but also such notions reinscribed and reaffirmed the "natural" inferiority of women. And for the relatively smaller cost of continued submission to white men, white women became willing participants and contributors to this ideology for the simple reason that they could reap a significant portion of the material benefits of sexualized race, despite the fact that doing so reinforced gender ideologies of domination and submission in order to enslave non-whites and plunder their territories.

Another added benefit to colonial powers of sexualized race was the reinforcement of sexual placements. Gobineau, Vogt, Klemm, and Carus could develop the Enlightenment thought that races have genders precisely because doing so supported the gendered heterosexual norm that authorized dominance. If, as many of them argued, the white race is masculine/dominant and the non-white races feminine/subordinate, colonization reiterated a heterosexual norm that supports both sexualized race and racialized sex. Heterosexual ideologies based upon a naturalization of heterosexual desire legitimated white colonization as "marriage" in which rape could not occur regardless of the violence of "penetration." Masculinized whiteness, which equates dominance with an identity, is thereby reinforced in heterosexual terms. So the modern ideology of sex, just like ideologies of race and gender, came to reside primarily in the arithmetic of white supremacy, and colonization-as-marriage became the means of its reproduction.

As part of this arithmetic, the institution of marriage itself was usually an economic necessity for both lower- and upper-class women aspiring to some measure of class (and so race) success in Europe and the colonies. Marriage also furthered the sex-gender-race co-constitution, making femininity and masculinity necessary sexual corollaries of one another and so necessary markers of race success, grounded in "nature." The well-documented public sexual brutalization of black women in slavery, and particularly the legal prohibitions against slave marriage, further distanced slaves from dominant, colonial practices of sexualized gender (not to mention their own inherited gender practices). The result was to racialize gender all the more, in this case through prohibitions on gender practices for certain *races*. Such prohibitions served further to "feminize" slave men except where they could dominate slave women, and to "masculinize" slave women, except where they could submit to slave or free men. Most of all, such prohibitions helped to construct the "natural" rightness of white upper-class sex and gender practices as paradigmatic of true and originary human ideals, thus racializing those practices and solidifying them in a class structure.[22] Enforcing limitations on all of these gendered practices to upper-class white people made evident both the whiteness of legitimacy and the legitimacy of whiteness at every level of social interaction.

THE IMPLICATIONS

If modern concepts of race are fundamentally and ineluctably co-constituted by gender and sex ideologies, and if modern concepts of gender and sex are fundamentally and ineluctably co-constituted by race ideology, it begins to make sense that white supremacy retains a kind of tenacity even among those who claim to be opposed to it, or that sexism and heterosexism persist among those who claim to be opposed to them. White supremacy is structured throughout the modern constellation of race, sex, gender, and class and can take up residence in any of these ports of meaning to weather occasional anti-racist storms, only to reemerge as soon as "success" is proclaimed. In her argument that whiteness and nonwhiteness define each other, Vron Ware points to the tricky issue of sexualized race, suggesting that the "different elements in this system of 'race' and gender identity have no intrinsic meaning; they work only in and through differentiation."[23]

Working in and through differentiation means that the terms of whiteness and blackness (as paradigm of not-white) and of femininity and masculinity are so interdependent that they cannot signify anything except the shape of their opposition. And in extremity, as Asian, Hispanic, Native American, and mixed-race scholars have noted, those who are neither white nor black exist in ambiguity or, worse, not at all. According to the vestigial colonial thinking on which "race" depends, however, to the extent that non-black non-whites can display gender, they can gravitate to a race. In an economy of oppositions, one must claim a pole or vaporize. And it is the economy of three-dimensional oppositions between race, sex, and gender that stabilizes white supremacy, in the past and into the present.

In other words, without femininity to define it, masculinity collapses on itself and vaporizes like Oz's Wicked Witch of the West. Likewise femininity cannot hold without masculinity to define it, and whiteness collapses in on itself and vaporizes without blackness, and vice versa. But even more dramatically and to the point here, without masculinity whiteness collapses, and without femininity blackness collapses. Like a trick drawing that contains two different pictures that you can see only by changing what you look for, one comes into focus on the back of the other and cannot exist except in that relation. Eve Kosofsky Sedgewick has made this argument clearly in terms of sexuality when she argues that the homosexual closet is a feature of heterosexuality, not of homosexuality. The closet, or exclusion of that which exceeds heterosexuality, limns and makes possible the heterosexual claim about itself.[24] It is for this reason that Hammonds admonishes white women to "refigure (white) female sexualities so that they are not theoretically dependent upon an absent yet ever-present pathologized black female sexuality."[25]

The core of this work for white people, I believe, lies in attention to our investments in *gendered* whiteness, meaning deep-level investments in sexualized and even eroticized assumptions of dominance and submission, authority and passivity that make reconstruction of whiteness a deconstruction of gender and vice versa. To recognize whiteness masquerading as masculinity that understands itself in terms of strength, voice, leadership, vision, direction, and authority may force some of the more tenacious and self-effacing aspects of white supremacy to emerge into public view. One of the reasons that white people have great difficulty undoing our own practices of white supremacy is that the co-constitutive aspects of race, sex, and gender make the practices of whiteness very difficult to perceive in oneself, particularly when they also function as gender and sex. Gender identity is so powerfully reiterative and self-reinforcing that even men who recognize the atrocities of masculinity constructed as dominance tend to suffer deep anxiety over the prospect of "unmanning" themselves and struggle to imagine a nondominant or dominating masculinity that remains both fulfilling and satisfying. It is easier, many men have said to me, to imagine nonsubmissive femininity than it is to imagine masculinity in terms other than dominance.[26]

This is one way of looking at the stickiness of supremacy in whiteness. It is profoundly difficult and anxiety producing to imagine whiteness in any other terms than dominance precisely because of its co-constitution with a particularly deep ideology of sex and gender that comes not only from the recent history of colonialism but from the imaginative depths of medieval and early modern Christian theology. It is not insignificant that God stretches out his powerfully male, languidly superior, and vividly white arm across the vastness of the Sistene ceiling to meet the supplicating white arm of his truest mirror image in Adam. There is sex, gender, and race in that construction, and it is not without allure. It is one of many moments that tie whiteness up in masculinity and masculinity up in whiteness, for God is the original white male and Adam is a mere first step down.

The argument that I have laid out here makes the work of disrupting white supremacy much more complicated and difficult, particularly for whites but also for non-whites. However, without this piece of the puzzle, the work against white supremacy may function like a stretched rubber band: if it is not unhooked on *all* points, it will simply rebound with a bitter bite. To put it most bluntly, can we unman ourselves enough to begin to take the supremacy out of whiteness? What would this look like in practical terms? What specific practices, responses, and expectations might have to change in my work and in my interactions to effect a reconstruction of whiteness that does not rest on sexualized race? This is the first question that we must ask ourselves, and we must ask it daily. Can I unman my whiteness enough to seek the guidance of non-whites on issues unrelated to race? Can I unman my whiteness enough to listen? To accept direction and supervision? To take up what James Foreman called "janitorial research"?[27] To what lengths am I willing to go to take the gender ideology, the supremacy, out of my whiteness?

Ultimately, I suspect that whiteness has to disappear altogether, since it was created and exists solely on the basis of exclusion for colonial gain. This does not mean that as a white person I must disappear or renounce my family. It also does not relieve me of responsibility for white supremacy and its continued benefits to me and the white members of my family. I also suspect that the demise of white supremacy will take much longer than I believe it should, and so I must resign myself to small steps and build up my faith in their importance. Right there I poke a pinhole in the balloon of whiteness-as-dominance. I take up the very un-white suggestion that Sharon Welch makes, namely, that I let go of my need for control over the results of my efforts and credit for their completion.[28]

Letting go of that need is letting go of one brick in the edifice of white supremacy that masquerades as masculinity, and of masculinity that functions as dominance. Welch calls this an "ethic of control" and advocates instead, based on her own study of African American women's writings, a pragmatic "ethic of risk" that does not pretend to control outcomes but keeps on anyway, believing in the value of actions that may not win wars or conquer evils, but that keep possibilities open for the next generation. That much we can do, and by valuing that, letting go of such deeply ingrained needs to direct, to lead, to chair, to receive credit, to determine priorities, to win arguments, we begin to take the supremacy out of whiteness and the dominance out of masculinity.

NOTES

1. See "The Human Genome," *Science* 291, no. 5507 (February 2001): 16. For a lay discussion on the complexities of interpreting the human genome project in relation to race, see Steve Olsen, "The Genetic Archaeology of Race," *Atlantic Monthly* (April 2001).

2. Anne McClintock, *Imperial Leather: Race, Gender and Sexuality in the Colonial Contest* (London and New York: Routledge, 1995), 8.

3. Robert J. C. Young, *Colonial Desire: Hybridity in Theory, Culture and Race* (London: Routledge, 1995), 91.

4. Evelyn Brooks Higgenbotham, "African-American Women's History and the Metalanguage of Race," *Signs* 17, no. 2 (1991–2): 251–74.

5. Young, *Colonial Desire,* 91.

6. Higgenbotham, quoted in Evelynn Hammonds, "Black (W)holes and the Geometry of Black Female Sexuality," in *Feminism Meets Queer Theory,* ed. Naomi Schor and Elizabeth Weed (Bloomington: Indiana University Press, 1997), 136.

7. McClintock, *Imperial Leather,* 5.

8. Hammonds, "Black (W)holes," 136.

9. Abdul JanMohamed, "Sexuality on/of the Racial Border: Foucault, Wright, and the Articulation of 'Racialized Sexuality,'" *Discourses of Sexuality: From Aristotle to AIDS*, ed. Domna Stanton (Ann Arbor: University of Michigan Press, 1992), 94–116.

10. Helen Scott, "Was There a Time before Race? Capitalist Modernity and the Origins of Racism," in *Marxism, Modernity and Post-Colonial Studies*, ed. Crystal Bartolovich and Neil Lazarus (Cambridge: Cambridge University Press, 2002), 167–82.

11. John Milton, *Paradise Lost, Book IV*, lines 295–308, from *Paradise Lost and Paradise Regained*, ed. Christopher Ricks (New York: Signet Classic, 1968), 88.

12. M. Shawn Copeland, "Body, Representation, and Black Religious Discourse," in *Postcolonialism, Feminism and Religious Discourse*, ed. Laura E. Donaldson and Kwok Pui-lan (London and New York: Routledge, 2002), 184.

13. Young, *Colonial Desire*, 101.

14. See Scott, "Was There a Time before Race?" passim. Also Lerone Bennett, *The Shaping of Black America* (Chicago: Johnson, 1975).

15. Young, *Colonial Desire*, 93.

16. Scott, "Was There a Time before Race?" 174.

17. Young, *Colonial Desire*, 111.

18. McClintock, *Imperial Leather*, 55.

19. Ibid., 75–180.

20. Young, *Colonial Desire*, 109–11.

21. Kadiatu Kanneh, "Feminism and the Colonial Body," in *The Post-Colonial Studies Reader*, ed. Bill Ashcroft, Gareth Griffiths, and Helen Tiffin (London and New York: Routledge, 1995), 347.

22. For a relevant biblical case study in an ancient Mediterranean context of race/sex/gender co-constitutiveness, see Ken Stone, "Queering the Canaanite," in *The Sexual Theologian: Essays on Sex, God and Politics*, ed. Marcella Althaus-Reid and Lisa Isherwood (New York: Continuum, forthcoming 2004).

23. Vron Ware, "Defining Forces: 'Race,' Gender and Memories of Empire," in *The Post-Colonial Question: Common Skies, Divided Horizons*, ed. Iaian Chambers and Lidia Curti (London and New York: Routledge, 1996), 142–56.

24. Eve Kosofsky Sedgewick, *Epistemology of the Closet* (Berkeley: University of California Press, 1990).

25. Hammonds, "Black (W)holes," 141.

26. For an interesting discussion of nondominant masculinity and satisfaction, see Scott Haldeman, "Receptivity and Revelation: A Spirituality of Gay Male Sex," in *Body and Soul: Rethinking Sexuality as Justice-Love*, ed. Marvin Ellison and Sylvia Thorson-Smith (Cleveland: Pilgrim Press, 2003), 218–31.

27. See Robert Coles, "Method," in *The Call of Service: A Witness to Idealism* (New York: Houghton-Mifflin, 1993), 9–13.

28. Sharon Welch, *A Feminist Ethic of Risk* (Minneapolis: Fortress Press, 1987), see esp. chap. 1.

Six

EL TESTIGO VERDADERO LIBRA
LAS ALMAS*

The Central America Peace Movement and Anti-Racism

BECKY THOMPSON

FOR MANY ANTI-RACIST ACTIVISTS, "doing our first works over" includes reckoning with early messages that most of us learn that English is the dominant and most valuable language, that the United States is the most important country in the world, and that white people are the best qualified to run it. White people learn these lessons in little and big ways from when we are very young. We learn English elitism when English is enforced in nursery school rhymes and kindergarten classes. We learn ethnocentrism when the histories of countries other than the United States are considered electives at best in grade school and on up the educational ladder. And we learn white supremacy when the media, family, and schools reinforce white power in theory and practice. Resisting white supremacy and its partners, ethnocentrism and English elitism, involves confronting racism as a global phenomenon. We can't understand slavery in the United States, for example, without knowing about the international slave trade. We can't comprehend the assault on unionized jobs and labor in the United States without grappling with U.S. colonialism, which left many Latin American countries vulnerable to Free Trade Zones, labor exploitation, and NAFTA.

---

*"The true witness liberates souls." *Santa Biblia,* Proverbs 14:25 (New York: Sociedad Bíblica, 1960), 516.

My interest in the extent to which contemporary anti-racist activism has incorporated a global perspective and an awareness of imperialism led me to analyze the Central America Peace Movement of the 1980s. Interviewing activists who were involved in initiatives to stop U.S. intervention allowed me to examine the extent to which the Central America Peace Movement upheld an anti-racist politic. This question required me to be explicit about what an anti-racist politic looks like in this context. Keeping an analysis of race and racism at the center of the movement's agenda and building cross-racial alliances both domestically and internationally emerged as the key requirements.

This movement was built to oppose Ronald Reagan's foreign policy, which hinged on asserting control over the political and economic structures of Panama, El Salvador, Nicaragua, Honduras, Guatemala, and Costa Rica — all countries that Reagan, and many presidents before him, considered the backyard to the United States. Since 1900, the United States has invaded Latin America thirty-six times.[1] According to historian William Chafe, "Reagan insisted on committing military advisors and millions of dollars to bolster a reactionary regime in El Salvador, while making the overthrow of the Sandinistas by Nicaraguan 'Contras' his top foreign policy objective."[2] Anti-intervention activism took several forms, many of which drew upon faith-based communities for its support. Prior to the recent national organizing against the invasion of Iraq, the Central America Peace Movement was the most significant struggle against U.S. imperialism since the anti–Vietnam War movement of the 1960s. The sanctuary movement provided resources and safety for Guatemalan and Salvadoran refugees forced to flee from their countries to the United States. Transnational activism included trips from the United States to Central America made by activists who sought to be witnesses to U.S. aggression in the region and then to educate people in the United States about this violence.[3] The Sanctuary Movement and the Witness for Peace campaigns both reveal complicated political relationships between North American activists, Central Americans living in the United States, and Central Americans in their own countries.

While there has been useful documentation of the organizing strategies of U.S. activists in general, this research is the first to examine the extent to which faith-based organizing did uphold an anti-racist politic. Activists' accounts of this period highlight the strengths and limitations of this movement in terms of anti-racism and offer useful insights for activists seeking to build race-conscious, multiracial international alliances now and in the future.

SANCTUARY: A BIG TERM

A key strategy in response to U.S. intervention in Central America involved the building of a regional and national network of churches, synagogues, and Quaker meeting houses that offered a safe haven to refugees. This initiative, which began in 1981, soon became known as the sanctuary movement. North Americans involved in this initiative defied federal immigration laws by providing housing and other resources to Central American refugees who otherwise risked deportation and death. Through this effort seventy thousand U.S. citizens provided support for between two thousand and three thousand Central American refugees over a several-year period.[4] Beginning in Tucson, Arizona, and then spreading to Chicago and throughout thirty-four states, the public sanctuary movement comprised more than three thousand churches, synagogues, and Quaker meeting houses by 1984.[5] Although most of the sanctuary locations were white, Black and Latino churches were involved as well, including the Hispanic Church of Cristo Rey in Racine, Wisconsin; Cross Lutheran Church of Milwaukee (a Black church); Operation Push in Chicago; and Riverside Church in New York City.[6]

What is deceptive and racially biased about identifying "the sanctuary movement" with predominantly white congregations, however, is that the lion's share of the work with refugees was done clandestinely by Mexicans in Mexico and Latino and multiethnic communities in the United States who took in and sustained hundreds of thousands of refugees.[7] Although it is hard to pinpoint the number of refugees who entered the United States, it is estimated that half a million entered each year.[8] As of 1986, 350,000 Salvadoran refugees were hiding in California alone. There are more Salvadorans living in Los Angeles than any other city in the world outside San Salvador.[9] Churches in these Latino and multiethnic communities played an essential role in making this unnamed sanctuary movement possible. One branch of the Mohawk nation in New York State also offered its sacred land as a sanctuary.[10] The Seminoles in Florida also harbored hundreds of Guatemalan Indians.[11]

The work done to make a home for refugees in these communities, however, is not typically included in research on the sanctuary movement, although clearly it formed the basis of the grassroots response to the U.S. war in Central America. Just as the Black community had been the "receiving network" that harbored slaves during slavery, Latinos living in the United States have largely provided the protective communities for Central American refugees. According to sanctuary activists and researchers Renny Golden and Michael McConnell, the historical invisibility of the Black community

> is due to the bias of the Western interpretation that focuses on individual heroism and overlooks the social courage of a people. Such a perspective succumbs to the attraction of white, male, clerical heroism, losing sight of the anonymous Black community. . . . The inspiration and infrastructure for the railroad — and, in fact, the abolitionist movement itself — was created by Blacks.[12]

The same can be said about the enormous effort of Latino communities in response to the influx of refugees from Central America.

A key difference between the Latino-based sanctuary movement and what is typically called "the sanctuary movement" is that whereas the first was necessarily clandestine, the second initially saw the media as its best protection once the refugees had arrived safely.[13] The public movement depended upon the media to spread the stories of refugees in sanctuary and the word that a growing number of largely mainstream congregations were harboring refugees. In its early years, sanctuary work was chronicled extensively in *Time* and *Newsweek,* on *60 Minutes* and PBS's *Frontline,* and in other national media. Meanwhile, media attention was the last thing people wanted in the communities that absorbed the overwhelming majority of refugees. For example, a small Protestant church in a Hispanic neighborhood in Chicago decided not to declare itself a sanctuary, given that 60 percent of its congregation were undocumented refugees.[14] This difference further supported the invisibility of the unnamed sanctuary movement.[15] Differences in class and legal status had an enormous impact on how these congregations responded to the refugee situation.

Recognizing both responses to refugees avoids the common mistaken portrayal of white sanctuary workers as the sole architects and heroes in the story. Characterizing the public sanctuary movement as "white" makes invisible the refugees whose lives and stories catapulted many North Americans into action. Were it not for the testimonies of the Central American refugees, media attention would have been far less effective.

From the point of view of Central American refugees, recognizing both movements is also important. Many refugees have been forced to stay in the United States far beyond the years the public sanctuary movement was in operation. In the process, Salvadorans and Guatemalans in Los Angeles, Chicago, New Jersey, and elsewhere have continued to draw upon and connect with larger and longer-standing Latino and multiethnic communities. Many Salvadoran refugees in the United States were in a long-term legal holding pattern because of 1990 legislation that granted them Temporary Protected Status (TPS). Under this status, they run the risk of being denied reentry to the United States if they travel to El Salvador. At the same time, there are few legal mechanisms available for them to obtain permanent residency in the United States.[16]

Another common misconception about the sanctuary movement relates to its origins. Although the public sanctuary movement is typically portrayed as an overwhelmingly white initiative, its origins were cross-national (between Mexico and the United States) and biracial (Latino and white). The story of its origins begins with Jim Corbett, a Quaker rancher living in Tucson, whose grandmother was a Blackfoot Indian.[17] A friend of Corbett's had picked up a Salvadoran hitchhiker who then was picked up and taken away with no explanation by the border patrol. Disturbed by his friend's story, Corbett tried to find the Salvadoran. Eventually Corbett contacted Manzo, a private social service agency in Tucson that had long assisted undocumented Mexican immigrants and had recently begun working with Central Americans.

Manzo's staff in 1981 included two political organizers, Margo Cowan, who had been trained by Cesar Chávez, and Lupe Castillo, an activist of Mexican descent.[18] Manzo staff suggested to Corbett that he continue to track down the Salvadoran hitchhiker, a process that eventually put him in touch with hundreds of Salvadoran and Guatemalan refugees fleeing repression. Corbett then contacted and began working closely with John Fife, the minister of a church in a Tucson barrio whose congregation was African American, Latino, and white. Fife's first parish had been in a Black church in Ohio, and he had participated in the Selma to Montgomery march in 1965. He spoke Spanish and had long been involved in progressive issues — opposition to against computer sales to Argentina and Chile, antiapartheid organizing, and the Nestlé boycott.

Corbett and Fife began working closely with Manzo, the newly formed Religious Taskforce on Central America, and an activist priest, Ramon Dagoberto Quiñones, in Nogales, Mexico, who had been working with refugees. The first collective rescue of Central Americans from a horrendous detention center in the United States culminated in sending two busloads of refugees to "a black church in Watts that offered temporary shelter for about eighty people."[19] John

Fife then approached his mixed-race congregation, which decided to become the first church to officially declare itself a sanctuary.

The fact that these various people knew each other and worked together is what initially made sanctuary (as a concept) possible. Without the work of the activist Catholic church in Nogales there would have been no organized place for refugees to go before crossing the border. Without Manzo, there would have been no organization to initially encourage Corbett to get involved. In other words, the two white men credited with initiating the sanctuary movement both drew extensively on their ties to Mexican religious activists and Chicano activists in order to begin setting up a pathway for refugees.

Understanding the multiracial, cross-national roots of the sanctuary movement makes it possible to identify how race and nationality played themselves out in the initial organizing. Soon after Corbett and Fife began setting up sanctuaries for Central Americans, Manzo decided to focus full time on Mexican immigrants. Ann Crittenden reports:

> As Margo Cowan and Lupe Castillo saw it, sanctuary was primarily a tactic to educate middle- and upper-class American church goers on the Central America issue. In their view, most refugees didn't need gringos helping them across the border. . . . They needed more help in the tedious and unglamorous work of fighting their cases through the courts.[20]

Another core conflict facing sanctuary workers involved the precarious situation of deciding which Central Americans would be taken into sanctuary. Sanctuary workers were overwhelmed by the number of people seeking asylum and knew the small but growing chain of churches and synagogues could not sustain them all. The workers also reasoned that the legitimacy of their movement in the eyes of the media and U.S. public rested upon its portrayal as helping only those refugees whose lives would be threatened were they to return to Guatemala or El Salvador. Sanctuary's publicity rested on distinguishing between those needing asylum for political reasons and those immigrants seeking to cross the border for economic reasons.

As the number of refugees seeking asylum increased, sanctuary workers (in Tucson and other locations) began interviewing Central Americans in an attempt to identify those refugees who were at "highest risk" — those whose stories clearly demonstrated they would be killed if they returned to their country. From the sanctuary perspective, clarifying that they were working with "high risk" refugees also provided the rationale they needed to explain why they were not working with the U.S. government — since the Immigration and Naturalization Service (INS) was refusing to recognize asylum as a legitimate category for Central Americans. According to one of the activists I interviewed, Darlene Nicgorski, who was one of the sanctuary workers in southern Arizona, the people chosen for sanctuary were those who wanted to and could speak publicly.[21] The two-tiered system (those fleeing for their lives versus those leaving for other reasons), however, meant that U.S. sanctuary workers had the power to decide, often based on an interview of only a few hours, whether a Central American individual or family would be taken into protection.[22]

Frequently, white privilege is what made it possible for early workers to help Central Americans across the border. Early on, for example, Corbett pulled together "housewives, students, professional men, and retirees" who carried binoculars for "bird watching" as they guided people across the border with no interference from the border patrol.[23] That same white privilege and U.S. citizenship was responsible for the central contradiction in U.S. sanctuary workers' power to decide who did and did not qualify as a refugee. Clearly the urban communities in Los Angeles and Phoenix that initially absorbed the lion's share of the Central American refugees did not "screen" the candidates; nor did the Catholic churches that many Salvadoran refugees attended as they got settled in these communities call themselves "sanctuary churches."

Those refugees taken in by the public sanctuary movement were afforded resources and legal protection not available to those in the unofficial movement. Again, the class privilege and legal status of the sanctuary locations in the official sanctuary movement far outweighed resources available to those in the underground movement. And yet, as Susan Coutin reports, based on interviews with Central Americans and Anglos involved in sanctuary, the political position of refugees in sanctuary was precarious.[24] From the beginning, Central Americans considered sanctuary a North American movement. As a critical mass of refugees came together in San Francisco, Tucson, and Los Angeles, they formed their own organizations such as CRECE (Central American Refugee Center) in San Francisco and El Comité in Tucson. Coutin asserts that, while the relationships among sanctuary workers and members of refugee organizations were often respectful, "sanctuary itself, however, remained a movement *about,* rather than *of,* Central Americans."[25]

Despite significant differences in the public and the underground sanctuary movements, both recognized that defiance of U.S. immigration laws was necessary. In 1984, the U.S. granted only 0.4 percent of applications for political asylum from Guatemalans and 2.5 percent from Salvadorans.[26] From the U.S. government's perspective, recognizing Central Americans as political refugees would mean acknowledging the political conflict that was fueled by the U.S. government itself. The Refugee Act of 1980 was supposed to bring U.S. policy in line with U.N. guidelines. However, the Refugee Act excluded people fleeing from military repression or natural disasters. Thus, as Crittenden explains, U.S. officials would argue that "most Salvadorans do not qualify for political asylum in the United States because they are fleeing a generalized climate of terror and violence, rather than specific threats to their lives."[27]

Although the U.S. government did little initially to stop the public sanctuary work, by 1984 the government stepped up its arrests of refugees and began arresting North American activists, infiltrating organizations, and creating dissent among movement activists. Ironically, this crackdown had unintended positive consequence, in terms of anti-racism; it led those involved in sanctuary to create a national organizational process for making decisions. At the 1985 national convention of sanctuary workers, refugees from different regions met for the first time and were thus able to collectively urge the sanctuary movement not only to defy existing immigration laws and to support refugees individually, but also to oppose the government intervention in Central America.[28]

With this assertion, refugees were challenging a tendency among sanctuary churches to see their work as done once "their" refugees were safe. For those seeking asylum, accountability meant not only harboring refugees but also recognizing that the United States was an imperialist nation. Refugees maintained that activists needed to both make the United States safe for refugees and ensure that Central America was safe for Central Americans. One Salvadoran explained, "We want to go back home. We want El Salvador and Guatemala to be sanctuaries."[29]

Many people first became involved in the sanctuary movement after hearing refugees' testimonials about the repression that forced them to leave El Salvador or Guatemala, typically after family or friends had already been threatened or killed. Opening a church or a meetinghouse to a refugee family was an act of conscience that took into account the resources available to the community of faith (usually money and access to safe haven) not otherwise accessible to the refugees. However, a comprehensive account of the decision making in faith communities about sanctuary also reveals complicated attitudes toward property rights and U.S. citizenship. One of the activists I interviewed became involved in Central America solidarity work after many years of activism for other causes. In the 1980s she began attending a local church where she proposed that it become a sanctuary for refugees from El Salvador. A group of twelve people from the congregation studied whether the church should become a sanctuary — a process that involved intensive consciousness raising among church members, some of whom had a history of activism and some of whom were new to activism.

Some congregation members were concerned about possible reduced property values and the wear and tear on the church building. Eventually, church members scaled back their original proposal that the church itself would provide a sanctuary. A compromise was reached: the church building would not be a sanctuary, but the congregation would instead raise money to pay for housing for refugees in a nearby town.

The implications of this church's decision are complicated. On the one hand, providing resources for refugees to live in a neighboring town gave the refugees autonomy not afforded to refugees in congregations where all their needs were addressed. The major differences in language, culture, and class between refugees and many people in sanctuary groups often led to communication problems that were exacerbated when refugees had few ties outside the congregation. On the other hand, the church's worry about property taxes and the responsibility of tenants in the church building is a troubling reminder of two parties coming to the table with extraordinarily different resources. A willingness to compromise came from accepting the church's decision that to do something was better than doing nothing. Clearly, one of the strengths of the sanctuary movement was its ability to involve people at varying stages of risk taking. Its inherent limitation, however, was that North Americans always maintained the upper hand in deciding the direction of the movement.

Although refugees recognized the risks sanctuary workers took to make safe journeys and resettlement possible, Central Americans also often wrestled with patronizing North American attitudes, huge gulfs in understanding because of cultural differences, and North American expectations that refugees be model citizens — by North American standards. Golden and McConnell report:

At a Presbyterian-sponsored conference on sanctuary, a refugee in sanctuary in Minnesota said, "We don't want you to treat us like we were your pets." Two others from upper New York State wrote to sanctuary organizers that "the great majority of the members of the church still maintained their racism." In their case, the refugees were never consulted about upcoming plans and the congregation went so far as to tell them when they could take a shower.[30]

Not surprisingly, those sanctuary workers with a history of involvement in Central American communities were often the best prepared to develop relationships with refugees based on equality and mutuality, rather than on condescension and a false sense of superiority. For Nicgorski, who lived in Guatemala in 1980 before beginning sanctuary work at the border in 1982, a key challenge was identifying how best to use her resources and knowledge to support refugees. In her twenties, Nicgorski had become a member of an order of nuns who were committed to justice. She moved to Guatemala in 1980 and began to run a preschool in 1981. At that time, the Guatemalan military were killing whole villages of people, sometimes including church leaders (nuns, priests, and ministers) who the military considered dangerous simply because they were working with poor people.

When Nicgorski's parish priest was killed in cold blood, she and the other nuns knew they had to flee for their lives. Nicgorski worked in a refugee camp in Honduras for a year before returning to the United States in 1982. Soon, Nicgorski became a key figure in the sanctuary movement in Arizona, working closely with Central Americans to help prepare them for what they might face once they arrived in a church in Rochester, New York, or in Portland, Maine, or in other locations throughout the country. During this period, Nicgorski was angered by some sanctuary churches' attitudes of entitlement. In her biography of Nicgorski, Julia Lieblich writes:

> Sometimes the problem lay with the sanctuary churches, which amazed Nicgorski with their special requests. Some specified the nationality of the refugee they wanted; others requested children

by age. One congregation asked her to send a nonsmoking vegetarian. Refugees were people, not pets, she reminded them. The point was to shelter people in need.[31]

Nicgorski also saw that white people had an easier time remaining committed to Central Americans in an abstract way than they did working with peoples of colors in the United States. Nicgorski remembers that, increasingly, it became an issue and priority to have leadership from Central Americans in sanctuary meetings (locally, regionally, and nationally). At no time, however, "do I recall it being an issue about whether sanctuary should be more grounded in domestic communities of color."[32]

BEARING WITNESS

Another key initiative against U.S. intervention in Central America took the form of what became known as witnessing tours to El Salvador, Nicaragua, and Guatemala. While having a religious affiliation was not a requirement to participate on these tours, many of those who became involved considered their witnesses as an act of faith, often tied to their religious communities. Witness for Peace was the largest group that organized these tours. This organization believed that placing North Americans in Central America alongside the religious people, health care workers, and union workers who were being persecuted would limit government repression.

Among those who participated in Witness for Peace, many were feminists, lesbians, or both, as was true about Central America solidarity work in general.[33] This was made possible in part by multiracial feminism, which included significant attention to the United States as a colonizing country — a critique brought home in part by feminists of colors from previously colonized countries (such as Trinidad, India, and Argentina) now living and active in the United States.[34] Multiracial feminism encouraged women to think about themselves as activists who were raced and classed and who had a national affiliation that, in Audre Lorde's terms, was on the wrong side of every liberation struggle.[35] Multiracial feminism led by women of colors encouraged anticapitalist, anti-imperialist activism. This analysis, along with the anti–Vietnam War protests that many women had been involved in through the early 1970s, readied them to stand up against U.S. imperialism in Central America in the 1980s.

For anti-intervention activists with a feminist agenda, attempts by the United States in the 1980s to overthrow the Sandinista government were particularly egregious; there had been more feminist involvement in the Sandinista revolution than in any other in the history of the hemisphere.[36] One-third of the Sandinista army had been women.[37] One of the earliest decrees by the new government prohibited the use of images of the female body to advertise products. The government encouraged domestic servants to organize for job security, and women's offices were established to attend to women's legal problems.

In some ways, the Sandinista government of the 1980s was more feminist than the U.S. government. The 1987 Constitution in Nicaragua assured equal rights for women, a parity yet to be achieved in the United States. The Sandinista government abolished wage differences based on gender, which made an enormous difference for families, given that women have always been a large part of the workforce. The government set up dozens of rural infant centers where there had been none, supported the emergence of two thousand unions (up from fewer than two hundred), funded what became a flourishing arts and poetry movement, redistributed land to farmers, and lowered the illiteracy rate dramatically (which was substantially higher among women than men).[38]

From the perspective of many feminists in Nicaragua, as the 1980s progressed, the Sandinista government backed off from genuinely supporting women's rights on many levels. In response feminists created an autonomous movement that flourished in the 1990s and did not (and still does not) depend upon the Sandinistas or the 1990s

National Opposition Union (UNO) government.[39] For feminists in the United States, contact with their Nicaraguan counterparts was invaluable — in terms both of Nicaraguan feminists' involvement in the Sandinista revolution and their increasing assertion of autonomy from the government in order to build a multidimensional movement.[40]

Dawn Gomes, an activist I interviewed, went to Nicaragua twice in 1983 and 1984. She went with the first wave of solidarity workers and picked coffee along with "brigades of people from all over the world."[41] In 1986 she went again, this time to build houses with the Nicaraguan Solidarity Committee. Gomes was enthusiastic about and felt affirmed by the Nicaraguan Revolution, partly because of the emphasis among many of the Sandinistas upon building an egalitarian society and breaking down class barriers. The Sandinistas were trying to organize a society based on principles Gomes had not seen in her previous work in a mixed-gender Black Power and white solidarity organization. She was also grateful to feel a sense of being "selfless and breaking away from white supremacy while really wanting to do something worthwhile for other people."[42]

Gomes believed that much could be said for "looking horrors and inhumane acts against people in the face" — a witnessing that thousands of people from the United States did and then came back to publicize. She also saw limits to the activists' approaches. From Gomes's perspective,

> some of the drive or impetus clouded our judgment and created this magical thinking — essentially idealizing the Nicaraguans and Salvadorans. We didn't have a sense of our own selves so we would idealize them, which I think came out of our own low self-esteem. When you idealize, then you are sure to do the opposite, when the clay begins to crack. We will surely then assault them or attack them or put them down.[43]

In this reflection, Gomes identifies two sides of the same racist coin: either romanticizing or demonizing Nicaraguan leaders, while failing to account for the way many U.S. activists' limited experience with working across race and culture blunted their abilities to recognize Nicaraguans as equals and to anticipate and guard against ethnocentrism.

This tendency to romanticize Central Americans was widespread among North American activists. Anthropologist Susan Coutin writes:

> Central American poor were seen as closer to God, as examples to emulate, as victims of "our gluttony," and as representatives of the authenticity "we" once had. Such images of Central Americans were made possible despite efforts to create personal relationships with Salvadorans and Guatemalans — by the *distance* between sanctuary workers and refugees.[44]

Coutin asserts that the romanticized portrayal of Central Americans was yet another version of "what Edward Said has termed 'Orientalism' — the tendency of Western societies to produce authoritative and power-laden images of the non-Western other."[45] Typically, Orientalism involves Western representations of non-Westerners as inferior and culturally deficient.

In the Central American–North American dynamic, North American activists often glorified Central Americans as a way of showing their dissatisfaction with their white middle-class cultural values (based on individualism, consumerism, and competition). Ironically, though, as Coutin explains, by idealizing Central Americans, North Americans still reproduced "culturally ingrained Orientalist tendencies to know, define, and create representations of non-Western peoples."[46] Meanwhile, the power differentials between Central Americans and North Americans remained essentially intact.

Jeanine Cohen, who also traveled to Nicaragua for extended periods during the mid-1980s, came to see ethnocentrism as one of the most substantial problems for the movement.[47] Jeanine came to an interest in Central America through her organizing work with gay and lesbian Latinos in San Francisco. After her first year of traveling to Nicaragua, Cohen became concerned that North Americans were rarely addressing cross-cultural issues. She began to ask, "What would it require for people to go to Nicaragua with all 'our relative privilege' and provide a service to people without having an arrogant assumption that we were helping people and they needed us?"[48]

Cohen also asked what it meant when people from the United States became sexually involved with people in Nicaragua. From her perspective, "It was not clean. It was not okay in my book. We need to talk about the implications of what we were doing. What was the effect of women getting involved with Nicaraguan men who were most probably married and had children?"[49] According to Ellen Scott, a sociologist who organized brigades to Nicaragua in the mid-1980s, both heterosexual men and women and lesbians were part of the problem. Some North American women who were working in Nicaragua became involved in relationships with lesbians there. Their affairs caused many problems. Most Nicaraguan lesbians were deeply closeted at that time, and many were often already in other lesbian relationships when they began seeing North American women. In addition, these affairs usually took place in small towns, so the impact of these liaisons was rarely anonymous. With regard to sexual relationships between North Americans and Central Americans Scott adds:

> The North Americans would then, typically, return home, leaving the mess to be picked up by others. In the meantime, they had sexualized and romanticized their work in Nicaragua. They were there for business, doing political activism and community service. They weren't there to get involved with people who would be there for the long haul.[50]

Scott's concern about the power dynamics involved in Central and North American lesbian relationships certainly applies to heterosexual affairs as well, given the long history of U.S. and European heterosexual oppression of Central American women.

Over time, some feminists who were doing long-term work with Nicaraguans began to include attention to ethnocentrism and the ethics of cross-cultural work in training for those traveling to Nicaragua. For Cohen, taking this work seriously began by scrutinizing her own behavior. Sometimes she found herself getting angry with the Nicaraguan organizers. She would assume they did not have proper plans when their plans were merely not apparent to her. She found herself wondering what was "wrong with these people" when they did not do things as she would have. Cohen believes her attitude, even when unspoken, was apparent in her behavior. "It is arrogant, feeling like it is great, what we are doing, but then in our actual practice, we might have been undermining the very things we were trying to create."[51] From these lessons, Cohen began doing much more preparatory work with people interested in cross-cultural activism and tried, with others, to openly identify how ethnocentrism among U.S. activists compromised long-term alliances.

LISTENING FOR THE LESSONS

While the success of the Central America U.S. peace movement is hard to measure, many believe that activist initiatives deterred Ronald Reagan from escalating the war to the extent that Presidents Johnson and Nixon had in Vietnam. The peace movement made clear that while Reagan may have wanted to get beyond the "Vietnam syndrome," activists in both eras refused to allow the war to continue unabated. U.S. peace initiatives took clear stands against U.S. aggression in which thirty thousand people were killed in Nicaragua, one hundred thousand killed in El Salvador, and as many as 1.5 million Central Americans were driven from their homes.[52] The protests, harboring of refugees, and activist trips to Central America all made public a war that the U.S. government hoped to keep "technological, clean and distant."[53] Between its official start in 1982 and when it tapered off in 1986, the sanctuary movement provided thousands of refugees with contacts and resources that might have otherwise been unavailable to them. Between 1982 and 1986, less than 1 percent of all the asylum cases were granted. By the middle of 1987, half of the Salvadoran applications in Arizona had been granted.[54]

Both the sanctuary movement and Witness for Peace present concrete instances of people who did not agree with U.S. policy and were willing to put their lives on the line if need be. In that way, those involved broke open the notion of a monolithic U.S. citizen. This break was important for Central Americans whose images of people in the United States otherwise might have been monopolized by Reagan-supported military men. Protests by people from the United States also raised the consciousness of others who, upon learning from those working with refugees or those who traveled south, joined in opposing the war.

While organizing efforts in the United States were clearly substantial, and in many ways effective, the limitations of the movement from an anti-racist perspective are troubling. Certainly, the fact that there has been little analysis of the racial dynamics of the movement is a telling reminder of how the use of a color-blind approach to social movement history renders invisible how race, racism, and ethnocentrism limited the movement. The activists I interviewed give many reasons that anti-racism often fell off the movement's radar screen. Few of the white activists who participated in Witness for Peace had existing networks with U.S.-based Latino and Black organizations. Those activists who saw multiracial ties as crucial ran the risk of being dismissed by other whites and potentially accused of slowing the momentum of the movement. According to Salvadoran activist Mario Davila, the overriding goal for Salvadorans was to stop the war in Central America.[55] That meant influencing public policy, an undertaking that required a funding base. From the perspective of Salvadorans, white people were those who had the wealth to fund such activism. For them, building multiracial alliances was less of a priority than changing public policy, a task that was largely in the hands of white people. These dynamics and the Salvadorans' views of North Americans were only exacerbated by the reality that, for most white activists, the whiteness of their organization and their lack of multiracial ties was simply unremarkable.

The fact that most white North American activists had little contact with Black and Latino activists in the United States also limited cross-race alliances in the sanctuary movement. The most depressing aspect of this research, for me, was discovering that there was virtually no communication between the above-ground sanctuary movement and the much larger underground movement within Latino and multi-racial communities. For significant alliances to have flourished, many more white activists would have needed to have been bilingual and have had longstanding ties to Latino and multiracial churches and community organizations. It has long been said that the most segregated hour in the week in the United States is on Sunday mornings when people pray, think, and preach in church. White sanctuary workers played into and exacerbated this segregation by not developing alliances with Latino faith-based communities. Power inequities between refugees and the North Americans who provided sanctuary and a lack of alliances between the white sanctuary locations and communities of colors (outside of the Southwest) undermined the ability of the movement to address race and racism adequately.

Another factor that may have limited cross-race alliances was that white-dominated organizations rarely knew how either to identify or confront their own race and class privileges. The solidarity that North American activists spoke about typically involved multiple contradictions that were rarely adequately resolved. For white sanctuary workers on the border between Mexico and Arizona, standing in solidarity meant dodging the border patrol and literally walking and driving alongside of refugees. Over time most North American activists became aware of the limits of that shared act. Refugees getting caught crossing the border ran the risk of deportation and possible death upon return to their countries. For North American activists, the risk was a possible arrest and, in a very few cases, imprisonment.

For many activists, "solidarity" meant being willing to risk arrest for civil disobedience, an act of defiance that largely depended upon having U.S. citizenship. Refugees simply could not afford to commit such acts. They not only had to forfeit their right to civil disobedience, but also as refugees, their very existence in the United States was under threat. For people who traveled to Central America on brigades or with Witness for Peace, standing in solidarity meant making a commitment to take what they learned back to the United States in order to push for changes in foreign policy. Travel to Central America could also mean being in physical danger, although North Americans were generally much less at risk than those living in Central America. Most travelers, however, were aware that the choice to travel to Central America could not be compared with the forced "decision" of hundreds of thousands of Central Americans to travel from their homes to avoid being tortured or killed. Refugees in the sanctuary movement potentially faced being infantilized by their host communities or idealized and stretched beyond capacity in terms of providing inside knowledge about political strategies and historical background about their countries. Neither tendency nurtured equal, powerful, cross-cultural political relations.

The enormous difference in the risks and costs highlights the limits of transnational, cross-racial solidarity. This does not mean that the actions are not worthy, but damage was done when these differences were not acknowledged openly. In some instances, white idealization of Central American culture and religion served as a distraction from dealing with power inequities. The geographical distance between the two cultures kept that idealization intact, another reason that, in the 1980s, many white activists seemed more interested and willing to confront poverty and repression in Central America than to confront it as it affected working-class peoples and people of colors in the United States.

There are still many questions to consider about what might have strengthened the Central America peace movement. What might it have taken to make the movement multiracial from the beginning — not just in pockets, as in the Southwest, but nationally? What kinds of education, reflection, and change need to occur in White-dominated churches so that multiracial faith-based alliances can flourish? What might it have taken to build organizations in the United States such that early brigades going to Central America could have developed and sustained relationships with Black and Latino organizations in the United States? I am left wondering whether, if white activists in the late 1960s and early 1970s had been better able to respond to the increasingly multiracial composition of activist organizations of that period — The Brown Berets, the American Indian Movement, Puerto Rican independence activists — the white activists might have been better prepared to participate in Latino-Black-white alliances in the 1980s. Sociologist Christian Smith reports, "More than one half of [white] Central American peace activists had participated in civil rights, anti–Vietnam war, environmental and anti-poverty campaigns."[56] These are all locations where lessons might have been learned about the limits of all-white groups and the problem of opposing imperialism without paying commensurate attention to anti-racism in the United States.

One lesson that emerges from this and other organizing is how important it is to create multiracial alliances from day one when a new organization begins or a crisis hits and to maintain these alliances across the life span of the organization. Had Witness for Peace activists worked closely with Black and domestic Latino religious organizations in the beginning — in 1982 and 1983 — who knows how much more powerful a coalition against U.S. intervention might have been formed. In many ways, the racial and class divides evident in the anti–Vietnam War movement manifested themselves again in the 1980s, and to some extent in the organizing against the U.S. invasion of Iraq. The anti-imperialist thrust of organizing must go hand in hand with an anti-racist agenda in the United States.

Among the multiple lessons to be learned from Central American solidarity work of the 1980s is the need to build a multiracial base in the United States while nurturing ties to progressive movements internationally. Building a progressive multiracial base remains a significant challenge and goal for activists standing up against the

World Trade Organization and other international financial centers of power. Not surprisingly, debates about strategy for organizing continue, as do conversations about pacifist vs. militant protests and the approaches required to build multiracial alliances that must be, by necessity, increasingly international.

NOTES

1. Renny Golden and Michael McConnell, *Sanctuary: The New Underground Railroad* (Maryknoll, N.Y.: Orbis Books, 1986), 5.

2. William Chafe, *The Unfinished Journey: America since World War II* (New York: Oxford, 1999), 477.

3. A third initiative was the Pledge of Resistance that led over eighty thousand people to protest, commit civil disobedience, or both. Of the three initiatives, this one was the least overtly faith based. For this reason I have not included it in this chapter. For an analysis of the anti-racism efforts within this wing of the movement, see Becky Thompson, *A Promise and a Way of Life: White Antiracist Activism* (Minneapolis: University of Minnesota Press, 2001).

4. Susan Coutin, *The Culture of Protest: Religious Activism in the United States Sanctuary Movement* (Boulder, Colo.: Westview Press, 1993), 187; Golden and McConnell, *Sanctuary,* 3; Robin Lorentzen, *Women in the Sanctuary Movement* (Philadelphia: Temple University Press, 1991), 14–15.

5. Golden and McConnell, *Sanctuary,* 53.

6. Ibid., 5, 53.

7. Ibid., 61.

8. Lorentzen, *Women in the Sanctuary Movement,* 15.

9. Golden and McConnell, *Sanctuary,* 48.

10. Ibid., 60.

11. Ibid.

12. Ibid., 61; Ann Crittenden, *Sanctuary: A Story of American Conscience and the Law in Collision* (New York: Weidenfeld and Nicolson, 1988).

13. Golden and McConnell, *Sanctuary,* 53.

14. Lorentzen, *Women in the Sanctuary Movement,* 29.

15. Some activists/writers merely treat the public "sanctuary movement" as the only movement. See, for example, Christian Smith, *Resisting Reagan: The U.S. Central America Peace Movement* (Chicago: University of Chicago Press, 1996), 171. Others, notably Golden and McConnell, and Ann Crittenden, are careful to specify that the U.S.-based Latino response to refugees far outweighed the number of people harbored through churches and synagogues. At the same time, although Golden and McConnell devote an entire chapter to the clandestine movement in Mexico, they do not take the next step and analyze the clandestine movement in the United States or consider a possible relationship between the two forms of sanctuary.

16. Coutin, *The Culture of Protest,* 223; Adrian Bailey, Richard Wright, Alison Mountz, and Ines Miyares, "Transnational Salvadoran Geographies: Space-Time and the Production of Permanent Temporariness," paper presented at the American Studies Association Conference, Montreal, Canada, October 30, 1999.

17. For the story of John Fife's and Jim Corbett's background and events leading up to the first sanctuary church, see Crittenden, *Sanctuary,* 3–83.

18. Ibid., 26–28.

19. Ibid., 47.

20. Ibid., 78.

21. For a lengthy and sensitive account of Nicgorski's life, see Julia Lieblich, "Daughter of Prophecy: An Activist Takes the Lead," in *Sisters: Lives of Devotion and Defiance* (New York: Ballantine Books, 1992), 203–81.

22. Crittenden, *Sanctuary,* 120.

23. Ibid., 54.

24. Coutin, *The Culture of Protest.*

25. Ibid., 11.

26. Golden and McConnell, *Sanctuary,* 77.

27. Crittenden, *Sanctuary,* 22.

28. Ignatius Bau, *This Ground Is Holy: Church Sanctuary and Central American Refugees* (New York: Paulist Press, 1985), 25–26.

29. Golden and McConnell, *Sanctuary,* 165.

30. Ibid., 55.

31. Lieblich, "Daughter of Prophecy," 233.

32. Ibid., 169.

33. For a first-person narrative by a white Jewish lesbian who traveled to Nicaragua with Witness for Peace see Rebecca Gordon, *Letters from Nicaragua* (San Francisco: Spinsters/Aunt Lute, 1986). For essays and poetry by a white lesbian who was a member of a Witness for Peace delegation and was captured (and released) by the Contras in 1985, see Judith McDaniel, *Sanctuary: A Journey* (Ithaca, N.Y.: Firebrand, 1987).

34. M. Jacqui Alexander and Chandra Talpade Mohanty, eds., *Feminist Genealogies, Colonial Legacies, Democratic Futures* (New York: Routledge, 1997); Chandra Talpade Mohanty, Ann Russo, and Lourdes Torres, eds., *Third World Women and the Politics of Feminism* (Bloomington: Indiana University Press, 1991).

35. Audre Lorde, *Sister Outsider* (Freedom, Calif.: Crossing Press, 1984).

36. Margaret Randall, *Sandino's Daughters Revisited: Feminism in Nicaragua* (New Brunswick, N.J.: Rutgers University Press, 1994); Margaret Randall, *Gathering Rage: The Failure of the 20th-Century Revolutions to Develop a Feminist Agenda* (New York: Monthly Review Press, 1992); Norma Stoltz Chinchilla, "Feminism, Revolution and Democratic Transitions in Nicaragua," *The Women's Movement in Latin America,* ed. Jane Jaquette (Boulder, Colo.: Westview Press, 1994); Minor Sinclair, ed., *The New Politics of Survival: Grassroots Movements in Central America* (New York: Monthly Review Press, 1995).

37. Randall, *Sandino's Daughters Revisited,* 5.

38. Ibid., 12, 87.

39. Randall, *Gathering Rage;* Randall, *Sandino's Daughters Revisited;* Karen Kampwirth, "Confronting Adversity with Experience: The Emergence of Feminism in Nicaragua," *Social Politics: International Studies in Gender, State and Society* 3, no. 2/3 (Summer/Fall, 1996): 136–58.

40. While I am highlighting Nicaraguan feminism here, there was significant activist organizing by women in Guatemala and El Salvador in the 1980s as well. See Jennifer Schirmer, "The Seeking of Truth and the Gendering of Consciousness: The CoMadres of El Salvador and the CONAVIGUA Widows of Guatemala," in *Viva: Women and Popular Protest in Latin America*, ed. Sarah A. Radcliffe and Sallie Westwood (New York: Routledge, 1993), 30–64.

41. Dawn Gomes grew up in California where she has been a social justice activist since the late 1960s. She helped to spearhead the first affirmative action plan for San Francisco's transportation system, and she worked extensively with a white group in solidarity with a Black liberation organization (from 1977 to 1982), with a nonprofit homeless coalition in the 1980s, and with a group opposing violence against women in the 1980s. In the 1990s, Gomes worked with a nonprofit multiracial coalition that helps communities prepare for disasters.

42. Dawn Gomes, interview by author, Oakland, California, April 1999.

43. Ibid.

44. Coutin, *The Culture of Protest,* 187.

45. Ibid., 154.

46. Ibid., 187.

47. Jeanine Cohen was raised by antiapartheid parents in Johannesburg, South Africa. As an adult her activism has included working in the squatters movement in England; working with a San Francisco–based Black nationalist organization; participating in the battered women's movement and with Lesbians Against Police Violence; and making documentary films/videos on interracial lesbian couples, butch-femme relations, and white racial identity.

48. Jeanine Cohen, interview by author, Oakland, California, April 1999.

49. Ibid.

50. Ellen Scott, interview by author, Cincinnati, Ohio, August 1999.

51. Cohen, interview.

52. Sinclair, *The New Politics of Survival,* 12–13.

53. Golden and McConnell, *Sanctuary,* 80.

54. Crittenden, *Sanctuary,* 347. In 1990, the Justice Department settled a lawsuit brought forward in 1985 by eighty immigrants' rights and church groups against the INS. The settlement granted temporary legal status to Salvadoran refugees. It required the INS to rehear 150,000 cases in which asylum had been denied and to hire new INS agents who would be knowledgeable of conditions in Central America. Lieblich, "Daughter of Prophecy," 280.

55. Mario Davila is a specialist in Central American affairs with the American Friends Service Committee in Boston. He was an activist in El Salvador before coming to the United States as a young adult and became a leader in The Pledge for Resistance; in establishing sister cities, unions, and universities; and in organizing with Salvadoran activists nationally.

56. Smith, *Resisting Reagan,* 175.

Seven

"WE MAKE THE ROAD BY WALKING"*

Reflections on the Legacy of White Anti-Racist Activism

SALLY NOLAND MAC NICHOL

THE SIN OF WHITE SUPREMACY:
STRUGGLING WITH RACISM, WRESTLING WITH WHITENESS

Racism is based on the concept of whiteness — a powerful fiction enforced by power and violence.[1]

FOR MORE YEARS than I can remember I have struggled with the ghosts of my racialized past and present. As a white woman raised in the Midwest, with deep roots in the southern United States, I have tried to reconcile the contradictions of a loving family with the fact that I, like most of my white brothers and sisters, was indoctrinated from my first breath of life with the notion that white people are more intelligent, more moral, more human, more valuable than anybody deemed Black, red, yellow, or brown. As a single white mother in New York City, I worked hard to figure out ways to raise healthy and strong anti-racist white children in a segregated city with a viciously racist public school system. As an anti–domestic violence advocate, my anti-racist feminist commitments have brewed, for almost two decades, in the cauldron of day-to-day work with women and children struggling to survive both the violence of intimate partners and the violence of a white male supremacist state.

---

*"We Make the Road by Walking": This is an adaptation of the title of a poem by Antonio Machado quoted in Louise K. Schmidt, *Transforming Abuse: Nonviolent Recovery and Resistance* (Philadelphia and Gabriola Island, B.C.: New Society Publishers, 1995), 1.

This chapter is grounded in these dimensions of my experience and represents one effort to name and take responsibility for the complexities of my past and the contradictions of my present. In permanent rebellion against the white supremacy that distorts all human persons who live within its defiling and destructive grasp, I write in anger and in sorrow, and *against* the fear that I will reproduce the same old white racial narcissism I wish to escape. Finally, I write to offer hope, however fragile, grounded in the fact that there are white people who have gone before us — race traitors and anti-racist activists — who were courageous enough to resist living an unexamined white life and strong enough to live out that resistance. The good news is that, although it has been assiduously concealed, there have always been white people who have supported the continuous resistance of peoples of colors in this country. These ancestors, and sisters and brothers struggling for justice in the here and now, can guide those of us looking for models of human resilience and ongoing commitment to justice in the face of unspeakable evil that must be spoken about and confronted.

White supremacy in the United States is a pervasive social, political, and economic phenomenon. It is not only a personal ideology based on racial prejudice, but a *system* that involves complex and insidious cultural messages, institutional policies and practices, as well as the beliefs and actions of individuals.

Theologically, we can speak of white supremacy as an idolatrous faith, a spiritual disease;[2] Martin Luther King wrote that the American people were "*infected* with racism."[3] We can speak of it as a corrosive and deadly sin that subverts creation and salvation. Indeed, it has been called America's *original sin* against the Holy Spirit.[4] Biblically, we might speak of racism as an active and aggressive principality, a demonic "power" that appears to move, adapt, and grow with a life of its own. From this perspective, the sin of racism is "an individual and collective collusion with established evil. It is willing complicity with our own enslavement to privilege (and limitation). It is giving ourselves over to an animate system of domination. It is thereby distorting our humanity, and...submitting ourselves to an idol."[5]

Because white supremacy is saturating, it is useful to analyze it as a power, defining it as structural and spiritual, visible and invisible. As Walter Wink writes:

> The New Testament's "principalities and powers" is a generic category referring to the determining forces of physical, psychic and social existence. These powers usually consist of an outer manifestation and an inner spirituality or interiority. Power must become incarnate, institutionalized, or systemic in order to be effective. It has a dual aspect, possessing both an outer visible form (constitutions, judges, police, leaders, office complexes) and an inner invisible spirit that provides its legitimacy, compliance, credibility and clout.[6]

Following Wink's concept of visible and invisible forms, I suggest that racism and whiteness can be seen and understood as dual aspects of the single reality of white supremacy. Racism is the visible pole, the outer form, manifest in our institutions and systems: for example, church, governmental structures, the economy. We see racism concretely in the prisons and on death row; in the cruel inequalities and inadequacies of health care, education and housing; in cultural and economic discrimination; in the economic and political violence of the state.

Whiteness is the "invisible pole, the inner spirit or driving force that animates, legitimates and regulates racism's physical manifestation in the world."[7] It is the reason that three decades after the Civil Rights Movement and endless commissions and legislation, white supremacy persists in forms that are perhaps less glaring, but as virulent, vicious, and insidious as ever. James Cone names whiteness evil, satanic in nature, a symbol of the Antichrist. James Baldwin concurred, "If you think you are white, there is no hope for you." And, in the words of race traitor Patricia Eakins, *"Whiteness is a death trip and the attempt to break out of it is an attempt to gain life."*[8]

Understanding the relationship between racism and whiteness in this way demands that white people committed to resisting racism confront the "powerful fiction" of our whiteness. Whiteness has given us privileges, which Peggy McIntosh has compared to an "invisible weightless knapsack of special provisions, assurances, tools, maps, guides, codebooks, passports, visas, clothes, compass, emergency gear, and blank checks."[9] Confronting whiteness and resisting racism, however, mean lamenting and coming to terms with the fact that, despite the benefits and advantages of the privilege, we have been crippled by white supremacy. Our spirits have been stunted, our souls profoundly harmed by living the lies of white superiority. We must work hard to exorcise consciously the driving force of whiteness within us as we attempt to transform unjust systems and oppressive institutions outside of us. But how?

James Baldwin has counseled white people who want to recover our humanity and honestly participate in the struggle to end racial injustice "to reexamine everything. Go back to where you started, or as far back as you can, examine all of it, travel your road again and tell the truth about it. Sing or shout or testify or keep it to yourself: but *know whence you came.*"[10]

"To do our first works over" — and over and over — is a critical practice in the struggle to transform white supremacist consciousness into a deep and abiding commitment to an active, everyday, long-haul struggle against racism. Most white people know, however — because we have been taught in every way imaginable — that a praxis of self-awareness and historical responsibility is strictly forbidden by the rules and regulations of white supremacy. Nor is a praxis of self-awareness and historical responsibility encouraged by white Western patriarchal Christianity. As Manning Marable argues, this Christianity has evolved as a "philosophy of self-deception," the purpose of which is "not to change the world, but to alter the prejudices and emotions of those who dwell within the world to tolerate their real conditions."[11] Most mainline Protestant churches, including the Southern Baptists, and the U.S. Catholic bishops have declared racism a sin and announced their intentions to repent. Despite this fact, however, confessional rhetoric has not translated into programmatic commitments to eliminate white supremacist structures in church and society. At this very moment, few Christian churches whose pews are filled with predominantly "white" faces take seriously the sins of white supremacy. Few are committed to the work of self-criticism and repentance that is necessary to resist and transform that which continues to cause so much suffering and injustice. If genuine repentance is known by "concrete signs of conversion, changed behavior and reparations," then there exists little evidence of repentance when it comes to white Christianity and the vast majority of white Christians.[12]

The discrepancy between the statements of synods, assemblies, and conventions, and the praxis/actions of local parishes and congregations is a continuation of white Christianity's "long and ugly history of worshipping at the altar of the status quo of white supremacy."[13] A majority of white Christians still worship at that altar, still glorify a white male Father, a white Mary, and a white Jesus. For many of us the association of blackness and evil, so deeply internalized, is created by what we grew up hearing in church: that everything that is holy, good, pure, beautiful, and true is white or light. (We should not forget that in the past and still to this day to be "American" means to be white *and* Christian; these two descriptors of citizenship are synonymous.)

We *learn* to be white.[14] Of course we learn to be white in a variety of ways, and there are many kinds of white people. All the particulars make a difference about the way we are white: whether we are straight, whether we are gay, male, female, what kind of work we do, how educated we are, how much money we have, what our religious affiliation is, how old we are and where we live. It is very different to be white in Utah than it is to be white in New York City, for instance, or to be white in Mississippi or Minnesota. It makes a difference whether you were born in 1947 or 1977. Some of us come from families that have been white longer than others. Even how we look and, yes, even the shade of pale we are, and the kind of hair and body we have makes a difference.

Regardless of significant differences and a broad diversity of historical and contemporary experiences, however, fundamental and common characteristics of whiteness — the inner spirit and driving force that keep white supremacy alive — are discernable. A deeply embedded false consciousness of goodness and purity — the "rightness of whiteness" — persists. It does so unconsciously and consciously, in the vast majority of white people, and reinforces the historical amnesia of the larger political culture that functions to keep structures of sin and domination tightly woven and in place. The denial of unearned privilege, the relentless blaming and scapegoating of victims of injustice, the minimization of oppression and suffering, the erasure of history: these are all dynamics of a supremacist logic that legislates the practices and policies and consciousness of white individuals, families, and communities, and the white male–dominated institutions of the state.[15]

The cultural obstructions keeping white people from exploring what it means to be white are legion. Questions about how racist white cultural norms have impacted one's identity and sense of self are fiercely prohibited. Most white children are strongly encouraged to "not notice" race, lest they make their white parents uncomfortable. The consequence of "not noticing" is profound disconnection from one's own racial experience.[16] Liberation psychologists Helene Shulman Lorenz and Mary Watkins write about what they call "silenced knowings." By this they mean:

> understandings we carry that take refuge in silence, as it feels dangerous to speak them to ourselves and to others. . . . Once silenced, these knowings are no longer available to inform our lives, to strengthen our moral discernment. Once pushed to the side these knowings require our energy to sustain their dissociation, and our numbing to evade their pain.[17]

Our habits of denial run deep — deep and wide — back through our white childhoods, our white educations, our white neighborhoods, white clubs, and white churches where "gaslighting" is the modus operandi of daily life. "Gaslighting" is a term used by domestic violence activists to describe a specific tactic of power and control, subtle and terrifying, that is meant to make its victim question her/his own perceptions and sense of reality.[18] It is so effective because the person perpetrating the deception is someone you trust: a lover, a parent, a friend, or someone in authority — like a teacher or a pastor who seemingly offers love, security, wisdom, safety, and survival. Not to accept the definitions of those you trust and depend upon is dangerous to a child's (and an adult's) sense of psychic, emotional, and spiritual survival. So, in order to be loved, in order to be accepted and protected, in order to belong, we become strangers to ourselves. We dissociate. This self-estrangement becomes habitual, something that seems like a natural part of being human. We become accustomed to "standing outside ourselves in ignorance," and thus it is easy to ignore the consequences of what we do.[19] The consciousness and logic of white supremacy alienate us from ourselves as well as others.

"To do our first works over," confronting where we come from, what we have been taught, and what we have become, is a painful and confusing process. Yet it is a necessary endeavor for white people struggling to recover our humanity. What happens when we are no longer blind, when we open our eyes and begin to actually *see* and *feel* the sorrow and suffering our white skin privilege has brought to others, and the sin-sickness it has produced in ourselves? Guilt, shame, and anger are inevitable. What then? What keeps us from retreating and falling once again into the ceaseless rounds of avoidance, delusion and denial, self-hatred, rage, and despair? What keeps us from guilt-ridden paralysis once we realize the depravity of "the history we carry inside of us, the history that is present in everything we do"?[20] What keeps us — to borrow Mab Segrest's words — from washing it down with gin and violence?[21] What keeps us from being *so* desperate for forgiveness and redemption that we repeat the insidious patterns/history of white supremacy, *using* Black people, Black culture, Black struggle for our own spiritual emotional purposes, while believing that cheap grace has washed us clean — white as snow? — of our sin and guilt?

James Baldwin has written, *"No curtain under heaven is heavier than the curtain of guilt and lies behind which white Americans hide."*[22] Emerging from behind the curtain requires that we truly lament what has been done in our name and what we have perpetuated because we were not willing to confront the truths of our experience. For white people, to lament and truly to mourn the tragic and evil realities of history, including that so many of our advantages, comforts, benefits — material and psychological — have been bought with unspeakable horror and cruelty, is part of the process of liberating ourselves from the quagmire of individual and collective guilt that serves to maintain the very reality in which we feel so uneasy.

"Mourning," as psychoanalyst Alice Miller has pointed out, "is the opposite of feeling guilt; it is the expression of pain that things happened as they did and *that there is no way to change the past."*[23] Without mourning, without authentic sorrow for the injustices that we benefit from, yet are deeply wounded by, we are alienated from ourselves, out of touch with who we are and who others are. *"Guilt is a dragon that guards the toxic waste of the past."*[24]

In fact, denial of pain, be it personal or collective, is one of the root sources of guilt; repressed feelings of shared responsibility is another. Anxiety, neuroses, and even more serious psychological dysfunctions do not derive from the experience of mourning but, to the contrary, grow from a desire to cohabit with historical wounds and the willingness to allow oneself to be fed by their destructive power. In essence, guilt is the debilitating force of repressed memories.[25]

The "physiology of racism" which, in Segrest's words, "encodes itself in our consciousness, closing the doors of perception," presents a profound methodological challenge.[26] How do we talk about race, racism, and white supremacy in a way that encourages and empowers white people to go beyond the confessional rhetoric, paternalism, and death-dealing logic of white supremacy? How do we move from what Ruth Frankenberg has called race-cognizance — the recognition that race makes a difference — to "racism-cognizance" — an active, everyday, long-haul struggle against white supremacy?[27] Where are the roadmaps for the work we need to do to begin to be present, clear-eyed, and mindful about the part we play in the nightmares of our current world? How do we live out our lives in such a way that our words and actions are in accord with one another?

"EVASION HISTORY"[28]

We are what we know. We are, however, also what we do not know. If what we know about ourselves — our history, our culture, our national identity — is deformed by absences, denials and incompleteness, then our identity — both as individuals and as Americans — is fragmented.[29]

The suppression of white anti-racist activism, the erasure of stories of "race traitors," has been one of white supremacy's most powerful tools for maintaining and sustaining white supremacy.[30] The erasure has worked well to keep white folks holding strong to the "lies, secrets, and silences" that surround our white existence.[31] Not knowing that there has been a solid and ongoing history of white anti-racist activism contributes to our inability to break the silence about the dynamics of our white racial experience, and our subsequent spiritual paralysis and political immobility. Not having access to the stories and the histories of anti-racist white women and men, we have little ground on which to imagine a white identity not bound by domination, exploitation, and injustice.

The invisibility of white anti-racist activism in U.S. history is ultimately tied to the largely missing and hidden story of progressive social movements in general, and the history of the extraordinary resistance efforts and ceaseless activism of peoples of colors, in particular. In his important study of American History textbooks, *Lies My Teacher Told Me: Everything Your American History Textbook Got Wrong,* James Loewen exposes the whitewashed "Disney" version of history that shapes most white U.S.-Americans' sense of the past and thus their own historical identity.[32] *The habits of denial we learn from our family and communities and the habits of denial we learn from church and state are mutually reinforcing.* Thus, like the textbooks we read in school, we can talk about slavery without addressing racism.[33] We can talk about racism without addressing genocide.[34] Think of the many state and federal commissions and task forces on racism that issue reports and recommendations without ever acknowledging white supremacy and the attendant violence, both past and present.

In the context of history's distortions and denials around all matters of race, it makes sense that the names of anti-racist activists and race traitors would be unknown to the majority of white people. Few people have heard of anti-racist/race traitors Lydia Maria Child, Moncure Daniel Conway, Lillian Smith, Anne and Carl Braden, or Jesse Daniel James, to name only a few, or of the white organizations that directly addressed racism's costs, such as the Association of Southern Women for the Prevention of Lynching.[35] Even those race traitors of the more recent past have disappeared. The names of murdered white civil rights workers like Viola Liuzzo, Mickey Schwerner, Andrew Goodman, and Jon Daniels seem to have long since disappeared.[36] Even more obscured are the names of living anti-racist revolutionaries — all of whom were once and/or still are incarcerated — Rita Bo Brown, Marilyn Buck, Linda Evans, Raymond Luc Lavasseur, Susan Rosenberg, and Laura Whitehorn.[37]

This summer I asked a group of white college students what they thought about when they heard the term "race traitor." A dull silence and blank stares ensued. Then suddenly a young man said "John Brown! Yeah isn't he, like, the crazy guy who was against slavery and led some kind of rebellion?" Indeed John Brown, one of

U.S. history's most powerful foes of white supremacy, resides in the popular imagination (if at all) as a madman, a terrorist, a religious fanatic. In some of the textbooks Loewen reviewed, Brown is described as "deranged," "gaunt," "grim," "terrible," "crackbrained," "of unsound mind." One textbook asserts that "thirteen of his near relatives were regarded as insane, including his mother and grandmother."[38] Even the textbooks that refrain from using this kind of language treat Brown in a perceptibly unsympathetic tone. The fact that Brown's commitment to ending slavery was rooted in strong religious belief, his guidance coming from the biblical mandate for justice, is rarely explored and more often belittled and disdained. His religiosity is generally held against him. Though the more neutral textbooks may not use the word "fanaticism," they suggest it in sentences such as, "Believing himself commanded by God. . . . "[39] No American history texts used in U.S. public high schools relay the fact that Black leaders like Harriet Tubman, Frederick Douglass, Henry Highland Garnett, and Martin Delaney knew John Brown and had profound respect for him. A far cry from the isolated and ignorant madman he is made out to be, Brown was well traveled among, and in touch with, the Black and white intellectuals of his day.[40] Executed on December 2, 1859, Brown was the first American since the Revolution to be hanged as a traitor. The message is clear. If John Brown is the prototypical race traitor, then the rest of us had better be quiet. For a white person to confront white supremacy, and to stand against its iniquities at all costs, bespeaks a madness that can only end in failure and destruction.

The silence and invisibility — and ascriptions of, at best, instability; at worst, insanity — accorded to those who resist white supremacy are clear markers that powerful forces of social control are in operation. In her indispensable social history of white anti-racist activism from the 1950s to the present, *A Promise and a Way of Life*, Becky Thompson asks, "What is at risk in treating anti-racism as a historical reality and a current possibility?" "Might it be," she replies, "a way out of the hard work of naming how each of us is implicated and how we collectively might create a culture that is different from the one presently around us?"[41]

"The Sins of the Fathers Have Set the Children's Teeth on Edge"[42]

In doing our first works over, engaging a praxis of self-awareness and historical responsibility, it is incumbent on each one of us to confront the *particularities* of our racism and our whiteness, the visible and the invisible, and to scrutinize how the presence of the past in our own lives shapes our choices and commitments. The spiritual and theological demands of this work lead us to an uncomfortable confrontation with what Christians call sin and evil. As a white Christian feminist, juggling the contradictions of my race, gender, class, and religion in the context of a virulently racist and sexist society and a family history steeped in the atrocities of slavery, I have intimate knowledge of the confrontation with sin and evil. There is no way around the horrors upon which my many advantages rest.

Dorothee Soelle, the late German liberation theologian, reflects on a similar struggle with her fate and destiny as a German Christian living out the guilt and shame of her own sinful legacy of evil:

As a very young woman I went to the Netherlands for the first time and observed that some people did not want to talk to me because I was a German and their relatives had been killed by Nazis. There it became very clear to me that while I had not done anything — I was too young — nevertheless these others had a right to turn their backs on me and not speak to me because by language, culture, and heritage I belonged to a human society which lived in a complex of guilt. I cannot get out of this; it is just the case. And this piece of objectivity is part of the concept of sin. Sin is certainly my decision, my free will, my "no" to God, but it is also the destiny into which I was born and I am entangled in it through my parents, my teachers and my tradition. Even those born later cannot avoid this reality, and while it is inappropriate to speak of collective guilt, the sense of a collective responsibility for guilt is necessary. *I am responsible for the house which I did not build but in which I live.*[43]

White people in a white supremacist society are implicated from the day we are born. As Paul and Augustine say, we are *ruled* by the power of sin. We may be committed and active anti-racists, we may choose to sacrifice safety and security to stay true to these commitments, but we will have to live with the fact that the color of our skin means injustice, terror, and evil for African Americans (and most peoples of colors although in different ways). We will have to accept that there is always the great possibility that we can *never* be completely trusted, even by those we believe to be our friends and intimates. Our presence will most likely raise the specter of unthinkable violence, unspeakable sorrow and suffering. Our humanity may be ever called into question. We are born into a sinful situation. We inevitably participate in it, and are, in large part, defined by the sinful structures and consciousness of white supremacy. There is no escape from this.

I did not begin doing my own first works over in a critical and conscious way until the early 1980s when I studied Black liberation theology with James H. Cone. His spiritual analysis of whiteness woke me up to missing pieces of my own racial experience and roused my own "silenced knowings" from a deep, yet very disturbed, sleep. I was challenged to look at my experience as a white person, a *white* Christian in a new way. Cone's theological understanding of blackness and whiteness compelled me to delve more deeply into my own historical, political, and spiritual identity. "Blackness," Cone insisted, "is the ontological symbol and visible reality which best describes what oppression means in America." It is "a concept which includes both what the world means by oppression and what the gospel means by liberation."[44] In Black theology, blackness becomes the most accurate symbol pointing to the various dimensions of divine activity in America. "Whiteness" is the opposing ontological symbol standing as the very antithesis of blackness; a visible reality of what *doing the oppressing* means in America.

> Whiteness is the symbol of the Anti-Christ. Whiteness character-
> izes the activity of deranged individuals intrigued by their own
> image of themselves, and thus unable to see that they are what
> is wrong with the world. Black theology seeks to analyze the
> satanic nature of whiteness and by doing so to prepare all non-
> whites for revolutionary action.... It would seem rather that
> white rejection of Black theology stems from the revolutionary
> implications in its very name; a rejection of whiteness, an un-
> willingness to live under it, and an identification of whiteness
> with evil and blackness with good.[45]

At the time, these words evoked an old and yet unnamed rage and confusion, buried deep in my childhood, for which I would have no words until much further down the road. As I heard and read Cone calling for the destruction of whiteness, I was intrigued, excited, and uncomfortable. If Cone were right, if whiteness and humanity were indeed mutually exclusive, white people could only be liberated into their own humanity by destroying their whiteness, and through God's grace, becoming "Black with Jesus."[46] Cone argued that by radically reorienting one's existence in the world — by becoming members of an oppressed community — redemption through God's grace was possible. He wrote: "Whites will be free only when they become new persons — when their white being has passed away and they are cre-ated anew in black being. When this happens they are no longer white but free."[47]

This was good news. I was encouraged by confronting truths pre-viously buried, and, at the same time, more perplexed. How exactly would I do this? How would I "destroy my whiteness" and radically reorient my existence? Who would guide me, accompany me, hold me accountable? What would this mean for me as a single mother, as a woman, and as a human being?

Growing up in the 1950s and 1960s, in segregated America, whiteness was *not* — as is often argued in critical studies of whiteness — invisible to me. We were just supposed to pretend that it was. I grew up in northwestern Ohio, the home of my father's people. My family and the community in which I lived legislated an elaborate geography of boundaries and separations. These boundaries of race, religion, class, sex, and gender not only marked my outer world — the neighborhoods I could go into, the people with whom I could be friends and lovers with — but my inner world as well. The rules and regulations of my birth tribe (the WASP tribe) demanded that I, particularly as a female, *obey,* that I be silent. That obedience, that silencing necessarily required that I cut off certain parts of myself. Experience and consciousness split into pieces, while a gnawing sense of repression and deception, a kind of unnamed cruelty and the vague threat of violence, always lurked. I learned to keep many of my thoughts and beliefs to myself. I held feelings, emotions that needed to be expressed, very close to my heart. It was a way to keep the peace, but there was no peace in it for me.

I remember the deep shame I felt as a child when I learned that my mother had descended from southerners — people in Virginia who had owned slaves! I am not sure why I knew this was a very bad thing, but I did and I was very upset. Most likely it was because I knew that Abraham Lincoln had "freed" the slaves, and that this was a righteous act. Furthermore, through my religious experience, I had become a lover of Jesus very early on and knew that Jesus loved ALL the little children no matter what their color. Between Abraham Lincoln and Jesus, I knew that slavery was wrong, that the South was wrong, and that my ancestors were wrong. My confusion and horror at being descended from slave owners (I found out later that some of these ancestors were not only owners but traders of human beings) was exacerbated by the fact that I seemed to be the only one who was disturbed by this history. Their silence told me that my mother and father certainly didn't seem to mind. I asked questions. I got no answers. There were no attempts to explain or even address my troubled queries. The message was clear: *Don't think about it. Don't talk about it. That's just the way it is. Put it out of your head. Just enjoy the good things we have because we are good people.*

My Virginian ancestors were not the only ancestors I had, but they seemed to dominate the landscape. This was especially true of the one we knew as Robert "King" Carter (1663–1732). Robert Carter was nicknamed "King" Carter because of his vast riches and influence. My family seemed proud of his power and riches. I remember my father gleefully relaying the story of "King" Carter losing half of West Virginia in a poker game. The fact that he was a wicked, greedy, cruel, and violent man — even by the standards of Virginia's slave-holding aristocracy — was rarely mentioned. In a privately published book about our Carter ancestors, written by my grandfather in 1961, he wrote that at the time of his death, "King" Carter left his nine children "an estate of approximately 300,000 acres of land, 1000 Negro slaves, several hundred horses, several thousand cattle, sheep and swine and 1000 pounds of sterling." My grandfather hints, rather lightheartedly, at his wickedness by writing, "Naturally so rich and powerful a man had his enemies as well as a coterie of friends, and tradition preserves the following jibe found chalked on King Carter's tomb":

> Here lies Robin but not Robin Hood
> Here lies Robin who never was good
> Here lies Robin that God has forsaken
> Here lies Robin that the Devil has taken[48]

In July 1991 I read an article in the *New York Times* reporting a small celebration held at the gravesite of a long-forgotten Virginia planter, Robert Carter III. The article reported that on August 1, 1791, Carter had filed something called a Deed of Gift in which he set forth his plan for emancipating five hundred slaves, "perhaps the largest act of individual emancipation to occur in American history."[49] This Robert Carter, who was born in 1728, was, I was stunned to discover, the grandson of Robert "King" Carter! It seemed impossible that I had never heard about this. I read on. The *Times* reported that by the time the younger Carter was twenty-one years old, he owned eighteen plantations, sixty thousand acres, and hundreds of slaves. Among his friends, neighbors, and correspondents were the Washingtons, the Lees, Thomas Jefferson, James Madison, George Mason, and Patrick Henry. Few details are available about how Carter's conversion to emancipation came about, although his move away from the Anglican church of the landed gentry, to the Baptist one where he prayed alongside small farmers and slaves, very likely played a role.

On the first page of this document Carter III wrote, "I have for some time past been convinced that to retain them in Slavery is contrary to the Principles of Religion and Justice, and therefore it is my duty to manumit them." He explains himself no further, moving on with "intensity" to the practical and legal matters.[50] The remainder of the document is lengthy and detailed, including numerous pages of censuses and schedules for the "gradual emancipation" of 500 enslaved Africans. In his doctoral dissertation written at Duke in 1973, John Randolph Barden reports 280 manumissions. According to Andrew Levy, who has written the only article of any substance about Carter in the last two hundred years, other evidence in the form of a variety of documents suggest a much larger total of emancipated slaves, perhaps more than Carter initially planned.[51] Reading Levy's account of Carter's act, one senses that Carter was consumed with the work of his plan. Moreover, he concerned himself with how the newly freed slaves could sustain themselves. He rented out land to free Black people, hired Black people as artisans, often to the great displeasure of his overseers. By the end of 1793, perhaps exhausted by the bitterness of his sons and sons-in-law, and complex relationships with both white and Black neighbors and friends, Carter left Virginia and settled in Baltimore. He hired Benjamin Dawson, a Baptist preacher, to become his business agent. Dawson, although apparently somewhat financially inept, was diligent about ensuring that Carter's schedules on the Deed of Gift were closely followed.[52] When

Carter died alone in his little room in Baltimore in 1804, his sons tried to overturn the Deed of Gift and revoke Dawson's power of attorney. A Virginia Court of Appeals upheld the Deed of Gift, however, and Dawson continued to enforce it. Levy writes, "The Deed of Gift had a momentum of its own: as late as 1852, nine years before the Civil War, Carter's descendents were still freeing the descendents of Carter's slaves under the terms of his original document, as if he were somehow still watching."[53]

Why had I never heard about Robert Carter III and his extraordinary decision? Did the family think "King" Carter's cruelty and power were more noteworthy than his grandson's radical conversion and act? I was perturbed, angry, and then stunned again when I found out that my mother had never heard about Carter either. My family was one thing, but what about the history books? Nowhere in my undergraduate work in U.S.-American Studies had I heard about Robert Carter III. Why had the Deed of Gift almost completely vanished from the record? Even noted historians of slavery like Ira Berlin, who knew who Robert Carter III was and knew what the Deed of Gift meant, seem to have made a conscious decision to bury the information.[54]

What is the reason behind this deafening silence? Becky Thompson's question about what is at risk in treating anti-racism as a historical reality helps us to discern an answer. Carter's Deed of Gift contradicts a central "truth" of U.S.-American history: namely, that had there been any way Washington or Jefferson or many of the other slaveholding founding fathers could have practically emancipated their slaves, they would have. Erasing this "awkward evidence" of Robert Carter III's actions from the "master" narrative of U.S. history allows white people to adapt to and live quite comfortably with ambivalence and confusion about race and racism in the ways that Washington and Jefferson lived quite comfortably with slavery. How easy it is still to reconcile our ideals of democracy and freedom with the reality of the "savage inequalities" of racism. How destabilizing it is to think that there were peaceful, rational alternatives to ending slavery. Robert Carter III's radical act inspired nothing but silence because he "did something that transcends our ability to listen to our own past."[55]

PATHS OF RESISTANCE, CHANNELS OF GRACE

Haunted by my southern ancestors, I have been drawn to the work and lives of two white southern lesbians, Lillian Smith and Mab Segrest. Race traitors, writers, educators, and unrelenting activists, their lives are "theories in the flesh" for me as I wrestle with the "sins of the fathers" and with what it means to be "white" and "woman" in a society thoroughly shaped by the demonarchic structures and consciousness of white supremacy and male supremacy.[56]

Lillian Smith was born in the Deep South in 1897 and died in 1966. Her family was prosperous, civic minded, "decent"; her parents good, white, Christian (Methodist) people. She loved them and she loved "the South." Yet from her earliest childhood days she was profoundly troubled by the deep contradictions of the world in which she lived, the everyday "gaslighting," the "strange mad obsession" of white supremacy.[57]

Smith "did her first works over" in 1949 in *Killers of the Dream*, her influential racial conversion narrative, or what I might call a "narrative of critical resistance."[58] She wrote it, she explains in the foreword of the 1961 edition, because she wanted to find out what life in a segregated culture had done to her. She describes the "haunted childhood that belongs to every southerner," a childhood edged with "the sing song voices of politicians who preached their demonic suggestions to us as if elected by Satan to do so," and daily images of "the bitter faces on my father's and grandfather's friends... men who clung to their white culture like a cripple clings to his crutches."[59] She remembers "the church and the home that kept hate alive" and the early lessons about God and sex and race that taught her "that God so loved the world that He gave His only begotten Son so that we might have segregated churches."[60] She was taught "that it was possible to be a Christian and a white southerner simultaneously; to be a gentlewoman and a callous creature in the same moment; to pray at night and ride a Jim Crow car the next morning and to feel comfortable at doing both."[61] *Killers of the Dream* was Smith's confession of her own racial blindness, and her passionate lament about the sickness and cruelty that white supremacy and segregation visited upon *all* the people of the South, Black and white, particularly the children. She writes:

> I began to understand slowly at first but more clearly as the years passed, that the warped, distorted frame we have put around every Negro child from birth is around every white child also. Each is on a different side of the frame, but each is pinioned there. And I knew that what cruelly shapes and cripples the personality of one is as cruelly shaping and crippling the personality of the other. I began to see that though we may, as we acquire new knowledge, live through new experiences, examine old memories, gain the strength to tear the frame from us, yet we are stunted and warped and in our life time cannot grow straight any more than can a tree, put in a steel-like twisting frame when young, grow tall and straight when the frame is torn away at maturity.[62]

Smith knew that something was wrong with a world "that tells you that love is good and people are important and then forces you to deny love and humiliate people. I knew," she wrote, "but not for years would I confess it."[63]

When she made that confession public in *Killers of the Dream* she was inundated with criticism from all quarters. She was criticized, particularly by liberal white men like newspaper editors Hodding Carter and Ralph McGill, both of whom had won Pulitzer Prizes for their editorials challenging racial violence. Hodding Carter called Smith "a sex-obsessed old maid." McGill reviewed *Killers of the Dream* in the *Atlanta Constitution* with these words: "A woefully unsound book. Miss Smith is a prisoner of the monastery of her own mind. But rarely does she come out of its gates, and then, apparently, seeing only wicked things to send her back to her hair shirt and the pouring of ashes on her head and salt in her own psychiatric wounds."[64]

This virulently misogynist and racist response to Smith's work was the result of her insistence on writing about not just race but that other taboo of the white South: sex. Furthermore, she made it clear that lessons about race and sex were inseparable from lessons about God. She wrote:

> When we as small children crept over the race line and ate and played with Negroes or broke other segregation customs known to us we felt the same dread fear of consequences, the same overwhelming guilt we felt when we crept over the sex line and played with our body, or thought thoughts about God or our parents we weren't supposed to think. Each was a "sin" and "deserved punishment," each would receive it in this world or the next. Each was tied up with the other and all were tied close to God.... The lesson of segregation was only a logical extension of the lessons on sex and white superiority and God.[65]

Smith dared to put forth the taboo issues that Ida B. Wells had brought to public attention half a century earlier. She was relentless in her analysis of the intimate intertwining of race and sex in the psyche of the white South that was the cause of such unspeakable violence. In *Killers of the Dream,* Smith raised the peculiarly southern "ghosts stories," as she called them, of "the race-sex-sin spiral": that guilt, shame, fear, and violence of the white southern male, "his hatred of colored man and white woman," the mass rejection of Black children by their white fathers, and the relationship of Black women to the families for whom they worked and cared. Smith attended to the intersections of race and class, though less so than that of race and sex, and understood the kinds of psychological and financial bargaining going on, as she wrote, between Mr. Rich White and Mr. Poor White.[66]

Smith enraged her southern critics and foes so profoundly because she was the worst kind of race traitor. She was a white woman beholden to no white man or men. Perhaps her double detachment from the centers of southern power — not only as a woman but as a lesbian — was what made her such a bold and morally courageous white woman. Others have suggested that her being a lesbian "contributed to a perspective that allowed her to feel, in a manner white male heterosexual liberals never could, the pain of prejudice of any kind."[67]

Despite large numbers of detractors and enemies — there were death threats, arson, and ongoing hostilities — there were those who appreciated Smith and the value of her work. In 1950, Smith received an honorary doctorate from Howard University with the following declaration: "You are a dangerous revolutionist. There is enough dynamite in what you say to blow up the very foundation of segregated civilization."[68] At the end of her life, young civil rights workers, *Killers of the Dream* in hand, looked to Smith's courage and commitment to keep their own strong.

Race traitor Mab Segrest was seventeen years old when Lillian Smith died of cancer in 1966. Like Smith, she too is a southern white lesbian writer, educator, and anti-racist activist, except she claims her lesbian identity wholeheartedly and publicly, as Smith was never able to do. Her critical resistance narratives, *Memoirs of a Race Traitor* and her recent *Born to Belonging* (both of which contain opening epigraphs from Lillian Smith), are a treasure for all who struggle with our white racist/anti-racist identities. In *Memoir of a Race Traitor,* her "treatise on the souls of white folks," Segrest, like Smith, examines the experiential dynamics of race and white supremacy in her conservative family, and "the relation of private emotion to public event to history."[69] Like Smith, Segrest puts her body and her soul on the line. During the 1980s as she organized against the Klan and the neo-Nazis on the back roads and in the small towns and cities of North Carolina, she finds herself feeling "pretty irregularly white. Klan folks had a word for it: *race traitor.*" She continues, "I was in daily intimate exposure to the cruel, killing effects of racism. . . . I often found myself hating all white people, including myself."[70]

The work and passionate commitment of Lillian Smith and Mab Segrest originate in a deep horror, sense of injustice, and mourning over what white people and white supremacy have done to Black people. Their activism is also rooted strongly in their concern for what racism and white supremacy have done to their own humanity and the humanity of other white people. Remembering her conversations with many young college audiences, Segrest writes: "I had come to believe that only dealing with white people on giving up privileges was counterintuitive. There must also be some fuller range of loss and gain. Some deeper calculus to invoke."[71] For both Segrest and Smith the deeper calculus is this (in Segrest's words): "Racism costs us intimacy. Racism costs us our affective lives. Racism costs us authenticity. Racism costs us a sense of connection to other humans and the natural world. Racism costs us our spiritual selves."[72] We who call ourselves white theologians and ethicists are challenged to address these costs.

Adrienne Rich cautions that "breaking silences, telling our tales is not enough. We can value that process — and the courage it may require — without believing that it is an end in itself. Historical responsibility has after all to do with action — where we place the weight of our existences on the line, cast our lot with others, move from individual consciousness to a collective one."[73] What the stories of white people who have chosen to stand up against white supremacy have to teach us is that the antidote to guilt, self-hatred, and despair is *struggle,* collective struggle, a praxis of self-awareness and historical responsibility. It is "active engagement with real structures," in the "places that we live and love and work."[74] Segrest assures us (and I think Smith would concur) that this praxis "will engage us at the deepest spiritual level of meaning in our lives," and, if we are lucky, if we do not retreat into our whiteness, if we keep doing "the work," we may come to know in our deepest feeling "that neither I, nor you, are

born for segregation, separation, domination, subordination, alien-
ation, isolation, ownership, competition or narrow self-interest." We
are "born to belonging and we know ourselves as human in just and
mutual relationships to each other."[75]

NOTES

1. Paul Kivel, *Uprooting Racism: How White People Can Work for Racial
Justice* (Philadelphia: New Society Publishers, 1996), 17.

2. George D. Kelsey, *Racism and the Christian Understanding of Man* (New
York: Charles Scribner's Sons, 1965), 9.

3. Martin Luther King Jr., "Showdown with Nonviolence," in *Testament
of Hope: The Essential Writings of Martin Luther King Jr.,* ed. James Melvin
Washington (San Francisco: Harper and Row, 1986), 71.

4. Cheryl A. Kirk-Duggan, "African-American Spirituals: Confronting and Exorcising Evil Through Song," in *A Troubling in My Soul: Womanist Perspectives on
Evil and Suffering,* ed. Emilie M. Townes (Maryknoll, N.Y.: Orbis Books, 1993), 151.

5. See Bill Wylie-Kellerman, "Exorcising an American Demon," *Sojourners*
(March–April 1998); online at www.sojo.net/index.cfm?action=magazine.article&
issue=soj9803&article=980312.

6. Walter Wink, *Unmasking the Powers: The Invisible Forces That Determine
Human Existence* (Philadelphia: Fortress Press, 1986), 4.

7. Ibid.

8. James H. Cone, *A Black Theology of Liberation,* 20th anniversary edition
(Maryknoll, N.Y.: Orbis Books, 1986), 8; Patricia Eakins, "Manifesto of a Dead
Daughter," in *Race Traitor,* ed. John Garvey and Noel Ignatiev (London: Routledge,
1996), 88.

9. Peggy McIntosh, "White Privilege: Unpacking the Invisible Knapsack," *Peace
and Freedom* (July–August 1989): 10.

10. James Baldwin, *The Price of the Ticket: Collected Nonfiction, 1948–1985*
(New York: St. Martin's/Marek, 1985), xix.

11. Manning Marable, *Blackwater: Historical Studies in Race, Class Consciousness, and Revolution* (Niwot: University of Colorado Press, 1993), 36.

12. Jim Wallis, "America's Original Sin: The Legacy of White Racism," in *New
Visions for The Americas: Religious Engagement and Social Transformation,* ed.
David Batstone (Minneapolis: Fortress Press, 1993), 201.

13. Ivan A. Beals, *Our Racist Legacy: Will the Church Resolve The Conflict?*
(Notre Dame, Ind.: Cross Cultural Publications, 1997), vii.

14. Thandeka, *Learning to Be White: Money, Race, and God in America* (New
York: Continuum, 1999).

15. Kivel, *Uprooting Racism,* 40–48.

16. See Elizabeth Garrick Knaplund and Beverly Daniel Tatum, "Outside the
Circle/The Relational Implications for White Women Working against Racism," in

Work in Progress, no. 78 (Wellesley, Mass.: Stone Center Working Paper Series, 1996), 114.

17. Helene Shulman Lorenz and Mary Watkins, "Silenced Knowings, Forgotten Springs: Paths to Healing in the Wake of Colonialism," a paper presented at the annual conference of the National Training Laboratory, Bethel, Maine, July 20, 2001, 2.

18. This term is taken from the movie *Gaslight,* with Ingrid Bergman and Charles Boyer.

19. Susan Griffin, *A Chorus of Stones: The Private Life of War* (New York: Doubleday, 1992), 153.

20. James Baldwin, "White Man's Guilt," in *The Price of the Ticket: Collected Nonfiction, 1948–1985* (New York: St. Martin's/Marek, 1985), 409.

21. Mab Segrest, *Memoir of a Race Traitor* (Boston: South End Press, 1994), 4.

22. Baldwin, "White Man's Guilt," 412.

23. Alice Miller, *For Your Own Good: Hidden Cruelty in Child-Rearing and the Roots of Violence,* trans. Hildegarde and Hunter Hannum (New York: Farrar, Straus & Giroux, 1983), 250. Emphasis added.

24. Ralph H. Blum and Susan Loughan, *The Healing Runes* (New York: St. Martins Press, 1994), 78.

25. David Batstone, "Life on the Back of the Bus," in *New Visions for the Americas: Religious Engagement and Social Transformation,* ed. David Batstone (Minneapolis: Fortress Press, 1993), 242.

26. Mab Segrest, *Born to Belonging: Writings on Spirit and Justice* (New Brunswick and London: Rutgers University Press, 2002), 166.

27. Ruth Frankenberg, *White Women, Race Matters: The Social Construction of Whiteness* (Minneapolis: University of Minnesota Press, 1993), 137–90. See also Ellen Kaye Scott, "From Race Cognizance to Racism Cognizance: Dilemmas in Antiracist Activism in California," in *Feminism and Antiracism: International Struggles for Justice,* ed. France Winndance Twine and Kathleen M. Blee (New York: New York University Press, 2001), 125–49. This article examines the struggles of two multicultural women's organizations — one a rape crisis center and one a battered woman's shelter on the West Coast — to deal with the racial politics of their organizations. Scott discovers that while many of the white women were "race-cognizant" and were able to "problematize their white racial identity," they had "a great deal of difficulty identifying manifestations of racism and the ways in which they perpetuated racism." She concludes: "In other words, while some white women could recognize racial hierarchies and racial privilege, they were unable to identify its immediate effects" (134). It is at this crossroads where I often find myself and many of my white sisters, and it is at this nexus that turning to the lives of race traitors and white anti-racist activists can be enormously helpful.

28. Andrew Levy, "The Anti Jeffersonian: Why Robert Carter III Freed His Slaves (And Why We Couldn't Care Less)," *American Scholar* 70, no. 2 (2001): 29.

29. William Pinar, "Notes on Understanding Curriculum as Racial Text," in *Race Identity and Representation in Education,* ed. Cameron McCarthy and Warren Chrichlow (New York: Routledge, 1993), 61, quoted in Becky Thompson, *A*

Promise and a Way of Life: White Antiracist Activism (Minneapolis: University of Minnesota Press, 2001), xxvii.

30. The term "race traitor" refers to someone who "is nominally classified as white, but who defies the rules of whiteness so flagrantly as to jeopardize his or her ability to draw upon the privileges of white skin." Ian Haney López, *White by Law: The Legal Construction of Race* (New York: New York University Press, 1996), 189. See the periodical *Race Traitor,* or the book of the same name, edited by Noel Ignatiev and John Garvey (New York: Routledge, 1996). The motto of *Race Traitor* is "Treason to Whiteness is Loyalty to Humanity."

31. See Adrienne Rich, *On Lies, Secrets, and Silence: Selected Prose 1966–1978* (New York and London: W. W. Norton, 1979).

32. James W. Loewen, *Lies My Teacher Told Me: Everything Your American History Textbook Got Wrong* (New York: Simon & Schuster/A Touchstone Book, 1995).

33. A recent example of this is George Bush's reference to the Middle Passage as a "large migration."

34. Joy James, *Resisting State Violence: Radicalism, Gender, and Race in US Culture* (Minneapolis: University of Minnesota Press, 1996). See especially chap. 2, "Radicalizing Language and Law: Genocide, Discrimination, and Human Rights." James writes about the "semi-illiteracy" of the dominant discourse on race in the United States arising from "severing racism from its logical culmination in genocide and from restricting the referent from human atrocities to past holocausts that have been commodified for mass consumption as historical objects and moral reminders. The moral import of racism is virtually meaningless after it has been severed from genocide" (46).

35. Lydia Maria Child (1802–80) was an editor, writer, and social activist at the forefront of the Abolitionist Movement. Wendell Philips, William Ellery Channing, and Charles Sumner credited her essay *An Appeal in Favor of that Class of Americans Called Africans* for converting them to Abolitionism. See Carolyn L. Karcher, *The First Woman in the Republic: A Cultural Biography of Lydia Maria Child* (Durham, N.C.: Duke University Press, 1998). Moncure Daniel Conway (1832–1907), a Unitarian minister and fierce abolitionist, aided some thirty Africans in their escape from his family's Virginia plantation to what came to be known as the Conway Colony in Yellow Springs, Ohio. Lillian Smith will be discussed later in this essay. Anne Braden and Carl Braden committed race treason in 1954 when they bought a house on behalf of a Black couple in a white neighborhood in Louisville, Kentucky. This began their life of dedicated anti-racist activism — see Anne Braden's *The Wall Between* (Knoxville: The University of Tennessee Press, 1999). Jesse Daniel James was one of the leaders of the antilynching campaigns in the South in the 1920s and 1930s; see Jacquelyn Dowd Hall, *Revolt Against Chivalry: Jesse Daniel James and the Women's Campaign against Lynching,* rev. ed. (New York: Columbia University Press, 1993).

36. Viola Fauver Gregg Liuzzo was a Unitarian Universalist social activist and mother of five in Detroit, Michigan. Liuzzo felt called to the civil rights struggle, headed to the South to work in the movement, and was murdered by four white men — one of them an FBI informant — on March 25, 1965, hours after she had marched with demonstrators in a voting rights march from Selma to Montgomery.

A year prior, in June, Michael Schwerner and Andrew Goodman, young white men from New York City, were executed, along with fellow civil rights worker James Earle Chaney, who was African American, in Meridian, Mississippi. Jonathan Myrick Daniels, a student at the Episcopal Theological School, was killed by a white man in Hayneville, Alabama, on August 20, 1965, while doing civil rights work. See William J. Schneider, ed., *The Jon Daniels Story* (New York: Seabury Press, 1967).

37. See Joy James, ed., *Imprisoned Intellectuals: America's Political Prisoners Write on Life, Liberation and Rebellion* (Latham, Md.: Rowman & Littlefield Publishers, 2003).

38. Loewen, *Lies My Teacher Told Me*, 173–74.

39. Ibid., 177.

40. See W. E. B Du Bois, *John Brown*, ed. and with an introduction by David Roediger (New York: Modern Library, 2001); Russell Banks, *Cloudsplitter* (New York: Harper Perennial, 1998); Carolyn L. Karacher, "Lydia Maria Child and the Example of John Brown," *Race Traitor* no. 1 (Winter 1993), and "Brown Family Letters," *Race Traitor* no. 10 (Winter 1999); and David Roediger, "Non-white Radicalism: Du Bois, John Brown, and Black Resistance," in *Colored White: Transcending the Racial Past* (Berkeley: University of California Press, 2002), 97–102.

41. Thompson, *A Promise and a Way of Life*, xv.

42. Jeremiah 31:29–30; Ezekiel 18:2–4.

43. Dorothee Soelle, *Thinking about God: An Introduction to Theology* (Philadelphia: Trinity Press International, 1990), 55. Emphasis added.

44. Cone, *A Black Theology of Liberation*, 7.

45. Ibid., 8.

46. James Cone, *Black Theology and Black Power,* 20th anniversary edition (San Francisco: Harper and Row, 1989), 151.

47. Ibid., 97.

48. B. Noland Carter, *The Carters of Redlands: A Family History* (Cincinnati: Privately Printed, 1961). In the forward my grandfather writes, "One's family should be something of which to be genuinely proud. It should be a responsibility to live up to and a factor in one's way of life. I believe, therefore, that the more one knows of his background the more he will be influenced by it and it will be his desire to live in the traditions of the family."

49. Steven A. Holmes, "Virginians Remember a 1791 Emancipation," *New York Times*, July 29, 1991.

50. Levy, "The Anti Jeffersonian," 18.

51. Ibid., 25.

52. Ibid., 27.

53. Ibid.

54. Ibid., 17.

55. Ibid., 32.

56. "Theories of the flesh" is language taken from Cherrie Moraga and Gloria Anzaldúa, eds., *This Bridge Called My Back: Writings by Radical Women of Color* (New York: Kitchen Table: Women of Color Press, 1983), 20. "Demonarchy" is a concept articulated by Delores S. Williams. See "The Color of Feminism: Or Speaking

The Black Women's Tongue," *The Journal of Religious Thought* 43, no. 1 (Spring–Summer, 1986): 52.

57. Lillian Smith, *Killers of the Dream* (New York: W. W. Norton, 1994), 17.

58. Fred Hobson, *But Now I See: The White Racial Conversion Narrative* (Baton Rouge: Louisiana State University Press, 1999).

59. Ibid., 25, 27.

60. Ibid., 28.

61. Ibid., 29.

62. Smith, *Killers of the Dream,* 39.

63. Ibid., 30.

64. Lynne Olson, *Freedom's Daughters: The Unsung Heroines of the Civil Rights Movement from 1830–1970* (New York: Scribner, 2001), 70.

65. Smith, *Killers of the Dream,* 84.

66. See ibid., part 3, chap. 2: "Two Men and a Bargain."

67. Hobson, *But Now I See,* 22.

68. Olson, *Freedom's Daughters,* 71.

69. Segrest, *Memoir of a Race Traitor,* ix, and Segrest, *Born to Belonging,* 157.

70. Segrest, *Memoir of a Race Traitor,* 80. See also Becky Thompson, who writes that "for white people in a racist society, confronting self-hatred becomes an ongoing process, since we see and feel racism every day. Doing anti-racist work requires struggling against self-hatred that exposure to and complicity in racism engenders. . . . I am left believing that the psychological dynamics of self-hatred are ones we must reckon with carefully and persistently." Thompson, *A Promise and a Way of Life,* xix.

71. Segrest, *Born to Belonging,* 158.

72. Ibid., 171–72.

73. Adrienne Rich, "Resisting Amnesia," in *Blood, Bread and Poetry: Selected Prose 1979–1985* (New York: W. W. Norton, 1986), 153.

74. Segrest, *Born to Belonging,* 174, and Delores Williams, "Womanist/Feminist Dialogue: Problems and Possibilities," *Journal of Feminist Studies in Religion* 9, no. 2 (Spring–Fall 1993): 69.

75. Segrest, *Born to Belonging,* 2.

Eight

TO HEAR AND TO BE ACCOUNTABLE
An Ethic of White Listening

AANA MARIE VIGEN

WHAT DOES IT MEAN for white folk — including Christians, scholars, students — to listen fully to the truths articulated by members of those communities who have suffered so long, and so pervasively, at the hands of white supremacy? How might white people resist the tendency to co-opt that which peoples of colors tell us? Finally, how might our ultimate understanding as white people come at less of a cost to these communities than it often does? I encourage you to linger with these questions. Do not let your mind, especially if you are a white person, rush with an answer or retort. Allow them to stir around a bit. For those of us who are white, deliberately restraining the impulse to answer, or presuming to know the answer, is a fundamental part of responsible listening.

This one chapter cannot answer completely any of these persistent questions. Engaging them is part of the ongoing lifework of all white people. Yet, this chapter can describe emerging elements of an "ethic of white listening" which grow out of qualitative research with Black and Latina women with cancer.[1] The argument here is that white scholars need to incorporate a method into our way of being and working, which disciplines in a particular way how we hear peoples of colors. Simply put, not only the content of white theology, practices, and ethics needs to change, but *how* each is done ought to shift fundamentally as well. Through the lens of qualitative fieldwork, I explore how white scholars might decenter ourselves both in research and in theology and ethics.

Before pursuing this argument in any depth, two caveats merit a word. First is the matter of audience. Given the scope of this book, this piece pointedly addresses white Christian theologians and ethicists. It also welcomes critique by scholars of colors. Its analysis, however, is not confined to these specific academic realms, but is relevant to other disciplines and nonacademic endeavors as well. Indeed, the work that white folk need to do on white privilege and structural racism is not merely an intellectual pursuit. Scholarly work alone will not be able to uproot white privilege in any sector of the academy or society.

Serious, ongoing work on white privilege and racism is a vocation and responsibility of all white moral agents, not an "elective" to be chosen or not. In everyday decisions, regardless of class, gender, and other social locations, white persons either perpetuate or disrupt white privilege, prejudice, and presumption. White anti-racism work must, therefore, be integrated into our most basic self-awareness and mundane interactions. So, if you are a white reader who does not consider yourself a "white scholar, theologian, or ethicist," you might replace these terms in what follows with "white moral agent," "white person," or simply with "I, we."

I emphasize this matter because the future of interracial coalitions and relations — whether within a faith community, classroom, city hall meeting, grassroots organization, or even a U.N. summit — may very well be at stake. Integrally related to this reality is the undeniable fact that the complexity and magnitude of menacing social ills (global capitalism, militarism, environmental degradation, violence in various forms, and poor education and health infrastructures) demand that people of differing racial/ethnic backgrounds and socioeconomic classes work together to resolve them. When human beings work dynamically together to resist such realities, there is hope for survival of all life on this fragile planet.

In order to create such coalitions, however, white people must first attune our ears. Interracial dialogues and projects hearty enough to confront and withstand such daunting challenges only thrive when they are planted in the rich soil of honest self-reflection among all participants. Constructive dialogue across various kinds of difference is always difficult. Yet, white people have a distinct responsibility in these contexts to reflect inwardly and to listen deeply to communities of colors because of the pervasive history of white supremacy (and the political, economic, and social oppressions woven therein). For if we do not look directly at the ways in which we benefit from white privilege and structural racism — our "history's presence in the present"[2] — we will never really hear what peoples of colors are communicating (even if we sit and listen for hours or years in multicultural settings or diversity trainings). Consequently, for more interracial endeavors to be resilient despite the many internal and external obstacles they will inevitably face, white people need to listen more carefully than we often have.

The second caveat situates this individual chapter within the content of rest of the volume. The analytical substance of this piece assumes the foundation laid by the previous chapters, which interrogate the notions and realities of race, whiteness, and white privilege. What follows cannot be dissected from this theoretical context. If it is, this chapter may degenerate into feeble "tips" for multiracial conversations.

This chapter builds upon the previous analysis to explore how such theoretical underpinnings might inform concrete relationships and interactions experienced in qualitative research (or other avenues of applied learning). In what follows, I elucidate what I mean by "decentering" white theologians and ethicists in our research. Then I provide some background regarding my own qualitative research. The remainder of the chapter unpacks four important elements of an ethic of white listening.

A STORY

First, I need to tell a story. This story illustrates the sometimes subtle — but still serious — missteps that often hobble white attempts to listen.

My supervisor, who had become my friend, was having a difficult day. I did not realize how difficult. I called her to discuss when people would be coming to cook or to sit with her. Mine were among the few calls the Rev. Dr. Douglass would take.[3] She was gravely ill with cancer that had metastasized to her liver.

The Rev. Dr. Douglass was a pastor and an assistant professor of practical theology; I was her administrative assistant. My job description had shifted dramatically when she was diagnosed with a third recurrence of cancer. As her condition worsened, I served as a liaison for the community in which she served, and coordinated much of her home care and appointments.

On this particular March day, I wanted to talk about scheduling and the Rev. Dr. Douglass wanted to breathe. I was frustrated by a number of schedule changes I had not been made aware of and by not being able to tell how much assistance she wanted. I felt I had been getting mixed messages from her — alternating between wanting not to be alone and not wanting people around all the time. And, "I was trying to help her." So, I kept asking questions, even as she kept trying to tell me that she could not focus on them at that moment.

Later that day, I went to see her and we sat on her bed. I apologized if my call had been an intrusion. In my mind, though, I still felt a bit defensive and indignant — telling myself that my intentions had been good, that I had her best interests at heart, and that I was doing a "darn fine job" coordinating things. Somewhere deep inside me, I still presumed to know best. The Rev. Dr. Douglass looked me in the eye and spoke the truth in love: My priorities were not hers in that moment; I needed to listen to her; she needed to conserve her energy and when I asked her to turn her attention to the immediate things going on around her, that drained her. I learned that I needed to attune my ears so that I could make appropriate adjustments as best I could. Even more, I learned that although she counted on me, she was not asking me to figure it all out, to run the show, or to take care of everything. She was asking me to listen and to be present.

This bit of my history illuminates a pernicious problem I have experienced in myself, and witnessed in much white theology, ethics, and practice seeking to work with communities of color and to be informed by them: White people often do not listen — not fully, even when we think we are listening — yet we can be so quick to speak. At a minimum, good intentions pave the way to missed opportunities and inadequate understanding. At worst, they fatally wound attempts at right relationship between people of color and their white counterparts.

One might counter that this story has nothing to do with racial dynamics, but rather speaks more universally about how caregivers need to listen to those in their care. On one level, this is true. The critically ill and dying in the United States, across racial, socioeconomic, and cultural lines, often have difficulty getting their care providers to listen to them. On another level, however, presumptions and differing priorities have everything to do with differences in racial, socioeconomic, and cultural backgrounds. And these differences directly impinge upon dialogue and quality of care, even if they reside underneath the surface of what is being said.

Recent quantitative research indicates that racial and cultural bias and stereotypes interfere with the quality of health care for communities of colors. For example, the Institute of Medicine (IOM) reported in 2002 that there is substantive documentation that, even with comparable insurance and income, U.S. racial and ethnic minorities receive a lower quality of health care than whites.[4]

For example, the quality and availability of language translation services and of cultural competence profoundly affect numerous racial/ethnic communities across the country, even in urban areas. The care of Latino/a patients and families often suffers dramatically when their providers do not speak Spanish, and/or do not understand Latino/a cultures, values, and beliefs with regard to health. Recent studies find that Latino/a patients tend to be less satisfied with their care and comply less with treatment plans when there is a lack of communication and understanding — linguistic and cultural — between themselves and their physicians.[5]

Reflecting on my own experience, I lament that my presumption to "know best" got in the way of hearing and responding to the Rev. Dr. Douglass. While I cannot draw definitive conclusions regarding the origin of this presumption, it is important to note three possibilities. First, this presumption may stem from the fact that my personality (one, it is safe to say, often found among those in theology, ethics, and/or ministry) is one inclined toward the caretaking of others. Thus, it may be true that regardless of the racial/ethnic background of the Rev. Dr. Douglass, I may have done the very same thing — overstepped bounds in the desire to "fix, take care of, help." A second possibility is that my internal self-perception, even if not fully conscious, as "efficient, clear-headed, well-organized, knowing best," has something to do with being socialized as a white person in this society.[6] Third, the combination of a general caretaking personality and white socialization having enculturated me with the sense that I "am right, know best" may have been at work.

Regardless of its origin or my intention, the flawed presumption that "I know best" deprived me both of awareness of the Rev. Dr. Douglass's active decision-making skills *as well as* awareness of my own emotions and inner chaos stemming from the reality that someone whom I loved deeply was very ill. I did not fully honor what was going on within her or within myself. Instead, focusing on "knowing best and taking care of her" cost me my ability to be present to my own emotions as I instead identified only with the rational, problem-solving (in other words, the "safe") part of my being.

Even more important to acknowledge, my personal presumption to "know best" directly relates to a larger, collective history. For over two hundred years in the United States, Black people were associated *only* with their bodies — for the sake of white needs — for labor, for sex, to feel psychologically superior to another, or for financial gain. To the white mind and gaze, Black people were not ends in themselves. They were tools suited for the realization of white ends/desires. Black and Indigenous peoples were considered not fully human, but instead more akin to animals. They were not presumed to have, nor were they granted, the same human rights to dignity, respect, or freedom. Furthermore, whites, especially men, claimed the domain of rationality, civility, intellect, and even humanity.[7]

This history continues to breathe in the present. Thus, even if I do not consciously hold such violent beliefs, I need to be aware of *how the legacy of this history lives in contemporary relationships and contexts.* This legacy means white persons inherently bear responsibility for making sure we do not replicate, or participate in replicating, a false and destructive dichotomy that in any way (linguistically, symbolically, relationally) denies or subverts the moral agency and intellect intrinsic to peoples of colors.

Ultimately, whether or not my caretaking and presumption reflect individual personality or are linked directly to white socialization and identity (or both) matters very little. Regardless of my intentions, my actions and attitude had certain, real effects due to the knowable and concrete history that stands between white people and peoples of colors. This history continually infuses relational dynamics with particular meanings in the present. I may be by nature a confident, capable caretaker. But, while paternalism is never helpful, it is imperative I understand that it can have particular ramifications across racial lines. Part of responsible white listening and moral agency is being attuned to this fact.[8]

The notion of a "double consciousness" is something people of color live with in order to survive in a white supremacist society.[9] One interpretation of this concept is that folks of color need to understand the "white way of seeing the world and the folks of color within it" as well as to cultivate ways of seeing themselves that are not dependent upon, or infected by, white consciousness. In other words, communities of colors need to understand — in order to survive —

a white system that disparages "coloredness" as well as to understand themselves as inherently beautiful, precious, gifted persons and communities whose worth and identity are not at all what the white gaze sees.

I suggest that white persons also need a double consciousness, but of a different kind and for different reasons. White people need to cultivate the skill to be fully present in interactions and work with peoples of colors, while also being able to step back from the immediate dialogue and events in order to be cognizant of the larger picture and to check one's self. Part of being responsible requires self-reflection both on how one may be perceived in a present context and on the actual effects of one's actions and decisions, given the histories of the peoples involved and history's import for the current relationship, exchange, or project.

Subtle but toxic presumptions that carry cultural and racial freight can be operative — even in a relationship where there is also genuine, mutual love and respect. Such presumptions may drive a wedge that obstructs communication and right relationship. The Rev. Dr. Douglass and I worked hard to keep things honest between us because the relationship mattered a great deal to each of us. So, rather than give up on me and distance herself, she held me accountable. Imagine for a moment how much racial and/or cultural stereotypes and presumptions might interfere between people who do not know or trust each other.

In summary, white people are accountable for the ways in which we fail to hear and understand the needs and claims that other communities make upon us. The tragedy is that in so many cases, as was true in mine, white learning comes at the expense of those already multiply harmed by white interpersonal and structural failures in perception, sensitivity, and justice. I regret that in the midst of contending with cancer, the Rev. Dr. Douglass had to contend with my presumption as well. My learning came at a cost to her well-being during an acutely difficult time in her life.

STEPPING ASIDE:
DE-CENTERING WHITE THEOLOGIANS AND ETHICISTS

White scholars need to be both *more and less* focused upon ourselves as we work with communities of color and undertake research
that involves and/or impacts them. Much of substance has already
been articulated in prior chapters regarding why more, and what
kind of, attention is needed with respect to white identity, structures, history, and privilege. Doing our own work on these fronts
is crucial to cultivating a healthy self-critical stance. Such honest
assessment of our histories and ourselves is integral to seeing, hearing, and understanding more fully the personhoods and claims of
others.

Yet, ironically, there is also the danger that white scholars and communities can turn these endeavors inward, into a kind of narcissism
that fails to turn back outward to face, and be accountable to, another. The deconstruction of whiteness is not the end of what needs
to be done, but the beginning. White scholars might turn the "deconstruction of whiteness" into an investigation that ends up making
us, yet again, the center of attention; we might profit from "de-
constructing" ourselves, without offering constructive alternatives.
Consequently, even as white scholars need to be more attuned to our
history and the ways in which power dynamics infuse social relations,
we also need to step back from center stage.

What is meant by "decentering"? At the most general level, it
means an intentional casting off of both preemptive and presumptive attitudes and actions. First, white theologians and ethicists need
to curb overt, or even residual, tendencies to predetermine the terms,
frameworks, or action strategies when listening to and working with
communities of color. Second, we need to be aware of, and call into
question, any initial assumptions we may have regarding others or
particular realities when we enter the scene — whatever the scene
might be. If not consciously owned and examined, such assumptions
get in the way of accurate perception. Instead of seeing clearly the

complexity of a person or situation, we may very well see, hear, and observe what we expected all along.

A Theological (Re)Starting Point

Given that this text particularly addresses Christian theologians and social ethicists, I want to suggest that decentering begins with theology and, specifically, that a radical (root-altering) shift in theological anthropology is a fundamental place to start. "Theological anthropology" is a term used to describe a faith tradition's conceptualization of what it means to be a human being. One formal definition of theological anthropology, as understood within Christianity, is the "systematic reflection on human nature and destiny (Human and Civil Rights) in light of the biblical witness."[10] Theological anthropology asks questions such as, "How does a faith community's understanding of God, creation, redemption, sin, and so on, impact its understanding of what it means to be human?" A faith tradition's answer to such questions has a lot to do with its theology, interpretation of scripture, and its experience and embodied memory within history.

With respect to Christianity, the traditional (and *tired*) root of anthropology, found in the majority of Western theology and secular philosophy, needs to be dug up and torn out. This vision of the human being, historically engrained on much of the Occidental eyeball, tends to see humanity (explicitly or implicitly) in abstract, individualistic, European, white, male, rational terms. Such a definition of the human being is highly problematic. Many white feminist scholars have tenaciously tugged at much of this diseased root.[11] Womanist and other feminist scholars of color have also courageously questioned the subjective racial assumptions hidden within this "universal."[12] These labors have yielded important results. It is no longer second nature, for example, for theologians and ethicists to assume that the anthropology operative in Aquinas or Augustine, especially with respect to gender, is true or adequate for present understanding.

Still, more work remains to be done. Uninterrogated assumptions based on whiteness, socioeconomic class, and ethnic/national identity found in theological anthropology need further examination and rooting out, and white scholars need to do our share of the tugging.

A seismic shift in theological anthropology can aid this decentering process: the basis for understanding what it is to be human ought to take as its frame of reference the most vulnerable of a society. This claim emerges in the work of Roman Catholic womanist theologian M. Shawn Copeland, who argues that the only viable anthropological subject is the one situated among the bodies of the most despised, namely, "the exploited, despised, poor woman of color."[13] Rather than holding up an abstract ideal of what a person can be, essentially is, or ought to be, Copeland challenges theologians and ethicists to understand the meaning of human being-ness in light of the actual experiences of the ones most vulnerable, objectified, and likely to be disregarded. She argues that theological and ethical definitions of what it means to be human will only approach adequacy if they include explicit, substantive respect for these persons. The requirements of the most marginalized within a society, therefore, ought to be the normative starting point for an adequate understanding of what justice means in human relations.

When taken seriously, this theological anthropology audaciously inverts the whole enterprise of theological anthropology itself. Rather than beginning with an abstract notion of the human being and overlaying it upon all particular persons/peoples, this theological stance does something markedly different. It begins with a concrete, embodied human subject and then assesses adequate understandings of the human being and related requirements for human flourishing against this particular standard. It is an inductive anthropology, rather than a deductive one. The move is away from a universal theory and toward exploration of actual lives in order to understand what it means to be human in concrete contexts. Through study, reflection, and conversation with scholars of colors, I have come to the realization that an adequate understanding of what it means to be human may only come out of encounters with particular persons and communities who have been too often left out of the theoretical formulations and calculations.

Ultimately, within this particular theological anthropology, I argue, white folk have the opportunity to *become* human, something we cannot really be in the classic Western formulation. When white people are the given illustration beside the entry for "human being" in the common lexicon of a society (as conveyed in much of mainstream advertising, television, film, and news, for example), the full identity and intrinsic value of others is obscured, while that of white persons is elevated to the level of the norm. In contrast, in a theological anthropology in which we are no longer made "the standard of humanity," it might become possible for us to be human in the deepest sense — with an awareness of our intrinsic interdependence, relationality, and accountability to others within a world of varied and equally important persons. This theological and ethical shift strips away a deceitful and conceited distortion that prevents all people, in one way or another, from being (or being recognized as) fully human.

Even if a given theological anthropology seems detached from the lives of people who are not theologians, it still has concrete effects on their lives. More is discussed on this point below. For now, what is important to emphasize is that how a person or community conceives of what it means to be human matters for how she/it treats other persons and communities. This conception is part of the basic baggage one takes on the journey of encountering other human beings and may make a critical difference in how, if at all, the others are recognized.

STEPPING OUTSIDE: EXPERIENTIAL LEARNING FROM QUALITATIVE FIELDWORK

Before addressing the elements of an ethic of white listening born out of my research, I need to offer a bit of background on the research itself. The overall aim of my dissertation, in which this research has been pursued, has been to explore quality-of-care issues for Black and Latina women with life-threatening forms of cancer.[14] Specifically, I have asked: (1) When one is seriously ill, what contributes to a sense of being well cared for and respected as a full human being? (2) What dynamics frustrate such care and respect? (3) What might the concept of human dignity, when informed by a particular theological and social ethic that understands all people as beloved children of God and intrinsically interrelated, add to the caregiving imagination within U.S. society? Not surprisingly, given what has already been argued, the project contends that ethicists, sociologists, chaplains, health care providers, and theologians can only arrive at an adequate sense of dignity and personhood in the context of health care when they take seriously the experiences and voices of those most marginalized by societal/structural inequalities.

A desire to hear from Black and Latina women, in their own languages and voices, lies at the heart of my project. It is vital to learn from the experiences of those who most directly confront health care quality issues: racially/ethnically/culturally vulnerable women with cancer and those who care for them.[15] The purpose of qualitative, ethnographic fieldwork, then, is to create a vehicle for such listening. The rationale for choosing Black and Latina women grows from the particular theological anthropology and my own experience, noted above. My hope is that attentive listening to these communities might make U.S. health care more humane for all persons.

Fundamental questions quickly surfaced as I set out on this path: How can I (a white, relatively privileged Ph.D. candidate) be a credible listener to, and recorder of, the experiences of these women? Why should they talk to me at all, let alone reveal such intimate information? What kinds of practices build trust between white theologians/ ethicists and communities of colors — the very ones to whom many of us hope our research will be of service? How ought dialogue be structured in order for the process and all of the participants to maintain their integrity? I do not purport to have resolved all of these questions, but utilizing theoretical and practical field research to date, I can share a few insights that are relevant to an ethic of white listening.

STEPPING TOGETHER: METHODOLOGICAL INSIGHTS FOR AN ETHIC OF WHITE LISTENING

Four salient themes begin to elucidate an ethic that may contribute to shaping white scholars into responsible listeners when working with communities of colors. They are not foolproof guarantees that we will not "muck it up," yet they may help. They can be described under the rubrics of inductive learning; seeking collaborators; and the need for both reflexivity and accountability.

The Significance of Inductive Learning

Most scholars, across disciplines, would agree that all theories or truth claims must somehow be tested within lived realities and observed events. However, there is wide diversity in the methods proffered. Some researchers, often in positivistic sciences such as medicine and other natural sciences, favor deductive reasoning to the exclusion of any inductive approach.[16] In deductive research, one begins with a theory or proposition and then moves to explore actual events, interactions, and lives. This method is helpful to quantitative studies in which one wishes to test a hypothesis using large, random data collections and surveys. For example, if you want to test the efficacy of a new cancer drug, a deductive method will be essential to your work. Operating with a reasonable hypothesis, based on findings from prior research, you can test a large population using blind trials, a control group, and so on. If the sample size is large enough, and is replicated in other research, you will be able to make a fairly objective claim regarding the drug's usefulness and potential harms (barring any undue influence from the drug company sponsoring the new drug).

In contrast, the purpose of qualitative research, in an inductive approach, is to describe in textured detail what the researcher learns from the immersion within a particular context. This method seeks neither to quantify a given reality nor to compare it to another. Instead, an inductive approach begins in the street or in the hospital room and observes what is there. This learning then informs any subsequent formal reflection/analysis. Only after digging deeply into a small section of the ground does it move to a higher vantage point to survey a larger scene.

Rather than testing a prior assumption, an inductive method seeks to discover what is there when one has very limited assumptions of what one will find. Ethnographer James Spradley explains the distinctiveness of the inductive approach this way:

> Western educational systems infuse all of us with ways of interpreting experience. Tacit assumptions about the world find their way into the theories of every academic discipline — literary criticism, physical science, history, and all the social sciences. Ethnography alone seeks to document the existence of alternative realities and to describe these realities in their own terms. Thus, it can provide a corrective for theories that arise in Western social science....
>
> Ethnography, in itself, does not escape being culture-bound. However, it ... says to all investigators of human behavior, "Before you impose theories on the people you study, find out how those people define the world."[17]

Ethnography, as Spradley describes it, intentionally attempts to displace the "expert's" theory or knowledge, and by association, the "expert" herself. It does so in order to describe a reality, a person, or a people *well* — namely, in their own terms. An inductive, ethnographic method may help to chasten a researcher's assumptions and heavy-handed theories.

Practicing this kind of discipline may be immensely helpful to white scholars. As noted earlier, racial power dynamics and the active presence of social and material history are inherently operative whenever a white scholar works with communities of colors. An inductive method may, at least partly, correct broad generalizations and stereotypes made by white scholars — anthropologists, sociologists, physicians, scientists, or ethicists — that reduce (consciously or not) complex realities and human identities to woefully inadequate observations.

When acknowledging the presence of flawed and/or racist assumptions along with shameful abuses of power enacted by white researchers, white people often cite examples that reside comfortably in the past, such as the notorious eugenics of Nazi doctors. Less often do we remember and discuss the white assumptions and brutality that make tragedies like the Tuskegee Syphilis study or the forty-one shots killing Amadou Diallo possible.[18] Even as slavery and segregation are legally abolished, current ethnocentric and paternalistic assessments of African, Middle-Eastern, Eastern, and Latino cultures/peoples still often deny their full humanity. Such assumptions are presently active in both the beliefs and policies of much of white U.S.-America. For example, they help to enable and justify the prolonged detention of persons from the Middle East in both U.S. jails and Guantánamo Bay, along with the immigration policies and practices that police the Mexican-U.S. border. In light of these realities, white scholars in the United States have the responsibility to teach, confront, and own both historical and contemporary manifestations of racism particular to our own context and nation.

White theologians and ethicists interested in social and racial justice have our work cut out for us — both in terms of constructively owning this history and in building relationships with communities of colors. An inductive mode of study incorporated in the work of Christian theology and social ethics constitutes one way to help us resist presumption in our theories and interpretations. Rather than co-opting people's stories or describing them so that they fit into our view of the world, inductive learning represents one viable way to challenge ourselves to acknowledge and critique our (pre)assumptions at the methodological level.

Seeking Collaborators Instead of Subjects

Much of quantitative research, along with some qualitative research, uses the term "human subject" to denote persons participating in a given study. This choice of terminology is not value-free. How the researcher identifies the people with whom she is working signals a particular kind of relationship. For example, one might study or work "on" a subject. Other possible terms such as "collaborator" and "informant" imply a different sort of relationship. Spradley highlights the contrast:

> Social science research that uses subjects usually has a special goal: to test hypotheses. Investigators are not primarily interested in discovering the cultural knowledge of the subjects; they seek to confirm or disconfirm a specific hypothesis by studying the subject's response. Work with subjects begins with preconceived ideas; work with informants begins with naïve ignorance. *Subjects do not define what is important for the investigator to find out; informants do.*[19]

Language matters. Is the participant your teacher or an object of study? Hopefully, and most likely, a white scientist who uses the term "subject" does not think of, or treat, the individuals with whom she is working in any way similar to the way she does a lab rat. Yet, the choice of terms may indicate whether or not one thinks that the participant has a role in helping define what is important to learn. This choice, and the ethos invested within it, therefore does make a real difference to participants and researchers, even if on a subconscious level. If participants feel their insights and experiences are genuinely valued by the researcher, they are more likely to trust the scholar and to teach her more of what they know.

Moreover, how a researcher conceives of the role of the people with whom she speaks can make a great difference, not only in rapport-building, but in resituating the claims and importance of the researcher herself. The key in this kind of work is that the researcher is not the expert, but the novice. She needs to be taught by the people with whom she works. This attitude decenters the authority and presumptions of knowledge or expertise on the part of the researcher. Rather than becoming defensive, rationalizing, or flat out denying what peoples of colors tell us about the contemporary appearance and dynamics of racism and white privilege manifest in society, white scholars need to listen seriously to this testimony. This is a realm of experience that we ourselves have not personally confronted.

In this vein, "collaborator" is a helpful term because it emphasizes that the researcher needs to partner with the individuals interviewed. The goal of this kind of qualitative research is to learn from an engaging conversation with someone who has direct knowledge of something that the researcher does not. To have an insightful and meaningful conversation, one needs to be emotionally present, rather than attempting to be an authority. (In fact, trying to come off as an expert usually guarantees you will *not* have a good conversation!) Researchers need collaborators in a way that they do not need subjects. Collaborators are colleagues, not subordinates. They not only contribute information about something, but help to construct the questions, the method, the frameworks, and operational definitions.

While honoring the fact that participants have much to teach, it is imperative that this awareness is not used to deny or overlook the power dynamics inherently present in the collaborator/researcher relationship. A white researcher, doctor, or theologian in the United States is not in the same social positioning as a study participant of color. Even if she respects the participants as collaborators, she does not face the same risks as the participant, and she may benefit more directly from the research than the participant. In particular, white researchers must not forget that there is a cost to participants in speaking of their experiences, which often involve hurt, betrayal, violence, and or disrespect by white people. Moreover, on a wholly other level altogether, it is lamentable that I, as a white researcher, need to be, or am asking to be, taught about such things by persons of colors in the first place.

White researchers, doctors, theologians, and ethicists may very well know some rather important things and have particular expertise, yet we need the knowledge of others as well. And we need it in a way that does not simply fit into, accent, or nuance our frameworks and paradigms, but in a way that displaces and re-forms our knowledge. Even as we may have significant insights, still, no matter the medical, scientific, or theological expertise, we will never know more about the values, cultures, and personhoods of others than they themselves do.

Consequently, for any exchange or project to be authentically interracial and collaborative, a truly diverse coalition of energies, knowledge sources, and input needs to be present from the ground up. White scholars cannot simply set the table and then invite others to come and dine. In my work, I have come to realize that Black and Latina women are helping me to learn the questions I need to ask. I am searching for the right questions, and they are helping me to articulate them.

This insight is especially important because white people (especially those who are highly educated and/or are from upper-middle and upper socioeconomic classes) are often used to a certain "authority" and agency in carrying out their lives and work. Many of us take for granted that we will be treated with dignity, that our rights will be respected, that we will be heard. Nearly every week in the streets of New York, I witness white people becoming quickly indignant (and sometimes outraged) when we are not. Embedded within white identity is a sense of entitlement. I have also observed that white folk tend to assume we are knowledgeable, rational, skilled individuals. Many of us are socialized by white privilege and white identity to do so. Much of this enculturation must be *un*learned in order to learn while doing qualitative ethnographic research. Even more importantly, it must be unlearned if we are to become fully human.

The Imperative of Reflexivity and Accountability

Lest the above be taken to mean that white people simply need to "go talk to peoples of colors" or engage in "voyeuristic tourism" and call it practical study, I reflect upon two additional insights which speak to the concrete mechanisms and kind of engagement needed. Qualitative research methodology is anything but monolithic. Numerous approaches fall under its umbrella. Thus, it is important to specify the particular kind of qualitative study that is helpful to the project of white listening and responsibility.

Reflexivity

Pierre Bourdieu has made vast methodological contributions to the fields of anthropology, ethnography, and sociology. Though these cannot be discussed here in their entirety, one particular insight is especially pertinent to the present work. Bourdieu, among others,[20] has elaborated a reflexive method of study for these disciplines.[21] Stated simply, reflexivity means two things: first, self-reflection on the part of the researcher as part of an academic culture; second, a mutual give-and-take between a researcher and collaborator in such a way that not only do the researcher's actions/ideas affect the collaborator, but the collaborator's actions and information fundamentally affect the researcher as well.

According to Bourdieu, sociology that fails to reflect critically upon itself as part of the research will not learn much at all. "Ordinary sociology, which bypasses the radical questioning of its own operations and of its own instruments of thinking . . . is thoroughly suffused with the object it claims to know, and which it cannot really know, because it does not know itself. A scientific practice that fails to question itself does not, properly speaking, know what it does."[22] Bourdieu understands that work lacking reflexivity often reproduces itself — its biases, discourse, and presumptions — rather than learning from the contexts and persons it wishes to engage.

In contrast, a reflexive method holds itself accountable by being attentive to the way the researcher situates herself in the field study. It does so by being attentive to various biases that may get in the way of fully seeing and hearing the collaborators in their own voices and right. Loic Wacquant identifies three types of biases with which

Bourdieu is concerned. First are "the social origins and coordinates of the individual researcher" (race/ethnicity, socioeconomic class, gender, cultural background, sexual orientation, etc.). Wacquant believes this bias to be the most obvious and easy to correct via mutual and self-critique.

Wacquant thinks the second bias is not as often interrogated, namely, the specific location the researcher occupies within the academic field. Bourdieu and Wacquant find that the fact that sociologists and other academics are producing their work in order to advance careers in some form or other is not often addressed in a self-reflective way. All academics compete for jobs and grants, and this can impact how they/we write, for whom they/we write, and the ends served by their/our work. The results can become solely self-serving if this reality is not held up to critical self-reflection.

Wacquant credits Bourdieu with being the most original in terms of a third meaning of reflexivity that confronts academia even more directly. According to Bourdieu, in academic culture, there is an "intellectualist bias which entices us to construe the world as spectacle, as a set of significations to be interpreted rather than as concrete problems to be solved practically."[23] When such a bias is present and unchallenged, academics, even in the name of liberation or social justice, may fall into the trap of simply writing about people, without impacting their lives in meaningful ways. What may be a vexing intellectual question for an academic could mean life or death for a person living with the problem. White academics often do not directly live with the same harsh realities of substandard education, a lack of food and clean water, the pervasive presence of AIDS or cholera, and widespread violence that poor people and/or peoples of colors living around the globe do.

To add insult to injury, scholarship can be, intentionally or not, condescending to the ways of thought, being, and acting of the communities and contexts it seeks to engage. This danger is particularly important for white scholars because so much intellectual discourse and theory have been produced by white folk — and often either

directly or indirectly about others. Even when scholarship is not orig-
inally presumptuous, it can be used in presumptuous ways by other
white people.

Particularly for white theologians and other scholars committed to
racial justice, reflexivity means self-critique at these precise points: as
a white person; as an academic trying to stake out a career and name
within a specific field; and as part of an intellectual culture that tends
to objectify others and create theories about them without helping to
solve actual problems. A rigorous and ongoing commitment to critical self-reflection, as an individual and also as one located within
a larger academic culture, is one way to test assumptions and to
evaluate them based on what is learned through concrete work with
people who may be, in ways obvious or not, different from the academic. The subsequent section discussing accountability highlights
a few specific ways to embody such reflexivity. Here what is most
important to understand is that I, as a researcher and as a white,
educated woman, need to be intentionally conscious of my social location, of how I am writing and thinking, and of how I am situated
within academia.

A methodological reflexivity is also helpful because it emphasizes the dialogical relationship between the collaborators and the
researcher. Collaborators ought not simply answer the particular
question asked, as if they were circling a response on a survey. The
best interviews are the ones where collaborators trust enough to not
limit their feedback to narrow answers to the exact questions posed.
Collaborators are often the ones who identify the best questions.
Thus, a flow back and forth is needed, which can only happen when
there is adequate trust and accountability between the collaborator
and researcher.

At its best, reflexive, qualitative research decenters and tests preexisting theory and assumptions, often created by white scholars,
and critiques and evaluates them based on knowledge gained induc-
tively in a case study. The scholar's assumptions and abstracted theory
ought to be offset by the experiences and evidence in the field. This

kind of listening and reflexivity means white scholars cannot simply go into the field to extract what they want and then leave. I ought to be affected by the experience and these effects need to be evident in my research. Reflexivity implies a return. To be a responsible scholar or listener, I need to be informed and re-formed by what I see and hear. And I need to be aware of my responses — emotional, intellectual, physical — to the stories and persons to whom I am listening. Both ought to impact me in fundamental, and hopefully transformative, ways. Good qualitative research (and I would add substantive cross-cultural dialogue or coalition efforts) necessarily involves a cost to myself as a white person — a real investment. It costs these women of colors to speak; it ought to cost me to listen.

Accountability

Most likely any scholar, regardless of method or discipline, who engages in some kind of direct research with human beings will become well acquainted with an entity known as the "Institutional Review Board" (IRB). This is the most formal way in which scholars are held accountable. IRBs are charged with ensuring that human participants involved in research are not violated and are protected from unnecessary harm and unethical studies. IRBs came into being in the wake of scientific horrors such as experiments done on Holocaust victims during World War II and the Tuskegee Syphilis study. To test a new drug, treatment regime, or device, one needs an IRB's authorization. Moreover, if one wishes to interview people in institutional settings, such as prisons, hospitals, schools, or places of work, one usually needs IRB approval — especially if one intends to publish the finding in a medical, sociological, or anthropological journal or text.

While receiving IRB approval is a rigorous and important process, it alone does not suffice to ensure accountability between the scholar and the people with whom she is working. Indeed, there is more to accountability than compliance with IRB mandates. Above all, research is accountable to those interviewed or studied in some other way.

By accountability, I want to identify four distinct traits. First, any scholar engaging in qualitative fieldwork needs to make genuine commitments to some kind of follow-up and feedback loop with her collaborators. Vigorous guards against misappropriation and misinterpretation are absolutely essential. Perhaps collaborators might have the option of reviewing transcripts of interviews and conversations. This step is important because if the researcher missed or misinterpreted something, changes can be made before the project progresses further. Minimally, participants ought to be invited to hear the findings at some point and to discuss them with the researcher, and/or to have access to any writing that discusses them. Some people may not wish (or be able) to read anything, but would appreciate hearing an oral presentation, perhaps given to a group. Later, if anything is published, collaborators not only ought to be acknowledged somehow, they ought to receive a copy.

The exact nature and degree of reporting back may vary depending on the number of people with whom the researcher works and on the collaborator's age, health status, availability, interest level, or other variables. Yet, the principles of opening one's work to critique and revision by collaborators, honoring and acknowledging them for their wisdom and contributions, and transparency within the research findings are constant. This kind of relationship does not mean that the researcher will necessarily change every observation or interpretation with which a given collaborator does not agree. It does mean that a researcher's findings and method will be more credible and less likely to overinterpret or misrepresent others if she shares her work and solicits feedback she will consider. This kind of engagement embodies (rather than simply talking or writing about) respect.

A second form of accountability speaks to the nuance of description. Whenever a researcher sets out to engage someone or something, her first task is to describe it well, in detail and with regard for the person or situation's complexity. If the analysis overgeneralizes or essentializes individual or communal identities, making them into tropes or stereotypes, the scholar is guilty of objectification. In this event, not only does the quality of research suffer dramatically, but a kind of violence is done to the participants, even if the researcher refers to them as "collaborators." When white scholars describe persons of colors in such a way that they become identified as the representative of "the Black experience" or "the Latino identity" (as if there were any such thing), they violate the complexity intrinsic to any community and individual person.

Third, accountable research considers the collaborators first. It considers their physical, emotional, and social well-being, especially if they are members of communities who are in any way vulnerable within the larger society. Special attention needs to be given to a collaborator's particular interests, needs, and sensitivities. Is this person at risk of deportation? Is she in any kind of pain? Do her immediate needs conflict with my agenda? If so, her needs come first. No research is ethical if a collaborator's dignity is violated or if her privacy is not protected. Collaborators need to understand fully the reasons for your research, what you hope to accomplish. And they need to agree to help you without any pressure or subtle coercion. It is not justifiable to impose upon anyone, even if you are convinced that she has much to teach you. No one ought to serve simply as a means to another's career enhancement.

A final aspect of accountability is this: the research ought to matter in some way to the positive transformation of society. At the risk of sounding brash, and speaking especially (but not only) to those in theology and Christian social ethics, I want to argue that scholarship ought to be accountable to pressing needs and issues within society. There ought to be some connection between the intellectual work and the shaping of the world. Otherwise, too many trees are being cut simply to produce paper. Granted, some linkages may be more direct than others. Still, it is possible for scholars, and morally incumbent upon us, to articulate why a given theologian, theological notion, ethical formula, or qualitative field study matters to those outside of the discipline, or even in a nonacademic context.

Collaborators have the right to demand that the researcher answer the question: to what ends? Why is this research important? The researcher's questions and topic ought to correspond in some way with the palpable needs of people in a given society. Spradley suggests:

> One way to synchronize the needs of people and the goals of ethnography is to consult with informants to determine urgent research topics. Instead of beginning with theoretical problems, the ethnographer can begin with informant-expressed needs, then develop a research agenda to relate these topics to the enduring concerns of social science. Surely the needs of the informants should have equal weight with "scientific interest" in setting ethnographic priorities. More often than not, informants can identify urgent research more clearly than the ethnographer.[24]

Starting with "informant expressed needs" implies that some kind of relationship is present between the researcher and the particular population(s) from whom she hopes to learn. A researcher will not happen upon the needs or the right questions unless she is in dialogue — over time and in a sustained manner — with the communities she hopes her work will serve. In a sense, the collaborator, not the researcher, drives the questions that inform the process.

Given the relative privilege and high standard of living of white scholars in the United States and Europe, I think it is not only possible, but imperative that we ask ourselves, regardless of our disciplinary field, questions such as: to what am I contributing? What do I hope to achieve with my life's work? How does my work help to enlarge and enliven human imagination regarding how human beings might more fully, and together, thrive? What larger purposes, such as ecological sustainability, or advocacy for those left out of "bottom line" equations, are being served by this work? In the wake of tumult and tragedies in New York City, Afghanistan, Iraq, Israel, Palestine, does my work contribute in any way to interfaith dialogue, or intercultural/religious and international understanding, or to peace studies/endeavors? Might my work in any way matter to an African child living with HIV? These questions are meant to be not judgmental, but rather a tool for self-reflection. At its best and most fertile, intellectual work makes meaningful connections between the scholar/pastor and others—across disciplines and vocations.

A CONCLUDING WORD FOR BEGINNING: THE VALUE OF ACKNOWLEDGED IGNORANCE

James Spradley begins *The Ethnographic Interview* with a basic, but crucial distinction: "Rather than *studying people,* ethnography means *learning from people.*"[25] In order to learn from people, you need to assume you do not already know what they are going to teach you. Spradley goes on to acknowledge: "Ethnography starts with a conscious attitude of almost complete ignorance."[26] The value of this insight is multifold, and it is not limited to those in academia. First and foremost, I, whether I am a white scholar, activist, teacher, social worker, doctor, friend, or church member, will learn more if "what I think I know" does not get in the way of learning and listening. An even bigger payoff, especially in terms of the formation of the white scholar, is that when one is not overly focused on being an expert, but rather on being a person, there is great potential to cultivate humility both within one's endeavors and within one's inner spirit.

Moreover, there are ramifications here not only for individuals, but for entire disciplines. To put it bluntly: White scholars may profit greatly if/when we spend significant, sustained time and energy *outside* of libraries/offices and *inside* a variety of relationships and activities. My time with the Rev. Dr. Douglass indicates not only *why* I chose a particular dissertation topic, but *how* I learned about it in the first place. I came upon inequalities in health care not primarily by deducing the problems from books of social theory, ethics, and theology, but by listening to patients, loved ones such as the Rev. Dr. Douglass, and staff, and by working in relationship with them.

In a related vein, it would be helpful if more academics would push ourselves to speak and hear fluently second and third languages — not only to read or translate them. Moreover, even if English is the only common language among a researcher and the people with whom she is working, meanings cannot be taken for granted. Semantic differences ought not be overlooked.

For example, when I am doing qualitative research within communities of colors, I do not want participants to translate meanings for me, to cease speaking their own language and begin to speak in ways that are more familiar to the white and/or professional ear. If I want to hear people in their own voices, then they need to not alter what they are saying to overly accommodate me. The burden is upon me, the white scholar, to understand, or to learn to understand, what others are saying — their experiences, culture, worldview — in the fullest sense possible.[27] Of course, the persons with whom I am working will always be accommodating me to a degree and every description by a researcher is a translation. But the important point is that I must make every attempt possible to ensure that my descriptions flow as directly as possible from the concepts and meaning of the people with whom I am working/interviewing.[28]

For white theologians and ethicists to engage racism and white privilege adequately, then, we need to find avenues of contact and relationship with the people who most directly confront racial inequalities. Learning from scholars of colors is vital, and we need to ever expand our treatment of their texts. Yet we must not stop here. The incorporation of works by scholars of colors will be stronger and more credible if it bears out in relation to concrete movements, projects, and experiences. It not only matters whom I have read, but with whom I worship, eat lunch, volunteer on weekends or evenings, lobby politicians, and canvass the neighborhood. Learning to decenter ourselves in our work and daily interactions with persons of colors is more of an art than a science. And it takes time. It takes time and effort to cultivate the sensibilities and skills within ourselves which will curb the overeager, presumptive, self-righteous, preemptive qualities so often present within white identity.

While not all white theologians and ethicists will do formal qualitative fieldwork in their research, perhaps more ought to consider it. Moreover, there are other channels for similar involvement (volunteering with grassroots organizations or church programs that address affordable housing, poverty, environmental racism, education, prison reform, health care, or migrant labor issues). I am well aware of the pressure to increase one's "scholarly" credentials — to publish books and articles, to give public lectures, to get grants. But perhaps an additional measure of an accomplished scholar ought to be given more weight: the hours one spends working with community organizations and programs dedicated to social, economic, and racial transformation. Perhaps seminaries, colleges, and universities might more intentionally promote and support the notion of a public scholar, whose task, in whatever field, is not only to advance knowledge, but to contribute concretely to the shaping of people and communities in which the scholar lives and works.

In short, there is a claim upon all scholars (of whatever racial/ethnic background) to envision and create even just a small corner of the good society. Intrinsic to any such creation is a specific claim upon me, as a white person and scholar, to cultivate sustained, concrete relationships with communities of colors — not only outside of my discipline, but outside of the academy — in entirely different life situations and vocations from myself. These kinds of practical engagements and relationships are of paramount importance because if white people do not get it right in our day-to-day interactions and relationships, we won't get it right in our thinking, writing, or sermons.

Reflection on my own missed opportunities and mistakes has led me to want to do better. If we cannot, to paraphrase Nell Morton, "hear one another into speech," our efforts at coalition building will be continually and tragically undercut.[29] Real differences must be intentionally respected in the midst of seeking solidarity and creating coalitions.

I am still exploring what has to be in place before coalition building is possible, or is even seen as worthwhile by peoples of colors. But, one thing I know is that, fundamentally, racism is a white issue, just as homophobia is a heterosexual issue and poverty makes a claim upon the wealthy. White folk must deal with our own stuff and become more adept at recognizing racism. This keen eyesight and insight will in turn make the quality of our hearing, cross-cultural discussions, and coalitions much richer and more productive than prior efforts.

Much of this chapter could be summarized by one word: humility. There may have never been a time when we could less afford to separate our intellectual work from our daily practices and commitments. Engagement in messy dialogues, ethnography, or conversations in a second language will likely make white folk, especially "scholars," awkward and somewhat bumbling. But there is great learning to be had from such experiences. They may teach us what it is to be not the standard of humanity, but instead to be simply human.

NOTES

1. The terms "Black" and "Latina" are used because the study was not limited to African Americans or to women related to a particular Spanish-speaking country. Some Black women prefer terms such as "African," "Afro-Caribbean," "Jamaican," "Puerto Rican," etc. When speaking with women of color, I asked them how they define their identity and which term(s) they prefer when being described by others.

2. James Baldwin, "White Man's Guilt," in *The Price of the Ticket: Collected Nonfiction, 1948–1985* (New York: St. Martin's/Marek, 1985), 409.

3. Her name has been changed to protect her and her family's privacy.

4. See Brian Smedley, Adrienne Y. Stith, and Alan R. Nelson, eds., *Unequal Treatment: Confronting Racial and Ethnic Disparities in Healthcare,* Institute of Medicine (Washington: National Academy Press, 2002). The abstract of this report summarizes their findings: "Racial and ethnic minorities tend to receive a lower quality of healthcare than non-minorities, even when access-related factors, such as patients' insurance status and income, are controlled. The sources of these disparities are complex, are rooted in historic and contemporary inequities, and involve many participants at several levels, including health systems, their administrative and bureaucratic processes, utilization managers, healthcare professionals, and patients.

Consistent with the charge, the study committee focused part of its analysis on the clinical encounter itself, and found evidence that stereotyping, biases, and uncertainty on the part of healthcare providers can all contribute to unequal treatment" (1).

5. See Marilyn Aguirre-Molina, Carlos W. Molina, and Ruth Enid Zambrana, eds., *Health Issues in the Latino Community* (San Francisco: Jossey-Bass, 2001), 65–69. During a 1996 chaplaincy internship in California, I met many Latino/a patients and families who either felt ignored or who feared that they were viewed as illegal immigrants to be denied health care under Proposition 187, in effect at the time. Also, because of a lack of translation services, many did not fully understand what was happening to or around them. I, a white chaplain intern from South Dakota, was the only non-Latino/a staff person (present just eighteen hours a week) who spoke Spanish. When I was not there, family members (often children) or housekeeping staff or an ATT operator provided this vital service.

6. While not experienced uniformly, white people in the United States are often socialized in ways which encourage us to take charge, assume leadership, make decisions. Socioeconomic class and gender are variables that certainly qualify this experience. However, I nonetheless contend that, *relative to communities of colors,* white people are enculturated by social systems to assume a right to supervision or authority over others and/or recognition of special skills or expertise.

7. In the Western dichotomy of mind/spirit/intellect/purity vs. emotions/body/carnal/sin, women, of whatever racial/ethnic background, have been associated with the latter instead of the former. However, white women, through their association with white men, have accrued significant benefits over Native Americans, Blacks, Mexicans, Latinos and others. Kelly Brown Douglass offers an insightful analysis of this legacy and its significance for how the contemporary Black church often views homosexuality. See her article, "The Black Church and Homosexuality: The Black and White of It," *Union Seminary Quarterly Review* 57, nos. 1–2 (2002).

8. I wish to credit Jennifer Harvey, who proved to be a gracious dialogue partner who greatly assisted me in clarifying my thoughts and arguments related to these insights.

9. W. E. B. Du Bois first introduced this phrase in 1903. Since then, it has been theorized and expanded upon in different ways by numerous scholars. See W. E. B. Du Bois, *The Souls of Black Folk: Essays and Sketches* (New York: Blue Heron Press, 1953).

10. Dietrich Ritschl, "Anthropology: Overview," *The Encyclopedia of Christianity,* vol. 1, A–D, ed. Erwin Fahlbusch et al., trans. Geoffrey Bromiley (Grand Rapids: William B. Eerdmans Press, 1999), 69.

11. Numerous white feminist theologians have pointed out the cavernous deficits in androcentric (male-identified) anthropologies and have articulated powerful alternative theological visions. See, for example, the works of Mary Daly, Carter Heyward, Elizabeth Johnson, Catherine Mowry LaCugna, Sallie McFague, and Rosemary Radford Ruether.

12. See, for example, María Pilar Aquino, Daisy L. Machado, and Jeanette Rodríquez, eds., *A Reader in Latina Feminist Theology: Religion and Justice* (Austin: University of Texas Press, 2002); Virginia Fabella and Mercy Amba Oduyoye, eds., *With Passion and Compassion: Third World Women Doing Theology* (New York:

Orbis Books, 1998); Elisabeth Schüssler Fiorenza and M. Shawn Copeland, eds., *Feminist Theology in Different Contexts, Concilium 1996/1* (New York: Orbis Books, 1996); Ivone Gebara, *Out of the Depths: Women's Experience of Evil and Salvation* (Minneapolis: Fortress Press, 2002); Ada María Isasi-Díaz, *En La Lucha: Elaborating a Mujerista Theology* (Minneapolis: Fortress, 1993); emilie m. townes, *In a Blaze of Glory: Womanist Spirituality As Social Witness* (Nashville: Abingdon Press, 1995); emilie m. townes, ed., *A Troubling in My Soul: Womanist Perspectives on Evil and Suffering* (New York: Orbis Books, 1997); Delores S. Williams, *Sisters in the Wilderness: The Challenge of Womanist God-Talk* (New York: Orbis Books, 1993).

13. M. Shawn Copeland, "The New Anthropological Subject at the Heart of the Mystical Body of Christ," *CTSA Proceedings* 53 (1998): 30. See also Ivone Gebara, *Out of the Depths.*

14. The title of the dissertation is " 'To Count Among the Living': A Theo-Ethical Inquiry into the Social Dynamics Affecting the Quality of Care of Black and Latina Women with Cancer." Black feminist essayist and poet Audre Lorde wrote early in her battle with cancer: "We must learn to count the living with that same particular attention with which we number the dead." Audre Lorde, *The Cancer Journals* (San Francisco: Aunt Lute Books, 1980), 54.

15. The women with cancer who were interviewed were members of New York–area cancer support networks. Attention was given to differences in socioeconomic class, ethnic/cultural backgrounds, and religious traditions among them. Additionally, a secondary tier of interviews took place with hospital employees who work with cancer patients (a cross-section of doctors, nurses, social workers, case managers). These latter interviews helped to parse out how the issues raised by the women with cancer relate to constraints on providers and to larger health care structures.

16. Bent Flyvbjerg argues that the antagonistic debates and relations between natural and social scientists stem from a fundamental misunderstanding about what each contributes to knowledge and from judging one by the other's standards. See Bent Flyvbjerg, *Making Social Science Matter: How Social Inquiry Fails and How It Can Succeed Again* (New York: Cambridge University Press, 2001).

17. James Spradley, *The Ethnographic Interview* (New York: Holt, Rinehart, and Winston, 1979), 10–11.

18. In New York City, in February 1999, Amadou Diallo was killed by an "elite" police force designed to aggressively patrol "high-risk" drug areas. Mistaking his wallet for a gun, the officers shot Diallo forty-one times in rapid succession when he attempted to show them his identification.

19. Emphasis added. "By word and action, in subtle ways and direct statements, [ethnographers] say 'I want to understand the world from your point of view. I want to know what you know in the way you know it. I want to understand the meaning of your experience, to walk in your shoes, to feel things as you feel them, to explain things as you explain them. Will you become my teacher and help me understand?' " Spradley, *The Ethnographic Interview,* 34.

20. Loic Wacquant distinguishes Bourdieu's notion of reflexivity from others in this manner: "Bourdieu's brand of reflexivity, which may be cursorily defined as

the inclusion of a theory of intellectual practice as an integral component and necessary condition of a critical theory of society, differs from others in three crucial
ways: First, its primary target is not the individual analyst but the *social and intellectual unconscious* embedded in analytic tools and operations; second, it must
be a *collective enterprise* rather than the burden of the lone academic; and third,
it seeks not to assault but to *buttress the epistemological security of sociology.* Far
from trying to undermine objectivity, Bourdieu's reflexivity aims at increasing the
scope and solidity of social scientific knowledge, a goal which puts it at logger-
heads with phenomenological, textual, and other 'postmodern' forms of reflexivity."
Pierre Bourdieu and Loic J. D. Wacquant, *Invitation to Reflexive Sociology* (Chicago:
University of Chicago Press, 1992), 36–37. Emphasis in the original.

21. For examples of qualitative case study methodology, see also Michael Burawoy, "The Extended Case Method," *Sociological Theory* 16 (March 1988): 4–33;
Michael Burawoy et al., *Ethnography Unbound: Power and Resistance in the Modern Metropolis* (Berkeley: University of California Press, 1991); and Robert Yin,
Case Study Research: Design and Methods (Thousand Oaks, Calif.: Sage, 1994).

22. Bourdieu and Wacquant, *Invitation to Reflexive Sociology,* 236.

23. Ibid., 39.

24. Spradley, *The Ethnographic Interview,* 14.

25. Ibid., 3.

26. Ibid., 4.

27. Ibid., 18–22.

28. Ibid., 24.

29. Nell Morton, *The Journey Is Home* (Boston: Beacon Press, 1985).

Nine

CEREMONIES OF GRATITUDE, AWAKENING, AND ACCOUNTABILITY

The Theory and Practice of Multicultural Education

SHARON D. WELCH

WHO ARE YOU? Where do you come from? Who are your people? Show us. Draw a symbol of something you are proud of in your culture. Think about your home, the community, the landscape, the people, and animals that share your world. What are some of the things you cherish about where you live?

With these simple questions we begin. Crayons, white sheets of paper — laughing, naming the sources of land and place, of people, friends and family that ground us, that grace our lives with a sense of belonging and purpose. We honor our ancestors, our companions, human and other-than-human, on the journey of life.

Now, grounded in gratitude for all that sustains us, we prepare ourselves for a journey into another world. We explore worlds of horror, of cruelty and exploitation, of conflict, of centuries-long struggles for integrity and freedom.

We acknowledge that the way will be hard. We will disagree, and disagree deeply, about things that are of the utmost importance. Although our intent is to learn together, we will say things that are offensive and hurtful.

I am deeply grateful for the many helpful suggestions I received from Suzanne Burgoyne, Mary McClintock Fulkerson, Jennifer Harvey, and Elaine Lawless.

Given the costs, and given the risks, how do we take the conflicts we will have, the pain we will cause, and learn from them? How do we work the alchemy through which conflict and pain, honestly faced, bring the deepening of community and relationship, and not the end of relationship?

We examine guidelines for our task developed by other people and add suggestions we have derived from our own attempts to talk about and learn from difficult conflicts.[1] The guidelines are simple. Respect each other enough to ask why someone says something that you disagree with. When you are offended, say something immediately, realizing that this is not an interruption of our work, it *is* our work. Keep in confidence personal stories that people tell — trust is not easily won and someone may tell something in a small group she or he is not ready to tell even the class, much less the wider world. Take risks, try new interpretations and strategies, knowing that we will respect each other enough to challenge each other if and when these ideas are inadequate or harmful.

Now, as students in my class on the theory and practice of multicultural education, it is only fair that they know the assumptions I bring to this work. I do not expect that they will agree with these assumptions, nor will I try to persuade the students that these assumptions are right. They include:

1. *People and institutions do grow and change.* Sometimes change is positive, but it can also be negative. There is not a linear path to social justice; gains can be made and gains can be lost.

2. *Oppression, bias, and discrimination hurt all, albeit in vastly different ways.* We will learn to see the ways in which injustice diminishes the humanity of both the oppressed and the oppressor.

3. *The motivation for deep-seated, long-lasting social change is gratitude and accountability, not guilt.* Why gratitude and accountability? I firmly believe that it is far better to see and

empathize with suffering than it is to be oblivious or indifferent to human loss and misery. The ability to care for others is itself a precious gift, one we have received from those who first loved and cared for us.

4. *Democracy is both a worthwhile goal and extremely difficult to implement, practice, and maintain.*

We begin by recognizing who we are: experienced teachers who have chosen to undertake further study of multicultural education. Most are working for graduate degrees, and have from five to fifteen years teaching experience. While a few teach at community colleges or private colleges, the majority work as teachers and principals in public schools, from preschool through high school.

In this course we study five models of multicultural education that cover a wide spectrum of political perspectives and views of human nature.[2] Before we study the work of others, however, we begin by clarifying our own views. Each student writes a short paper, answering the following questions, based solely on their previous experience, education, and insights: What is the purpose of multicultural education? What are your goals as a teacher? What aspects of your cultural background affect your teaching? What strengths and limitations do you bring to teaching? What do you think motivates academic excellence? What do you think motivates students to become active citizens? How do you define the following terms: bias, prejudice, discrimination, oppression? Give examples of each in American society and in American schooling (examples may be from the past or present).[3] How just is American society? How close are we to fulfilling our ideals of liberty and justice for all?

While the responses to these questions vary slightly, Sandra's are quite typical of the commitments and opinions that students bring to the class.[4] Sandra has taught social studies to nine- and ten-year-olds for eleven years at a public school in a small Missouri town. She is also the social studies coordinator for her elementary school of 435 students. Her commitment to her vocation is clear: "From the beginning, I feel that my purpose has been to teach children. My...main goal is to try to teach each and every student in my classroom to love themselves...and of course I always strive for students to value reading and to improve in reading skills."

In her teaching, Sandra tells us that she "passes on the values" she gained from her parents, "honesty, kindness towards others, patience, tolerance of others, the value of self and hard work...These qualities are things that my parents instilled in me as a child and still today I get reinforcement from my seventy-eight-year-old father, who still works two jobs, and my seventy-one-year-old mother, who is retired."

Sandra states that she "grew up in a white, small, rural middle-class farming community in Central Missouri. There was no other ethnicity represented in our community except white." Because of this lack of exposure, she writes that "the one positive thing, if there would be one, is that I did not have any negative experiences with any ethnic group as a child....I didn't have any positive experiences with other ethnic groups to build upon either except for the baby-sitter's daughter surprisingly having a biracial baby (half black and half white). I loved her and accepted her just like she was a sister to me."

Sandra's students are predominantly white and middle class, but she is "disturbed" by the "growing number of students in the poverty level." Sandra acknowledges that she has not always seen the value of multicultural education: "It has taken many years to begin understanding the importance of seeking multicultural knowledge in order to better meet the needs of my students."

She now sees multicultural education as important in redressing the injustices of American society: "American society is not as just as our government would like us to believe. We are far from our founding fathers' intentions in many areas. If things are so just, then why are so many children starving in the United States? If things are so just, then why do the rich keep getting richer and the poor continue to struggle in our society? If things are so just, then why are there so few women that lead in the country's decision-making process? We've come so far in many ways, however, fall short in others. *I've never thought much about this,* but people definitely don't have equal chances to succeed with the hurdles of poverty, race, and gender just to name a few [emphasis added]."

Sandra is a committed, loving teacher. As she readily admits, however, she has not thought much about injustice. Over the course of our work together, a class of twenty-one meeting for four hours a day, four days a week for two and a half weeks, Sandra's views of justice and injustice change dramatically.

"In my first draft I wrote that 'We are far from our founding fathers' intentions in many areas.' However, I [now] totally disagree with this notion because our founding fathers slaughtered thousands of Native Americans, used women on a regular basis, tortured blacks routinely without guilt, watched as almost an entire race of Native Americans vanished. What was the intention of our founding fathers? Many wanted religious freedom and opportunities. Many were fueled by greed. Some were good-natured, hard-working people; however, things could have been so different. It hurts to think about all of the death and destruction that our history has experienced to put us to where we are today."

Sandra's sense of her whiteness also changed: "My cultural background as a White female affects my teaching more than I would have ever liked to believe!" In her first paper, Sandra wrote of being limited by being raised in an all-white community. She now sees further ramifications of that limited background: "my White culture taught me that the United States is a great, strong country full of opportunities for all.... I've always been very patriotic and proud to be an American and I still am. However, I am ashamed of the many groups that were oppressed by our forefathers during the settling of this country. Whites are so naive, and so was I before I completed my course work in this class."

Sandra's response to this new awareness is not cynicism or despair, however, but clarity and focus. Her awareness of the extent of her own power, and her ability to help move society toward greater justice, has changed as much as her sense of her whiteness. She now writes that her "main goals" as a teacher are: "to promote equality, self-esteem, equal opportunities in school, to reduce prejudice and stereotyping among parents and students, to encourage critical thinking and problem solving, and prepare citizens to work to promote change in society for structural equality and cultural pluralism. I definitely have my work cut out for me, but change has to begin somewhere."

Sandra's goal as a teacher is "to realistically strive to change the system as much as I can." She clearly rejects the model of multicultural education that fosters the assimilation of minority groups into dominant American culture: "[This model] maintains a society that consists of, encourages and promotes prejudice, bigotry, oppression, and three types of racism: institutional, cultural, and personal, as well as the exploitation of many cultural groups." Sandra is highly critical of all models of multicultural education that "do not deal with the inequalities that exist among groups."

In her first paper, Sandra described her students as being predominantly white. She now recognizes more diversity in her classroom, and describes the population of her elementary school as being 84 percent white, 15 percent African American, and less than 1 percent being from other racial groups. She also sees the need for specific attention to the needs of African American children in a largely white environment: "Many of the African American students have their first experiences being around White students and adults. . . . This can be quite uncomfortable and confusing for minority children who are trying so desperately to construct knowledge."

While Sandra only became aware of the extent of oppression through this class, she realizes that the experience of many minority students is far different from her own: "Many minority children have already learned the injustices of society and don't want any part of conforming to it. Cultural differences bring about a totally different set of experiences which children use to construct knowledge. These various experiences must be tapped into in order for an educator to get to 'know' the student and make a difference."

Sandra has learned to value multicultural education and recognize both the limits of her prior work as an educator and what she can do to rectify these limitations for herself and others. She has begun to "incorporate more cultural groups into my instruction including: people with disabilities, increased Asian American studies, more Native American research, just to name a few."

Through the course, Sandra has come to prefer the analogy of America as a "tossed salad" to that of America as a "melting pot." She also has a clear vision of what is required for her to reach that political and educational goal. Sandra knows that she can influence more than her classroom. She will use more politically sophisticated models of multicultural education in the in-service training that she provides for teachers. Her goal is to foster "cultural pluralism," and she cites approvingly Christine Sleeter's and Carl Grant's description of the tasks of cultural pluralism: an endeavor that "includes the maintenance of diversity, a respect for differences, and the right to participate actively in all aspects of society without having to give up one's unique identity." In her work as a social studies coordinator she "can encourage, inform educators and administrators of the need for curriculum revision to include multicultural education."

Sandra sees much that can be done within schools, but she is not convinced that the most politically radical model of multicultural education (multicultural and social reconstruction) is realistic: "It is not practical to believe that schools and educators have the power to change society independently of other institutions." She also thinks that this model of multicultural education lacks an "adequate research base." Despite her reservations about "utopian" social change, Sandra does "agree with implementing the part of this model that promotes involving democratic decision-making about school-wide issues, and promoting knowledge of how to go about peacefully challenging the status quo. I would probably lose my job if I promoted radical challenging!"

What led Sandra to move from a focus on individuals to seeing structural inequality? What enabled Sandra to see her whiteness and its impact on her teaching and on her view of the justice of American society? What enabled her to see her power as a teacher and social studies coordinator to creatively work for systemic change?

RESEARCH DESIGN AND COURSE DESIGN

In 2000, four colleagues — Suzanne Burgoyne (Theatre), Helen Neville (Counseling Psychology), Peggy Placier, and Karen Cockrell (Educational Leadership and Policy Analysis) — and myself began a research project on the pedagogical efficacy of Theatre of the Oppressed. This is a technique developed by Augusto Boal for enhancing both awareness of injustice and creativity in rectifying injustice.

Boal is a Brazilian author, director, and activist whose work was developed in concert with Paulo Freire's *Pedagogy of the Oppressed*. Boal first developed Theatre of the Oppressed in Brazil in the late 1960s and early 1970s as a technique to help workers and peasants clarify the nature of their oppression and imagine ways of challenging that oppression. Boal began by having actors portray a dilemma that was facing a community, and then took suggestions from the audience about actions to try in response. During one such performance, the woman in the audience who had posed the problem for the actors to resolve was not satisfied with any of their solutions. She asked if she could try something. Boal agreed, and Forum Theatre was born. In Forum Theatre people enact a dilemma being faced by the community, and members of the audience (spect-actors, rather than spectators) take over the role of the protagonist and try different responses.[5]

Boal's methods enable people to think in more innovative ways, helping them discover their own resources and the ways in which they can mobilize those resources for justice. Theatre of the Oppressed workshops begin with a substantial time of playing games, some of which are immediately relevant to issues of oppression, others of which are designed to facilitate nonverbal communication and thinking outside of established categories. Many of us have become accustomed to being primarily aware of the obstacles to our work for social change. Theatre of the Oppressed workshops circumvent such entrenched modes of analysis. For example, if the group involved in a workshop decides that a particular strategy is ineffective, the group simply moves on, and someone tries another response.

In addition to Forum Theatre, we used two other of Boal's techniques in our research: Image Theatre and Rainbow of Desire. In Image Theatre the community sculpts, without words, an image of an oppressive situation. Once there is agreement that the image reflects a situation shared by the group, they then sculpt an image of a desired state of affairs. The final challenge is to move, slowly, step by step, from the initial oppressive image to the image of freedom and justice. The third technique, Rainbow of Desire, was developed by Boal during his work in Europe. In Europe, Boal found, rather than facing arrest and torture by the police and the military, many people were oppressed by "the cops in the head." They had internalized structures of oppression, and could not imagine ways of moving beyond fear, cynicism, despair, guilt, or inertia. Rainbow of Desire was created to elicit an awareness of these internalized obstacles to social action, and enable people to overcome them through creativity and courage.[6]

Our research team assessed the efficacy of Boal's techniques in three classes. The first section of the project involved collaboration between two courses, a course on Theatre of the Oppressed taught by Dr. Suzanne Burgoyne, and a course on the relationship between schools, community, and society taught by Dr. Peggy Placier.[7] The third class studied was my summer 2002 course on the Theory and Practice of Multicultural Education, of which Sandra was a part.[8] There were eighteen white women in the class, one white man, one Latina woman, and one Chinese woman from Taiwan. All were invited to participate in the research project, and eight white women agreed. They gave us permission to review their first and final papers, and their evaluations of the Theatre of the Oppressed exercises, which we incorporated during two different class sessions.

In the past, many students had found the summer course on multicultural education to be exhilarating but overwhelming. They were encountering, often for the first time, descriptions of the depth and range of oppression within the United States, and a multitude of competing theories of domination, prejudice-formation, racial identity development, and social change. Incorporating Boal's Theatre of the Oppressed exercises seemed as if it might offer an additional way of building community, and of learning to see and challenge oppression. In the summer of 2002, therefore, we included two sessions of Theatre of the Oppressed exercises, one on the second day of class, the other the last. During the first session, warm-up activities were followed by exercises in Image Theatre. On the last day, warm-up activities and games were followed by exercises in the Rainbow of Desire.

My approach to examining oppression and empowerment has been greatly informed by the work of Dr. William Jones. Jones's basic principle of engagement is that of internal criticism. He encourages activists to find the values that people already hold, the experiences that they already have, and begin with these as the basis for foundational social and political critique. His exercise, the grid of oppression, is an expression of this principle. I have used it in many courses, and found it to be extremely helpful in working with students who do not think in systemic terms. Most of my students resist attempts to tell them that oppression is systemic. The response to even the most passionate denunciation and call to action is often defensive resistance or simple disbelief. The world that I portray does not reflect the world they know. Herein lies the power of the exercise developed by Jones. Rather than telling people that oppression exists, we work together to look carefully at the power dynamics between social groups within their own communities.

On the first day of the course, we hear each others' stories. Most are quite familiar to me. I share with the class that I, too, grew up in a farming community, nurtured by a close extended family. Like most of them, my family lived a deep commitment to Christian faith, our social world encompassed by church and family. Like most of my students, I am white, and my background is working class moving into upper middle class. Unlike them, however, the community in which I was raised was racially diverse and racially divided. Almost half of the population was Latino/Latina, yet the ownership of land and businesses, the leadership in government and civic organizations, was exclusively white. Unlike the parents of most of my students, my parents were community activists. Their understanding of Christian faith led them to be advocates for social justice and institutional change. My father was instrumental in establishing and maintaining a hospital that could serve the needs of this largely poor and working-class rural population. Both of my parents were advocates of racial justice and, later in their lives, members of PFLAG and advocates of equality for people who are gay, lesbian, and bisexual.

I was raised in a community that was obviously fractured by racial injustice and class divisions, and by parents who modeled the joy that can be found in explicitly challenging injustice. None of my students in this class, and very few that I have worked with in the past, have had this kind of formation. They have not been taught to think systemically; they have not been exposed to the depth and costs of oppression. We begin our work, therefore, with helping them see more clearly the contours of power and oppression in their own communities. I do not tell them that their communities and American society as a whole are radically unjust. Rather, I ask a simple question: who has power in your community?

The class is divided into small groups to work through the exercise developed by Jones. I ask each group to name the most powerful institutions in their community. The answers fly: banks, large family-owned business, the police force, local and state government, schools, hospitals, military bases, the university, influential churches,

the newspaper, radio and television stations. I then ask them to analyze an institution of which they have personal knowledge, identifying
what person or group of people have the most power in that institution. The answers are obvious — the school board in the case
of the school system, the owners of media, the chief of police, and
so on. Then I ask them to identify by race, gender, class, and presumed sexual orientation the person or group of people who holds
such institutional power. The results are stark: while there are a few
women and peoples of colors in leadership positions, the majority
of these positions are held by white, upper-class, presumedly heterosexual men. We test these results. Are they a fluke, an accident of
this particular class? We try to think of institutions in which the majority of decision-making positions are held by women, by African
Americans, by Latinas/Latinos, by Asian Americans, by people who
are gay, lesbian, bisexual, and transgender. While there are some exceptions, the class quickly realizes that the distribution of power in
the United States, economically and politically, is far from equitable.
The students name institutions in which African Americans do have
power: a few mayors, some governors, black churches, the NAACP,
and historically black colleges. We then examine another question:
Under which of these institutions do whites have to live? With the
rare exception of the governorship, none.

After this period of discovery, the students are ready to examine
critically statistical measures of inequality and analyses of the causes
of that inequality. We take our work to a deeper level, drawing on
Iris Marion Young's definition of five faces of oppression. I present
Young's theory to my students as a question — asking them if they
see these forms of power imbalance and injustice in their communities. We first examine exploitation: "a steady process of the transfer
of the results of the labor of one social group to benefit another."[9]
The students readily list groups who are exploited: teachers, nurses,
janitors, small farmers, and fast-food workers. They also recognize
that many of these jobs are held primarily by women or by peoples
of colors.

The second form of oppression is marginalization: "Marginals are people the system of labor cannot or will not use."[10] In addition to not being employed, people who are marginalized are often treated disrespectfully by the social agencies designed to serve them. They are also often viewed as extraneous to the social and political system, their ideas having little weight or value.[11] The students, independently, list the groups also identified by Young, the elderly, people with disabilities, single mothers, people on welfare, the inner-city poor, and American Indian people on reservations.

The third form of oppression, powerlessness, is also one that they recognize: "The powerless have little or no work autonomy, exercise little creativity or judgment in their work, have no technical expertise or authority...do not command respect."[12] This class of experienced teachers is well aware of this form of oppression, as they experience attacks on their professional status. They find themselves with increasingly less autonomy and creativity, and more pressure to follow standardized curricula and gear their teaching to what they see as inadequate standardized tests. They are also able to cite other examples. Most of them come from working-class and middle-class backgrounds, and know firsthand the lack of respect for electricians, plumbers, and mechanics.

The fourth form of oppression is cultural imperialism:

Cultural imperialism involves the universalisation of a dominant group's experience and culture, and its establishment as the norm....To experience cultural imperialism means to experience how the dominant meanings of a society render the particular perspective of one's own group invisible at the same time as they stereotype one's group and mark it out as the Other.[13]

This, too, is a form of oppression they readily recognize — stereotypes of women, poor people, and peoples of colors in textbooks, advertising, and television. They are also struck by the ubiquity of the fifth form of oppression, violence: "Members of some groups live with the knowledge that they must fear random, unprovoked attacks on their persons or property, which have no motive but to damage, humiliate, or destroy the person."[14] They quickly name the instances of violence — racially motivated attacks against African Americans and Muslims, the fear that women have of rape, the fear that people who are gay and lesbian have of hate crimes.

In the course of a few hours, the students in the class see their own communities in a different light. Jones's exercise and Young's definitions have given them a vocabulary, a grid for holding together things that they already knew, but had not before brought together in a systematic fashion. After discovering the power imbalances and the forms of oppression in their own communities, students are then willing to evaluate critically, rather than simply dismiss, statistical information about oppression and theories of oppression.

We continue our process of discovery through videos, guest lecturers, and reading. In addition to gaining information about the ways in which people have been and are working for justice, we focus on different approaches taken by educators, examining their efficacy and suitability for different age groups and social contexts. We thoroughly examine the five models of multicultural education described by Christine Sleeter and Carl Grant. The goal of the first model, "Teaching the Exceptional and the Culturally Different," is to "help people fit into" society as it is now. Teachers are encouraged to do this by "building bridges" from the students' existing culture to the norms of the dominant culture.[15] The second model, "Human Relations," focuses on the promotion of "feelings of unity, tolerance, and acceptance within [the] existing social structure." Teachers work to "promote positive feelings among students, reduce stereotyping, [and] promote students' self-concepts."[16] Advocates of model three, "Single Group Studies," "promote social structural equality" for a particular group that has been oppressed (American Indians, women, gays, lesbians, bisexuals, people who are transgender, African Americans, Asian Americans, Latinos/Latinas). A single group, its history, and culture are studied in depth, and students are empowered "to work toward social change that would benefit the identified group."[17] The fourth model, simply called "Multicultural Education," is designed to "promote social structural equality" for all social groups. Teachers and the school system as a whole work together to "promote equal opportunity in the school, cultural pluralism and alternative life styles, respect for those who differ and support for power equity among groups."[18] The fifth model, "Multicultural Education that is Multicultural and Social Reconstructionist" is explicitly political. In addition to learning about the causes of social inequality, students are taught the skills of social advocacy as an integral component of responsible citizenship in a democratic society.[19]

For each model, students address the following questions: Which aspects of the description of culture and which aspects of the political perspective of this model do you agree with, if any? With which aspects do you disagree? Which theories of learning and of social change do you find helpful and accurate? With which do you disagree? We also examine the theories of power and knowledge behind each model, and critically evaluate the lesson plans that Sleeter and Grant provide for each.

RESULTS: EDUCATION AND SOCIAL JUSTICE

All of the students began the class with an understanding of multicultural education that corresponded neatly with either model one, Teaching the Exceptional and Culturally Different (assimilation redressing deficiency or cultural difference), or model two, Human Relations. These teachers focused on individual change, helping children gain academic skills, and helping children appreciate different cultures and learn to get along well with children from cultures other than their own. By the end of the course, all saw these models as inadequate, and argued, with depth and eloquence, for models four and five, the models of multicultural education that explicitly address structural change and prepare students to be citizens involved in structural change.

In her first paper, Janet, a professor of teacher education at a private Christian college, described her goals as an educator in some detail. She is training future teachers, and wants to "assist" them in meeting "the academic, emotional, physical and spiritual needs of their future students." She also wants to help them "use instructional and resource materials to help children attain educational objectives," and help them develop "appropriate teaching, classroom management, interpersonal and professional skills." She is also concerned with "developing character appropriate for a role model for children."

In her final paper, Janet wrote that she "was quite amazed...that there were no goals related to multicultural education," since her reason for taking the course was to "begin an emphasis on multicultural education within her doctoral program." Janet also saw herself as having "a better than average multicultural background" because of her lifelong "exposure to various cultures."

Despite this "multicultural background," Janet writes that she "did not have a clear picture of what multicultural education would include." As a result of the course, however, she developed a more nuanced understanding of the different models of multicultural education, and planned on incorporating elements of all of them within her work with preservice teachers: "I might be able to enhance their view of education by enabling them to see themselves as empowering agents and even in some cases, change agents." Janet writes that "in conclusion, I would say that I have a strong Model #5 streak, which often leads me into controversial situations!" Although she expresses a strong affinity with the model of multicultural education that focuses most explicitly on social change, she also recognizes the dangers of this model: "The multicultural and social reconstructionist model does provide a forum for teaching children that they can be proactive in changing culture. Empowering children is a good idea as long as the context remains developmentally appropriate and an effort is not made to promote a particular agenda to the exclusion of all others." The class spent much time closely evaluating lesson plans for model five, and became acutely aware of the significant difference between exposing students to a wider view of the world and political indoctrination.

With these caveats, Janet added the following three goals to her list of educational objectives:

Use student's life experiences as a starting point for analyzing privilege or oppression.

Promote involvement in student government as a means of working toward equal opportunity and decision making within the college.

Provide community involvement opportunities as a means of teaching social action skills.

Heather has just completed her degree in early childhood education and will continue to teach young children. Along with many other students, she entered the course with a positive vision of American society as a "melting pot." Her goals as a teacher clearly reflected this view, focusing on helping all people "understand and respect diversity.... If people have not been taught about different cultures, then these same people will be less likely to have positive interactions with people of different cultures."

By the end of the course, however, Heather had a greatly expanded view of the political ramifications of cultural differences. She now sees America as a "stew," and writes that "I wish to lead children to the view of cultural diversity as an essential aspect of living in American society." The result of seeing the integral role of such diversity is far broader than merely having positive interactions between individuals: "Due to the cultural diversity in the classroom, I feel that Models 4 and 5 are the only ones that would work well.... From Model 4, I would take the elements of promoting equal opportunity and respect for cultural diversity, building on different learning styles, and involving parents from all SES (socioeconomic) levels. From Model

5, I would use the elements of developing social action skills and involving children in making decisions about school concerns."

Heather now places respect for diversity in a wider political context, describing her goal as a teacher as "promoting social structural equality, while realizing that this is a goal that will take decades and is not something that can be rushed." In her concerns to not "rush" the work of social equality, Heather does not mean that we should avoid such work, nor be complacent in our efforts toward justice. It reflects, rather, a sober assessment of the magnitude of the task before us, and her recognition that she can be part of a larger movement for social change.

As they began to see how the students they already respected and nurtured are affected by social forces and oppressive institutions, the teachers redefined their goals. Jessica, a teacher of special education and an advocate for children with special needs, realized that her previous approach to multicultural education was inadequate. In the past, she had taken a "tourist approach," focusing on customs, foods, and festivals. Her goals now, however, are much deeper: "The purpose of multicultural education is to teach people of all ages how to respect and to listen to other people. It includes teaching about culture, race, gender, religion, disabilities, sexual preference, socio-economic status, personal preferences or beliefs that may contradict our own, and it addresses the structural nature of inequality."

Jessica became sharply critical of model two for its sole focus on helping people appreciate the differences and similarities of other individuals. While it "can be a good starting point," and can, when used in early childhood education, "provide a basis for more sophisticated approaches to multicultural education," its value is limited. It is valuable to the extent that it can be used "to reduce stereotyping" and "promote unity and tolerance." Jessica writes that other models, however, are needed to follow this one because this model "does not address the underlying issues of stereotypes, low achievement, poverty, powerlessness, or prejudice."

THE INJUSTICE OF AMERICAN SOCIETY

Throughout the course, the students recognized and increasingly adopted pedagogical strategies that addressed more explicitly the need for, and challenges of, structural change. This change in pedagogy was accompanied by a greater sense of the degree of injustice in American society. Five of the eight stated that through the course they had come to see that American society was far more unjust than they had previously imagined.

Heather began the course with a conviction that American society is not just, but "is making progress in that direction." She also believed that continued change would occur through the education of individuals. By the end of the class, however, Heather claimed that education of individuals was not enough, and described her work as an educator of young children as part of a larger movement to change society. Her words are blunt and to the point: "American society is not just. People are not treated equally. And until white men are not the ones who run everything from our country to our early childhood centers, then we will not be able to fulfill our ideals of liberty and justice for all."

Deborah is a teacher of a Title I preschool class, which she described in her first paper as "aimed toward students who are perceived as 'at risk' of failing in school." The majority of her students are "Caucasian, African American or Bi-racial" with students from South Africa, Nigeria, Korea, China, Vietnam, the Philippines, and the Middle East.

During the course, she became aware of the extent of injustice and the need for structural change: "Prior to this class, I thought American society was fairly just. I have been opened up to a whole new world. There is still a long way to go to fulfill the ideals of liberty and justice for all."

Deborah also sees the need for change in political structures and educational policies: "In our society today we are still focusing on the 'norms' of society. Many people in power are not aware or not yet ready to change those norms. Several elements of our society will have to evolve.... The political structure of our society will have to change. Different groups of people are going to need to be in power and then school systems will have to adapt in order to fulfill the needs of all students." Deborah recognizes that "these sound like overwhelming tasks" but believes that it is possible to "keep striving" and possible to come "closer to achieving [our] American ideals."

Of the five students whose ideas about the justice of American society changed, Leah's changes were the most dramatic. Leah is a teacher of young children who was herself raised in a poor family. She began the course with intense empathy for the pain and challenges that are faced by poor children, and an equally intense anger with parents who seemed to her to be unmotivated to change their lives:

> My father was an alcoholic, who never had a steady job. My parents divorced when I was 3 years old. My mom worked three jobs so that we would not have to go on welfare....I have a true respect for families that struggle to pay the bills....It is difficult for me to see able-bodied parents not working, while their children are suffering.... My weakness in this area pertains to my inability to tolerate parents that don't seem to care that they are raising kids in poverty. I have so much empathy for the kids, but so little for the parents. I had an inner drive and motivation that my kids would never ride in an old pickup truck with no passenger seat, and a hole right down to the street below (this was the truck my dad had). I realize the helplessness of these kids and it makes me feel bad.

Although she stated that she "valued diversity," Leah also claimed that American schooling was misguided in its emphasis on minority cultures:

> American schooling attempts to be just. Our teachers and administrators have become so careful not to offend anyone, that we don't get meaningful information much of the time. Young

elementary children don't get grades, just vague competency estimates.... We have English as a second language. We study a different country every year at my sons' school. Many religious holidays are discussed in public school, except the birth of Jesus. Some people feel in our attempt to include everyone that the white middle class protestant American gets ignored. There will always be the issue of the majority feeling that the minority is using more resources.

Leah's initial ambivalence, however, is indicated by the sentences that immediately follow her critique of a school system that focuses "too much" on minority concerns. She writes that Americans "need to value diversity and strive to include all of these people in the process of education. What a boring country we would have if everyone were exactly the same."

Leah sees the need to add diversity for the cultural interest that diversity provides. This view is congruent with her convictions about the fundamental justice of American society: "I believe we are fulfilling our promise of life and liberty for all.... We value our freedom. We have been welcoming of immigrants, but I do see a downturn since our recent terrorism events. This continually needs to be assessed and changes made. We are such a wonderfully diverse country.... Each family has a special history. I love that about America."

Two and a half weeks later, Leah wrote the following assessment of American society:

America is not a just society. Inequality exists all around us. Black men statistically are pulled over by the police more often than any other group. Women make less than men in the same job. Traditionally female-dominated jobs pay less than male-dominated jobs. States have laws that they are "English only." Many gays and lesbians still feel they must remain "in the closet" to function in our society. Welfare-to-work laws are celebrated, while single mothers work minimum wage jobs and the kids go hungry. Disabled people are underutilized in the job force.

Muslims fear retaliation from Americans. We have not fulfilled the ideal of liberty and justice for all. There currently is liberty and justice for the middle or upper class white male only.

Leah also underwent a fundamental reassessment of her own experiences of poverty. While not denying in any way the pain of that experience, and the lessons she gained from it, in her final paper Leah wrote that "the readings, films, discussions and debates taught me that my real-life experiences couldn't be generalized to all others in society. Many factors led to my ability to change the direction of my life. I am white; my family resources increased enabling me to attend college, and I had a large network of people willing to help me. Many of my students do not have these luxuries."

With this greater awareness of the factors that influence her life, and those of her students, Leah sees herself as poised to be a more effective educator and agent of social change: "My strength in teaching is that I am willing to look beyond my own experience and into the experience of the children from diverse backgrounds. I am also willing to learn and change for the better to provide a nurturing classroom environment that is multicultural and promotes social change."

WHITENESS, POWER, AND LIMITATIONS

Half of the students explicitly described ways in which they learned to see the significance of race in their teaching and in their place in society. At the end of the course, Janet recognized the racial significance of her college's core curriculum. Her institution has been cited by its accrediting agency for its lack of attention to multicultural needs. She writes that the administration is "basically unsure about how to correct this." She states that they plan simply on bringing in more minority students, and do not realize that the core curriculum is "Euro-American" and needs to be changed.

In her first paper, Heather acknowledged the limitations of "having lived in a very homogenous, white [rural] Christian town." By the second paper, she was more aware of the significance of her racial background: "Another limitation that I face as a teacher is that I am white. As a white person, I have not experienced many of the trials and tribulations that some of my future students may have faced."

Given her background, Heather is aware that she needs more education about specific cultures and more work with people from other cultures. She realizes that it is not enough to learn about others, but that learning is best when it occurs in the context of working together. She cites the example of Vivian Paley, a Jewish teacher "who met with a fellow teacher who was black in order to learn more about black culture and [her] views of integrated schooling. I think that if I were to incorporate this type of learning into my teaching that I would not only learn about a specific culture but build positive relationships with people of that culture."

Jennifer writes that her goals for multicultural education have changed, and her goals for her own continuing education have changed as well:

Even though I've expanded my experiences, my thoughts and the ways I view others, I know that I have not had many experiences with others from certain cultures. I still catch myself jumping to conclusions before I really know a person of another race. My job and this class have helped me to have a better understanding..., but I would still like to have more experiences with other cultures to be able to expand my knowledge and viewpoints.

A small sample, but the changes are not anomalous. I have observed a similar transformation in three-quarters of the people who have taken the course in the past three years: each teacher with a greater understanding of the structural dimensions of oppression; each teacher more prepared to continue the lifelong, the generations-long, work of social justice.

FACTORS THAT ENABLE CHANGE

How did these changes occur? What was the role of Boal's Theatre of the Oppressed exercises in enabling such creative transformation? The students themselves described several factors as salient in evoking change: certain guest presentations, videos, discussions, and the attitude of the instructor.[20]

Heather highlighted the presentation by Carol Lee Sanchez, a poet, artist, and writer of the Laguna Pueblo. Sanchez does not focus on American Indians primarily as victims, but describes the power, creativity, and resilience of contemporary American Indian nations. This helped Heather see how much she needed to learn about the "positive" aspects of marginalized groups. Sandra found the videos helpful: "Groups are oppressed on a regular basis in broad daylight. Equal opportunities do not exist for all races, genders, socioeconomic and religious backgrounds. There has been so much research done to confirm this fact, but why is it so sheltered from our 'White' society? The content of the videos that our class viewed needs to be seriously publicized and viewed by all Americans in order to close the gap that is vital to 'fulfilling our ideals of liberty and justice for all.'"

Leah attributed her dramatic change to the mix of readings, films, discussions, and debates: "The readings, films, discussions and debates taught me that my real-life experience couldn't be generalized to all others in society." Leah also highlighted the "nonjudgmental style of the instructor," and the attempt to include a "wide range of learning styles."

The students gave mixed, but predominantly positive, assessments of the Theatre of the Oppressed exercises. Jessica, for example, wrote that the Theatre of the Oppressed activities "really opened my mind." Sandra plans on adapting these activities for her classroom of nine- and ten-year-olds, and wrote that "these activities encourage people to engage and reflect on experiences that they've had and also try to understand our society better."

Suzanne Burgoyne, professor of theatre and instructor of Boal's work, and Sally Foster, a graduate student who had taken Professor Burgoyne's course on the Theatre of the Oppressed, led our class in several techniques from the work of Boal. During the first session we spent an hour on the activities designed to elicit creative thinking through the use of nonverbal communication. Deborah saw these as useful for "getting to know people in the class" and facilitating subsequent group work, but did not see the relevance of all the exercises to multicultural education. Heather found the exercises "nerve-racking in the beginning," but "entertaining." She did not, however, find them "relevant to this class."

While two students did not find the Theatre of the Oppressed exercises particularly relevant to the course, five did. They gave both general responses to the exercises as a whole, as well as specific responses to particular aspects of Boal's work. Janet, for example, wrote that "the reflection time after the exercise was my favorite. The insights from everyone were remarkable." Samantha stated that "I liked it [Theatre of the Oppressed] because it showed very good examples of power, nonpower." She also wrote that "it made many ideas more clear for me, and made me think about ideas that I wouldn't have otherwise." Leah wrote that the exercises were an "excellent ice-breaker for the beginning of a new group." She also said that "the first exercises, grouping each other, sculpting, etc. were very good activities to come to an understanding of your belief systems and other classmates. It was amazing what can be portrayed without words!"

Several activities involved Image Theatre. This is an exercise in which an individual silently groups people and arranges them in a configuration that represents some form of social power, a dysfunctional family, for example, or an oppressive classroom. After the scene was arranged, we were asked to merely describe what we saw, without interpretation. Sandra described how this type of activity "challenged me to think in a different way ... For example, the strategy to give concrete observations before interpretations was super because it *really* made it clear how *we* as a society are constantly interpreting and can often times misinterpret situations."

The last day of class we were once again led in exercises by Burgoyne and Foster. The final activity was especially transformative. Burgoyne and Foster led us in the Rainbow of Desire. In these exercises, the protagonist chooses a situation in which he or she feels oppressed. Someone is selected to play the role of the oppressor, and then the protagonist chooses people to represent different facets of his or her reaction to oppression (i.e., defiance, rage, fear, shame, or confusion). The protagonist and antagonist act out a brief scene that illustrates the oppressive dynamics, and then the "alter egos" take turns interacting with the oppressor. The oppressor is to remain the same, and the protagonist and alter egos are to change, trying out different strategies and responses.

We began with the students acting out a situation in which a young woman felt oppressed and misunderstood by her mother. She comes from a Christian family, and is becoming seriously involved with a man who is Muslim, and whose family is Muslim. Her mother does not approve of the relationship, and wants her daughter to marry another Christian. The exercise was intense, and slowly the dynamics began to shift. The woman selected at random to play the role of oppressor began to see the ways in which she, in her own life, *actually was* being oppressive to her daughter. First, she struggled to stay in character, but then broke the rules. Rather than the protagonist seeking ways of addressing and challenging her oppressor, we had the oppressor struggling to find different ways to change, and to reach out to the protagonist.

Leah gave a clear description of the power of the exercise:

Honestly, I was kind of dreading going to it [the second Boal exercise]....The first couple of exercises were okay — I didn't really understand how mirroring being beautiful, etc., pertained to oppression, but I did my best. The instructors are so positive and motivating, it is hard not to share their enthusiasm, and I slowly found myself getting involved and interested. I cannot tell you how moving the final exercise was. I felt the pain of the daughter (having been one), and the mother (being one now to a daughter)....I LOVED how the instructor let the mother lead, even when it was the daughter's exercise. Way to be flexible. I truly felt a resolution, and a peace. Hard to explain. Excellent.

Jessica described the impact of the final exercise:

The last day of class was extremely interesting. It made past experiences come alive for me and made me reflect on conversations I've had with my mother. It also helped me to see her side of the coin and that was hard....It was a good experience and will help me see the emotions that are involved in heated conversations more clearly. It will also help me to have a better understanding of where the other person is coming from.

Janet, the woman who was cast as the oppressor, had a poignant assessment: "I think the underlying idea of all the voices is an excellent demonstration of reality. It was just a little too real for me, but actually it was very good for me and has been a good thing in my relationship with my daughter. Maybe that is true of others too. If so, then embarrassment is a small thing."

Although the Theatre of the Oppressed is explicitly directed to helping those who are oppressed see ways of challenging oppression, we saw something else occur. A person who may be oppressed in some ways (exploited as a teacher, discriminated against as a woman) also saw her power, and the ways in which she was acting oppressively. She tried, with determination and encouragement, to face the "embarrassment" of seeing that reality, and then tried to do something to rectify it.

What would it mean to explicitly structure Theatre of the Oppressed exercises to elicit this process of awareness by "oppressors"? Is it crucial to begin with people exploring the ways in which *they* are oppressed or are relatively powerless before they can see their own power and oppressiveness? The changes in this group of students were significant, but are they long-lasting? Do the students find colleagues to support them in their work for social transformation? Do they find themselves isolated, or alienated, in their new sense of the political significance of their work as teachers? And, while the strategies that we have developed work well with these students, would they work as well in a more diverse classroom?

THE ETHICS OF MULTICULTURAL EDUCATION

What do we, the researchers, think caused such dramatic changes? We cannot isolate a single determinative factor. Rather, the use of Boal's Theatre of the Oppressed is congruent with an ethic of multicultural education and intercultural engagement predicated on gratitude, honesty, accountability, and respect. In Theatre of the Oppressed workshops, participants are invited to work together as allies in the search for justice. All work together to accurately depict the contours and costs of oppression. All work together to imagine realistic steps that move from oppression to empowerment.

The interaction of empowerment, oppression, and resistance is complex and ever-shifting. People can learn to see their multiple social locations, where they and their people have been oppressed, and how and where they have used power and can exercise power in ways that are exploitative or equitable and freeing.

How do we respect ourselves, how do we respect others as we challenge each other to greater accountability, to a fuller expression of our highest dreams and deepest aspirations for an equitable, vital, human community? I think it is possible to apply to our work for justice the insights of critical legal theorist Patricia J. Williams:

> To say that blacks never fully believed in rights is true. Yet it is also true that blacks believed in them so much and so hard that we gave them life where there was none before; ... This was the resurrection of life from ashes four hundred years old. The

making of something out of nothing took immense alchemical fire — the fusion of a whole nation and the kindling of several generations. . . . But if it took this long to breathe life into a form whose shape had already been forged by society, and which is therefore idealistically if not ideologically accessible, imagine how long the struggle would be without even that sense of definition, without the power of that familiar vision.[21]

We can take the best of people's desires to be fair, honest, and inclusive, and work an alchemy that expands our hearts, minds, imagination, and will.

As we learn that it is possible to find points of connection with those who appear to be only opponents and enemies, it is easier to remain open to the new challenges that face us. Work for social justice is not a linear process. Particular forms of injustice may be successfully challenged, only to be replaced by other forms, equally damaging, equally pervasive. It is important that we heed the warnings of Patricia Hill Collins and William Jones. Forms of oppression "mutate." One form of racism or homophobia may be suppressed, only to be replaced by another form of domination.[22]

We can remain vigilant without succumbing to cynicism or paralysis. The means of such resilience take time; they are practices of attention that can become part of each day, each hour. These bulwarks against cynicism and despair are not, however, arduous or draining. They are ceremonies of gratitude and wonder, gratitude to those who have given us the ability to care and to have empathy, and wonder at the richness of human life, the exhilarating beauty of art and music, the awe-inspiring resilience and courage of many people in the face of oppression and suffering.[23]

Gratitude and wonder exist in concert with full awareness of how much is lost, of how precious are the lives marred and destroyed by injustice. Our mourning and rage are as deep as our joy in being, our wonder in living. What cannot easily be held together in words and concepts is profoundly honored in art — in dance, in the music of jazz, spirituals, and the blues, in the exuberance of the visual arts.

As I learn to honor the openness of the students in my class, I no longer see work for justice primarily as the denunciation of injustice from the outside. Rather, it is a calling, an evocation, *a summoning of something else that we already are.* We are not just isolated, arrogant, cynical, or despairing. We are also open, imaginative, empathetic; capable of mourning, rage, and creativity. If we forego the glorious isolation of the prophet, and the satisfactions of jeremiad, we may discover the wonder of what Patrick Chamoiseau calls "knowing through which vices to rifle in order to stumble upon virtue."[24]

This is the work of multicultural education — to tap and nourish connections between peoples, to honor the stories of hope. This, not for a world without struggle, but for a world in which we are no longer the unwitting nor the defensive and determined bearers of exploitation and destruction.

We listen, we learn. We mourn, rage, and remain open to the suffering around us. We acknowledge, with wonder and joy, the rich threads of human connection that bind us to the past and to the future. We participate in the work of many generations — remaining open to pain, to possibility, and to change. As Chamoiseau would say, "Write the Word? No. But tie the knot with life, again, yes."[25]

NOTES

1. Many of us at the University of Missouri were trained at the Equity Institute, an organization based in Oakland, California, but no longer in existence. We modeled our "MU to the Future" training workshops on their methods. The guidelines and assumptions that we used are based on those developed by Equity.

2. See Christine Sleeter and Carl Grant, *Making Choices for Multicultural Education,* 3rd ed. (New York: John Wiley and Sons, 1999); Carl Grant and Christine Sleeter, *Turning on Learning,* 2nd ed. (New York: John Wiley and Sons, 1999). I have provided a more detailed description and analysis of these models in *Sweet Dreams in America: Making Ethics and Spirituality Work* (New York: Routledge, 1999).

3. The other essays in this volume use "U.S.-American" in order to signal that citizens of the United States are not the only Americans and to cut against the U.S.-centric tendencies of such language. This essay reflects analysis of a research project and, thus, for the integrity of the analysis, the language and sensibilities used in the course and of the students need to be reflected.

4. All students in the class were asked to participate in the research project, and eight agreed. The eight signed consent forms allowing their words to be cited in our research. The names of students are pseudonyms.

5. Augusto Boal, *Theatre of the Oppressed,* trans. Charles A. and Maria-Odilla Leal McBride (New York: Urizen, 1979).

6. Augusto Boal, *Games for Actors and Non-Actors,* trans. Adrian Jackson (London: Routledge, 1992); *Rainbow of Desire: The Boal Method of Theatre and Therapy,* trans. Adrian Jackson (London: Routledge, 1995); *Legislative Theatre,* trans. Adrian Jackson (London: Routledge, 1998).

7. For a fuller analysis of this subset of the research, see Karen Cockrell, Peggy Placier, Jite Eferakorho, Esteban Alejandro Renaud, Suzanne Burgoyne, Sharon Welch, and Helen Neville, "Theatre of the Oppressed as an Instructional Practice: Guide to Preservice Teachers' Knowledge and Understanding of Student Diversity" (forthcoming); Suzanne Burgoyne, Sharon Welch, Karen Cockrell, Helen Neville, Peggy Placier, Meghan Davidson, Tamara Share, and Brock Fisher, "Researching Theatre of the Oppressed: A Scholarship of Teaching and Learning Project" (under review).

8. I have taught a seminar on the theory and practice of multicultural education for eight years. The initial design of the course was developed by Dr. Peggy Placier.

9. Iris Marion Young, *Justice and the Politics of Difference* (Princeton, N.J.: Princeton University Press, 1990), 49.

10. Ibid., 53.

11. Ibid., 54.

12. Ibid., 56–58.

13. Ibid., 58–59.

14. Ibid., 61.

15. Sleeter and Grant, *Making Choices for Multicultural Education,* 38.

16. Ibid., 77.

17. Ibid., 111.

18. Ibid., 153.

19. Ibid., 189.

20. We examined the following six videos: (1) "Displaced in the New South," produced by David Zeiger and Eric Mofford, distributed by University of California Extensions, 1995; (2) "Can You See the Color Gray?" produced by Alexandra Corbin, distributed by University of California Extensions, 1997; (3) "Shadow Catcher: Edward S. Curtis and the North American Indian," distributed by Phoenix Film and Video, 1974; (4) "Out: Stories of Lesbian and Gay Youth," produced by National Film Board of Canada, distributed by Filmmakers Library, 1994; (5) "One Fine Day," words and music by Kay Weaver, Ishtar Films, Sherman Oaks, California, Nimue Publishing, 1984; (6) "True Colors," produced by ABC News, distributed by MTI Film and Video, 1992.

21. Patricia J. Williams, *The Alchemy of Race and Rights: Diary of a Law Professor* (Cambridge, Mass.: Harvard University Press, 1991), 163.

22. Patricia Hill Collins, *Fighting Words: Black Women and the Search for Justice* (Minneapolis: University of Minnesota Press, 1998).

23. For a fuller examination of the spiritual and political power of ceremonies of gratitude, see Carol Lee Sanchez, "Animal, Vegetable, and Mineral: The Sacred Connection," in *Ecofeminism and the Sacred,* ed. Carol J. Adams (New York: Continuum, 1993), 226. For a rich description of political activism modeled on respect and gratitude, see Ronald V. Dellums and H. Lee Halterman, *Lying Down with the Lions: Public Life from the Streets of Oakland to the Halls of Power* (Boston: Beacon Press, 2000).

24. Patrick Chamoiseau, *Texaco,* translated from the French and Creole by Rose-Myriam Rejois and Val Vinokurov (New York: Pantheon Books, 1997), 294.

25. Ibid.

AFTERWORD

WHAT IN THE PRESENT MOMENT will advance the struggle against white supremacy in U.S. society? What in the present moment will advance the struggle against white supremacy in my life, in the lives of those closest to me, and in the communities of which I am a part? How in the present moment can I best work within my spheres of influence to help overcome white supremacy?

These are key questions of moral, ethical, and political importance for all who are committed to racial justice. They suggest a need for close attention to long-term strategic thinking and organizing, toward which theory can merely point. The authors of this volume have not answered these questions, but they have explored some of the complexities of white anti-racist praxis so that readers may be better equipped to formulate their own answers.

We suggest that there are three arenas where much work needs to be done to resist white supremacy. These arenas are: (1) the development of anti–white supremacist theories in theology and ethics, (2) the strengthening of anti-racism work in churches, and (3) the beginning of sustained anti–white supremacist investigation and conversation in the theological academy. To close this volume, we outline below what we see as some of the major tasks in each arena.

A PROJECT FOR THEORETICAL DEVELOPMENT IN THEOLOGY AND ETHICS

Commitment to white anti-racist praxis — "emancipatory praxis," as Karin Case calls it — that is embodied in communities as well as explored in theory requires attention to complexities and problems within white identity. Those of us who are white live and move and have our being in a social reality permeated by supremacy, and thus we are formed in ways that make it seem all but impossible to move into effective multiracial coalitions. Shared political commitments and similar ideological perspectives are never enough to create, let alone sustain, coalitions. We bring the actions and behaviors of how we are formed as people, in a thoroughly white supremacist racialized landscape, into our ways of being with others. Attention to this most personal and, in some ways, most difficult work, is of paramount importance. As Aana Vigen says, "if [we] do not get it right in our day-to-day interactions and relationships, we won't get it right in our thinking, writing, or sermons."

At the same time, however, our ongoing development and formation as people is thoroughly linked to what we do. Thus, for white people, growth into a disruptive practice cannot be pursued by mere self-reflection. To become the kinds of people who might begin to "get it right" requires stepping into active participation at all levels of struggle against racism, even before we will be able to "get it right." This requirement for action pertains even to those whose vocational lives are focused on constructing theory.

Action at every level requires speaking up against expressions of racism in our families and most intimate settings, searching for ways to be in risk-taking solidarity with colleagues of color in our workplaces, and recognizing the violence of everyday racial life in the United States such that we take to the streets to protest and to express our outrageous commitment to a racially just future. Action shapes who we are. It is, thus, the means by which we take responsibility for how we are formed in a system that relies for its power on our remaining passive and discouraged. In the face of the social and personal stagnation that marks participation in white supremacy, acting our way into theory and theorizing our way into action are, simultaneously, essential.

Insisting on attention to both who we are and to the development of and engagement in strategies of resistance indicates how much more work is needed, as well as something about what kind. First, we need to know our entire history. We need to know both the historical realities and the "moral crisis," as Jennifer Harvey calls it, of what it has meant *to become* and *to be* white in the United States. And we need to know too about those "who have gone before us — race traitors and anti-racist activists — who were courageous enough to resist... and strong enough to live that resistance out," as Sally Mac Nichol writes. Such "knowing" requires digging below the erasure of resistance history and the manufactured idea that the reality of today is the only reality that could have been possible, in order to theorize and to live into a new non-white-supremacist tomorrow.

Second, we need to continue to develop complex languages, methodologies, and frameworks that do not collapse into monolithic notions of white identity itself, nor erase the multivalence with which white supremacy operates. As difficult as it may be "to digest" the complex relations among race, sex, and gender, as Laurel Schneider writes, we must be increasingly savvy about the "co-constitutive quality of race, sex, and gender... because of the support each construction gives in the modern West to the tenacity of white supremacy."

Complex analysis is the only way to describe well the *actual experience* of social reality in which we never live from only one node of our location. Delving into the complexity of our lived experiences is important, because it is the only way to develop theories that are adequate. Yet it is, perhaps, one of the most difficult aspects of this work, as intersections of privilege and oppression create what Elizabeth Bounds has insightfully called "flashpoints." Bounds points to how essential it is to keep it complex in order to think and speak about whiteness in ways that do not hinder work among differently located white folks. Moreover, as Sharon Welch shows in her analysis of Leah's story, when we are dealing with issues of oppression and privilege, we are talking about the most personal and poignant experiences of each of our lives. Thus, there are many good reasons to move with care.

This required complexity is a particular challenge to work being done in the academy, which is thoroughly racially stratified, and thoroughly economically classed as well, in ways that are enormously difficult to untangle, explore, and change. Meanwhile, the genuine need for highly developed and nuanced theory never exempts us from the responsibility to act.

We are aware of important matters not included in this book. For example, we do not address the international reality of white supremacy. And, yet, as Becky Thompson argues persuasively, "The anti-imperialist thrust of organizing must go hand-in-hand with an anti-racist agenda in the United States." Her remark is as relevant to theorizing as it is to organizing. The intimate interrelationship between imperialism and white supremacy also speaks to the most frequent erasure — in many ways perpetuated again in this book — of Native Americans in analyses of white supremacy. We cannot truly understand the operation of white supremacy without investigating imperialism in North America. Our sense is that this work, especially in critical studies of whiteness, remains thoroughly underdeveloped.

AS A PROJECT FOR THE CHURCHES

We are aware that this book does not address adequately white supremacy in the churches, or efforts already taking place among churches to resist white supremacy. Robin Gorsline exposes the failure of the white theological academy to provide white churches with anti–white supremacist resources. He asserts that existing resources have been developed, instead, by denominational and ecumenical bodies "because members of the [church] groups both recognize a deep wound within their own ranks, and are disturbed by the continuing racial insensitivity, injustice, and divides they see in their own communities." Becky Thompson's work suggests to us that there are significant historical precedents for anti-racist activism in church communities. Greater attention to the engaged activism of these and present-day faith communities — along with honest reflection of their strengths and weakness — remains an important task.

A larger enterprise for denominations — both Roman Catholic and Protestant — is to explore their histories and structures for clues about how white supremacy has shaped them. As Robin Gorsline states, the growth of the Black church resulted from white supremacy and results in the perpetuation of the white church. There is far more to this story, however. Its contours and details will be revealed as church leaders undertake thorough examinations of their histories and polities utilizing an anti-racist lens to focus on the points at which crucial choices were made to accommodate and even reify white supremacist practices and ideologies. Such work requires concrete attention to mission history, both in other parts of the world and on the North American continent.

Behind the history and structure of church bodies, moreover, lie theo-political constructions that support U.S.-American Christian-based ideas of exceptionalism and manifest destiny. The Puritan ideal of "the city on the hill," for example, contributed centrally to the belief that Native Americans were savages to be pushed aside and slaughtered in the name of God. This ideology is alive and well in the United States and in many of our Christian denominations and theologies. And while it manifests in different forms today, its persistence is cause for significant alarm. Each Christian religious body in the United States undoubtedly has roots in this web, and a project for all of us is to expose those roots and undertake the slow, painful process of ecclesial and theological change.

AS A PROJECT IN THE THEOLOGICAL ACADEMY

When we began this project, in conversation with a number of scholars, several pointed out to us that the project of anti-racist praxis requires ongoing, sustained attention. We must do our best to avoid the past pattern of sporadic, individual efforts that never achieve a critical mass. Many of the scholars with whom we consulted, therefore, suggested we think long term even as we began this book. They suggested that we consider convening a multiracial gathering to examine what critical whiteness studies offer for the project of liberation theology and ethics, as well as to explore the ground for active solidarity and coalition. Such a conference, they said, could form the basis of a second book.

These suggestions clearly reflect ongoing concern — most cogently, eloquently, and repeatedly raised by James H. Cone — that white participants in theological disciplines overcome our unwillingness to engage actively the reality of racialized oppression and white supremacy. More to the point, they reflect the reality that a theological academy, whose primary texts and greatest minds are so deeply implicated in the history and present reality of white supremacy, must somehow work its way out of the racist morass it continues to inhabit and sustain.

We do not suggest finger-pointing as a solution, unless the fingers point inward to ourselves. What we suggest is that each of us take responsibility for uncovering our own particular complicities. Then, we need to share them with others so that all receive additional resources for the work. We see the need for work that will directly impact theological education as a whole, and for scholarship that intentionally bridges the divide that so often bars engagements between academy and church. Moreover, we are certain that theologians and ethicists have much to learn from pastors and parishioners who are at work on these issues.

Perhaps our most ardent desire for this volume is that it be one spark among many others that are out there already; that it will help ignite a dialogue that is deep, broad, and sustained, as well as contentious, concrete, constructive, critical, and collaborative. In short, we long for a dialogue that reflects the crucial, foundational work before us.

IN CONCLUSION

We wish to close with this simple point: The urgent task of white anti-racist praxis requires ongoing work at multiple sites in order to fuel resistance and growth. At some of these sites our work is basic self-education and critical self-reflection. At some of these sites our work requires more direct engagement in multiracial conversations and coalitions. At some of these sites we must construct specific pedagogies, strategies, and plans for building stronger white participation in the project of racial justice. At some of these sites our work will be the advancement of theories that continue to clarify and scrutinize social reality, and develop new ways of thinking to compel anti–white supremacist action.

No one of these sites is separate; every site is intrinsically linked to the others. Nor is there a linear path to the emergence of white anti-racist praxis; true growth in one site depends on growth in the others. Foundational to them all, we continue to believe, is the necessity of recognizing the need to "do our first works over," and over, until we begin to see that our successive acts are increasingly free of and freeing us from the beast called white supremacy.

CONTRIBUTORS

Elizabeth M. Bounds is Coordinator of the Initiative in Religious Practices and Practical Theology at Emory University, where she is also Associate Director of the Graduate Division of Religion and Associate Professor of Christian Ethics. Along with the volume *Coming Together/Coming Apart: Religion, Community, and Modernity*, she has published articles on welfare reform, pedagogy, and racism.

Karin A. Case holds the Ph.D. in Christian Social Ethics from Union Theological Seminary in New York City. A minister in the United Church of Christ, she serves as a pastor in a local congregation and has worked as a hospital chaplain in Boston. Karin has been active in interfaith dialogue, and is currently involved in anti-racism work and racial justice concerns with the Massachusetts Conference of the United Church of Christ.

Robin Hawley Gorsline serves as Senior Pastor of Metropolitan Community Church in Richmond, Virginia. He earned the M.Div. from Episcopal Divinity School, and the Ph.D. in Systematic Theology from Union Theological Seminary in New York. His research, writing, and activism focus on the intersection within theology and religion of various forms of supremacism.

Jennifer Harvey received her Ph.D. in Christian Social Ethics from Union Theological Seminary in May 2004. The title of her dissertation was "The Moral Crisis of 'Being White' and the Imperative of Reparations." She is an ordained minister in the American Baptist Churches, USA, and has been actively involved with anti–police brutality issues in New York.

Dwight N. Hopkins teaches theology at the University of Chicago Divinity School. Some of his works include: *Heart and Head: Black Theology, Past, Present, and Future; Introducing Black Theology of Liberation; Down, Up & Over: Slave Religion and Black Theology; Global Voices for Gender Justice*, co-editor; *Loving the Body: Eroticism and Black Religion*, co-editor; and *On Being Human: Black Theology Looks at Culture, Self, and Race* (in process).

Sally Noland Mac Nichol received the Master of Divinity degree from Union Theological Seminary, where she is currently working on her doctoral dissertation, "Pharaoh's Daughters: Toward an Anti-Racist White Feminist Liberation Theology." She has been an antiviolence educator and activist for almost twenty years and is currently Director of Programs at CONNECT, a nonprofit organization dedicated to ending family violence in New York City.

Laurel C. Schneider (M.Div., Harvard; Ph.D., Vanderbilt) is Associate Professor of Theology, Ethics and Culture at the Chicago Theological Seminary. In addition to articles and chapter contributions in feminist theology, queer theory, and disarmament, she is author of *Re-Imagining the Divine: Confronting the Backlash against Feminist Theology* (Cleveland: Pilgrim Press, 1999).

Becky Thompson is Associate Professor of Sociology at Simmons College, where she teaches African American Studies, Women's Studies, and Gender and Cultural Studies. Becky is the author of several books, including *A Promise and a Way of Life: White Antiracist Activism; Mothering without a Compass: White Mother's Love, Black Son's Courage;* and *A Hunger So Wide and So Deep: A Multiracial View of Women's Eating Problems.*

Aana Marie Vigen earned the Ph.D. in Christian Social and Theological Ethics from Union Theological Seminary in New York. Her dissertation, "To Count among the Living," explores health-care quality issues for Black and Latina women with cancer. She is an active lay member of the Evangelical Lutheran Church in America.

Sharon D. Welch is Professor of Religious Studies, University of Missouri, Columbia, and the author of numerous articles and books on ethics and social change, including *A Feminist Ethic of Risk* and *Sweet Dreams in America: Making Ethics and Spirituality Work*. Sharon lectures widely on the ethical and political challenges of multiculturalism and works with an international coalition of peace groups developing regional centers for conflict resolution and mediation.